Congress, the Press, and the Public

Congress, the Press, and the Public

Thomas E. Mann *and*
Norman J. Ornstein, *eds.*

American Enterprise Institute
and
The Brookings Institution

WASHINGTON, D.C.

AMERICAN ENTERPRISE INSTITUTE FOR PUBLIC POLICY RESEARCH
1150 17th Street, N.W., Washington, D.C. 20036

and

THE BROOKINGS INSTITUTION
1775 Massachusetts Avenue, N.W., Washington, D.C. 20036

Library of Congress Cataloging-in-Publication data

Congress, the press, and the public / Thomas E. Mann, Norman J. Ornstein, editors.
p. cm.
Includes bibliographical references and index.
ISBN 0-8157-5462-0—ISBN 0-8157-5461-2 (pbk.)
1. United States Congress—Public relations. 2. United States Congress—Reporters and reporting. 3. Press and politics—United States. I. Mann, Thomas E. II. Ornstein, Norman J.
JK1140.C62 1994
070.4 '4932873—dc20 94-26580
CIP

9 8 7 6 5 4 3 2 1

The paper used in this publication meets the minimum requirements of the American National Standard for Information Sciences—Permanence of Paper for Printed Library Materials, ANSI Z39.48—1984.

Set in Times Roman

Composition by Harlowe Typography, Inc., Cottage City, Maryland

Printed by R.R. Donnelley and Sons Co., Harrisonburg, Virginia

Preface

This book is a product of the Renewing Congress Project, a joint effort of the American Enterprise Institute and the Brookings Institution designed to give an independent assessment of Congress and to offer recommendations for improving its effectiveness and restoring its legitimacy within the American political system.

The Renewing Congress Project has over the past two years issued three reports to provide members of the House and Senate and outside observers with a perspective on congressional reform. The first report, issued shortly after the 1992 elections, focused on the House of Representatives and emphasized the need to strengthen the ability of leaders to set an agenda and act on it, increase the quality of deliberation and debate, improve the relations between the parties, reform the campaign finance system, and clean up the House's internal support system.

In June 1993 the second report addressed the full agenda of the Joint Committee on the Organization of Congress, including ethics, committees, the budget process, floor deliberation, and staffing in both chambers, as well as relations between Congress and the executive, the courts, and the public. The report laid out a model for how Congress should operate and provided detailed recommendations for institutional renewal. A number of the project's specific recommendations were incorporated into the Joint Committee's final report, issued in winter 1993.

The Renewing Congress Project issued a third report in February 1994 in response to the Joint Committee's final recommendations. This report identified strengths and weaknesses in the Joint Committee's work and suggested how it could be strengthened and promoted by party leaders.

This book is an extension of the project's work, highlighting the important issue of public opinion toward Congress and exploring the relationship between news media portrayal of the institution and the current public animosity toward it. The book is based on a conference held in May 1993 that brought together some fifty journalists, congressional specialists, and media and public opinion scholars to discuss public and media attitudes toward Congress. The discussion explored the historical relationship between the press and Congress, the roots of current opinions and press coverage, and strategies for improving the image and public understanding of Congress.

Many people have contributed to this book, and to the other activities and products of the Renewing Congress Project, by participating in roundtable discussions and conferences, conducting research, writing memoranda and commissioned papers, and providing critiques of draft documents. We are especially grateful to the many members of Congress and their staffs who spent hours with us discussing the problems of the institution.

We thank the conference participants for their insightful comments and lively debate. Carey Macdonald, Kimberly Coursen Parker, Todd Quinn, and Amy Schenkenberg provided valuable research assistance. Judy Chaney and Inge Lockwood helped prepare the manuscript for publication. James Schneider edited the manuscript, and Julia Petrarkis compiled the index. Richard Fenno, Jr., Charles O. Jones, Nelson W. Polsby, Cokie Roberts, and Catherine E. Rudder serve on the advisory committee that provides overall guidance to the project. We are grateful to all of them.

Financial support for the Renewing Congress Project is provided by a number of private foundations, including the Markle Foundation, which was the prime sponsor of the conference and this volume, the Carnegie Corporation of New York, the Ford Foundation, the Robert Wood Johnson Foundation, the Henry Luce Foundation, Inc., and the John D. Olin Foundation, Inc.

The interpretations and conclusions presented here are solely ours and those of the authors and should not be ascribed to the persons whose assistance we have acknowledged, to any group that funded the research reported here, or to the trustees, officers, or other staff members of the American Enterprise Institute or the Brookings Institution.

THOMAS E. MANN
Director of Governmental Studies
The Brookings Institution

NORMAN J. ORNSTEIN
Resident Scholar
American Enterprise Institute

Washington, D.C.
July 1994

Contents

1 Introduction

Thomas E. Mann
Norman J. Ornstein

CONGRESS is under siege. The healthy skepticism that long characterized public attitudes toward the institution has degenerated into corrosive cynicism. The support it once enjoyed among the most politically active, which moderated the swings in mass sentiment and constituted a bedrock of legitimacy, also appears to have crumbled. Common critiques of Congress—that it is filled with unethical professional politicians out of touch with ordinary Americans, in bed with lobbyists, consumed with retaining lavish perquisites of office, and unresponsive to urgent national needs—are carrying the day and undergird the burgeoning movement to limit terms in office.

In some respects this hostility is unremarkable. In the past thirty years, traumatic national events have led to a general deterioration of trust in government. Recently, an angry populism has arisen in democracies around the globe to challenge traditional governing arrangements that appear to favor entrenched interests. In the United States, stagnant wages, job insecurity, and growing inequality, all associated with a globalizing economy, provide ample grounds for citizens to disparage the performance of their government. The struggles to grapple with huge budget deficits, waged by a government contending with polarized political parties, intensify an image of gridlock. And the well-publicized scandals that have rocked Capitol Hill in the past few years provide more than enough grist for the critic's mill.

It may be that the low repute of Congress is justified, that the poor performance of American government and congressional disarray and violations of ethics are more than sufficient to explain public contempt. Congress certainly has its share of problems; and the American Enterprise Institute-Brookings Institution Renewing Congress project has identified many institutional reforms that could strengthen its capacity to set an agenda and act on it, improve the quality of deliberation and debate, and promote more constructive relations with the executive and judicial branches. Nonetheless, we are increasingly struck by the disjuncture between the public criticism and the institution's real strengths and weaknesses. It would be wonderful if the criticism led to constructive change inside the institution. But instead of a healthy democratic response that provides a much needed stimulus for change in the membership and rules, this public revulsion could cripple Congress's ability to recruit and retain able members, engage in serious deliberation, and maintain the legitimacy that is essential if its decisions are to be widely accepted.

In 1993 the American Enterprise Institute and the Brookings Institution convened a conference to consider how serious the public's animus is and what part the press may be playing in fostering it. Participants from the news media, Congress, and the universities reacted to analyses of public opinion and press coverage of Congress and considered what might be done to improve public understanding of the institution. This volume is a product of that endeavor.

Trends in Popular Support for Congress

It is hard to imagine that Congress was ever perceived as a beloved or popular institution (Mark Twain struck a chord when he referred to its members as our "only native criminal class"). By its very design it is fated to be the least popular branch of government. Slow, conflictual, diffuse, open, and self-critical, Congress is more likely to evoke ridicule and scorn than affection or awe.

If scorn is the watchword, it is not maintained at a consistent level. As Herb Asher and Mike Barr point out in chapter 2, support for the institution of Congress (which usually runs 25 to 35 percentage points lower than the ratings of individual members) varies in response to economic conditions and international and domestic events. In recent decades support surged to 48 percent in August 1974 when Richard Nixon was forced to resign the presidency over Watergate and to 49 percent in January 1991 during the congressional debate on intervening in the Gulf War. Approval plummeted to an all-time low of 18 percent in March 1992 during the House bank scandal. The return of unified party government under Bill Clinton has produced some improvement in public ratings of Congress but not to the levels common in the 1940s and 1950s.

It is difficult to say whether the hard times Congress has fallen on represent another of those periodic downturns in public support that have occurred throughout its history or whether they represent a more fundamental shift of sentiment. Gallup poll approval ratings for the institution extend back only to 1974. But a comparison of responses to individual questions over longer periods suggests that the public today believes their senators and representatives are *less* honest, ethical, public spirited, and responsive to the interests of their constituents than they once were, in spite of objective evidence to the contrary. (See the discussion by Karlyn Bowman and Everett Ladd in chapter 3.) And there are other signs that the distrust of Congress should be taken seriously.

Ominously, Asher and Barr report that the more politically attentive, informed, and involved citizens are increasingly the most critical of the institution. These days, at least, familiarity with Congress seems to breed contempt. This partly but by no means entirely reflects the fact that educated Republicans are most hostile toward a Democratically controlled Congress.[1] Other signs of this phenomenon are the growing support for term limits among the most highly educated Americans, the intense animus toward the institution in evidence at town meetings and on radio call-in shows, and the loss of faith in Congress among other members of the political community. Those who once provided the most dependable support for an institution not easy to understand or appreciate now often lead the chorus of criticism. Sadly, their ranks include many members of Congress itself.

Media Coverage of Congress

It would be fatuous to attribute Congress's problems with the public entirely to the news media, but it would be equally foolish to ignore their critical role in presenting the institution to the public. The impression most people get of Congress and its members comes through the prism of press coverage—and the evidence suggests that the nature, volume, tone, and content of the coverage have all changed sharply in recent years.

Dramatic developments in the news business, including new communications technologies, intensified economic competition, and altered professional norms, have transformed the ways in which news is defined, produced, and received. Most visible have been the proliferation of television network newsmagazines and the blurring of news and entertainment that they represent, as well as the more general tabloidization of the mainstream press. The more intense focus on celebrity, sensationalism, and scandal have shaped the coverage of Congress and have probably colored the way the public views the institution.

Research commissioned by the Renewing Congress project examined press coverage of Congress in a variety of ways. In chapter 4 Mark Rozell reports on the content and tone of coverage in the national print media between 1946 and 1992. Using a qualitative content analysis of three newsmagazines, *Newsweek*, *U.S. News and World Report*, and *Time*, and three daily newspapers, the *New York Times*, *Wall Street Journal*, and *Washington Post*, during ten important periods since World War II, Rozell summarizes and analyzes the major themes in the coverage of Congress. Through repetition these themes create images or stereotypes that people come to perceive as the whole reality.

Negative, superficial coverage of Congress, Rozell discovers, is nothing new, but in recent years the tone of unfavorable coverage has become much more severe. Stories focus on scandal, rivalry, and conflict to the exclusion of policy and legislative process. They routinely portray members of Congress as self-interested, self-indulgent politicians who exploit the process for personal gain. The angle of coverage reveals that journalists have a strong preference for a reform-oriented, progressive, policy-activist Congress that works effectively with a strong, ambitious president. There is little appreciation for the special deliberative responsibilities of the legislative branch envisioned by the Framers, and there is no realistic portrayal of the actions taken on Capitol Hill that affect the lives of citizens. Priorities for stories on Congress are drama, colorful personalities, and pork-barrel projects. No wonder the public knows little about Congress and thinks very poorly of its performance.

Since most Americans receive their news about politics and government primarily from television, not from national newspapers and magazines, it is also important to document the changing news coverage of Congress on network television. In chapter 5 Robert Lichter and Daniel Amundson do just that: they examine the three networks' treatment of Congress during one month of each year from 1972 through 1992. Their findings could not be more dramatic. First, the amount of congressional coverage has declined precipitously—from an average of 124 stories a month on the three networks between 1972 and 1978 to 42 a month between 1986 and 1992. Since 1979, when the House began to allow proceedings to be televised on C-SPAN, the major networks appear to have lost interest in its ongoing activities.

Second, the focus of the shrinking coverage has changed: fewer stories than before on policy issues, more on scandal. Until the mid-1980s, the authors report, the networks broadcast about thirteen stories on policy matters for each report on ethical lapses. Since then the evening news has shown nearly one story involving scandal for every three focusing on issues. At the same time the news format has become more adversarial:

the proportion of stories featuring individual or institutional conflicts has doubled, by 1987 reaching two out of every three stories on Congress.

Finally, the tone of the coverage, long decidedly negative, has become even more disparaging in the past twenty years. By 1992 nine of every ten judgments about Congress aired by the networks were unfavorable. And these sound bites were increasingly provided by critics outside the institution.

How much these changes in coverage reflect an underlying reality of American politics and society and how much they reflect the subjective news judgments of network journalists is debatable. But it is hard to come away from this research without believing that the media are making an independent, and destructive, contribution to the public disaffection with Congress.

Why have press outlets covered Congress less and with a more jaundiced eye toward scandal? In chapter 6 Stephen Hess chronicles how a shift in power from bureaus to home offices, pressures from new owners to scale back news operations, changing video technologies, low consumer interest, and new definitions of news have diminished reporting on Congress, and on government and politics more generally. Fewer stories on Congress are being written; those that survive are increasingly negative and driven by events, especially scandals, with very little focus on Congress as an institution.

As our communications system becomes more specialized and fragmented, each channel appealing to a narrow segment of the audience, there will be even less emphasis on the institution. No amount of exhortation to news executives or reporters will alter the basic forces that drive this market-based system to produce less coverage and more critical coverage. The only way to increase and improve reporting on Congress as an institution, Hess argues, is to create an institutional voice for Congress.

In chapter 7 Kimberly Coursen draws on a survey of journalists commissioned by the Renewing Congress project to supplement these studies of press coverage with information on journalists' attitudes toward Congress. She finds striking differences between specialists in congressional coverage and media executives: the specialists are much more critical than the executives of the diminishing amount and poor quality of congressional coverage and of the more frequent focus on scandal. The executives are more critical of Congress as an institution and more inclined to deplore the influence of special interests and PACs. In other words, those with the power to set the national news agenda and dictate the extent and tone of coverage of Congress—executive producers and managing editors—are the most hostile toward Congress and the most contented with the current pattern of news coverage. Those most knowledgeable about the institution are frustrated with the diminishing and scandal-based coverage but in no position to do much about it.

Among groups of journalists, radio talk show hosts emerge as the most hostile to Congress. Although their range of political ideologies and opinions in no way fits the stereotype of Rush Limbaugh, they are united in their intensely acerbic view of American political institutions and public officials, especially Congress and its members. This hostility is shared by most of their viewers. These programs thus become stages for crystallizing and mobilizing anti-Congress sentiment in the country.

How Congress Presents Itself to the Public

Many of the papers in this volume concentrate on the role of the press in filtering information about Congress for the public and on the distortions produced by the peculiar characteristics of the media lenses. But journalists are surely constrained by the material they have to work with—what Congress is and does and how it presents itself to the public. In the concluding chapter Ronald Elving examines how Congress and its members contribute to the institution's low standing with the public.

During most of its history Congress scarcely presented itself to the public at all; the institution and its members were largely unseen. Although in recent decades Congress has become much more visible, it has not become more comprehensible or appreciated. It lacks the traditions, mechanisms, and mentality for effective presentation that might convert new communications opportunities into improved public understanding. The personal touch that members develop with their constituents through repeated appearances back home does nothing to elevate the standing of the institution. Members routinely use the Capitol's broadcast facilities to project themselves into the living rooms of their districts and states, but they seldom exploit the opportunity to teach the public something about Congress. Media strategies embraced by party leaders are designed to advance the programmatic objectives of their caucuses, not to represent to the public the interests of the institution.

Even televising the proceedings of the House and Senate on C-SPAN has worked more to the benefit of individual members than to the institution as a whole. The average viewer is likely to see an institution apparently hamstrung by its own arcane procedures, petty and harassing in its partisanship, and disrespectful of its own integrity and worth. When members routinely denounce their institution before C-SPAN viewers, why should news professionals be reticent about bashing Congress?

Elving calls on Congress to fashion a public relations strategy for the institution, one that makes the process of legislating clearer and more comprehensible, that facilitates the job of reporters, that presents Congress in a more realistic and, ultimately, more sympathetic light.

Improving Public Understanding of Congress

None of the contributors to this volume or the participants at the conference that inspired it see any obvious means of lifting the siege of Congress. If the news media's angle of vision has contributed to the record low levels of popular support of Congress, the levels also reflect economic, social, and political forces that are not susceptible to manipulation by the most dedicated reformers. Sustained economic growth accompanied by real wage gains across all income groups would probably do more than anything else to improve the public standing of Congress, but this is a condition over which reformers have little control. An extended period of productive relations between the president and Congress would also likely improve the public mood, but again this is a condition not expected very often, given our fractious and sprawling society and separated system of government. Periodic alternations in party control of the House would give the minority party a stake in the public standing of Congress and dampen internal attacks on the institution, but it is impossible to predict when the Republicans will be able to break their long drought. More aggressive competition for market share and other developments in the news business portend a continuation if not acceleration of contentious, sensationalized coverage. And as plebiscitary forces gather in the United States and around the world, the legitimacy of national political institutions, especially deliberative legislatures, will come under constant attack.

So what is to be done? A free press in a free society cannot and must not be regulated. The alternative, then, is to strengthen professional norms of journalistic behavior. Some such norms did exist, at least for a while, in recent decades. They included refusing to air rumors without solid, independent confirmation; distinguishing between the private behavior of public officials and their performance of public duties as subjects for news coverage; and emphasizing coverage of substantive performance over scandal-driven allegations. To be sure, the mere existence of norms did not mean that all news organizations adhered to them. But many, especially such journalistic opinion leaders as the *New York Times*, the *Washington Post* and CBS News *did* adhere to them and influenced the overall nature of coverage of Congress and policymaking in general.

But for all the reasons noted in this volume, the allegiance to the norms has eroded in the prestige press and disappeared entirely elsewhere. Under competitive pressure, and with a new generation of reporters trained in the Woodward-Bernstein investigative tradition and weaned on contempt for politics and politicians, the prestige news outlets have adopted the sensationalist approach of their less reputable counterparts. Coverage of the House bank scandal, for example, was as overdone and distorted in the *Washington Post* as it was on radio talk shows.

Those less reputable counterparts, from the *New York Post* to the *National Star*, *Hard Copy* to *Inside Edition*, are proud to flout the old norms. But it is much easier for them to do so, and much easier for scandal-driven stories to flourish if the prestige press lends legitimacy and encouragement to the methods of the real tabloids. The coverage of congressional perquisites and trips on *Hard Copy* develops a much greater legitimacy when it merely echoes, with a sleazier twist, the weekly reports on ABC's *Prime Time Live*.

Reestablishing journalistic norms is not easy. It requires aggressive proselytizing by reporters and editors who espouse them, people such as Jack Nelson of the *Los Angeles Times* and Tom Oliphant of the *Boston Globe*. It requires serious efforts by journalists and educators to focus journalism school curriculums on professional ethics—and to embrace the right ones. It requires changes in journalism award programs to reward more reporting of substance and less reporting designed to bring public officials down. Most of all, it requires the peers of editors, producers, and op-ed page editors, those they respect and interact with, to cry "shame" every time the code of behavior is stretched or broken. Of course, that in turn requires that journalists, opinion leaders in their own right, have more respect and understanding for Congress as an institution and for its members. And it requires at least some change in the public's eagerness to believe the absolute worst about elected representatives.

For that to happen, Congress must tend to its own behavior and the way it presents itself to the public, actions over which it has some control.

Although much of the democratic critique of Congress, particularly the diatribes against corruption and the pervasive influence of special interests, is wide of the mark, Congress must strengthen ethics enforcement, restructure methods of campaign financing, and apply employee protection and other national laws to its own bailiwick if there is to be any improvement in public assessments of it.

These changes should be implemented because they are right and necessary. But they will also remove the most obvious targets of neopopulist attacks on the institution as a bastion of privilege and corruption. It is an unfortunate reality that reforms themselves will not alter the attitudes or incentives of journalists, so-called public interest groups, and ideological forces, nor will they blunt their attacks on Congress. But the attacks lose some of their force if practices that are difficult to defend are no longer targets.

Accompanying this more visible reform agenda there should be an agenda of changes designed to make Congress more effective as a deliberative body. Many of these are detailed in *Renewing Congress*, three volumes (a first report, a second report, and a progress report) published earlier by our project.

Can Congress also present itself to the public in more effective ways? There are three public windows into the institution: the prism of the press, C-SPAN, and, for millions each year, first-hand impressions when they visit the Capitol. Beyond improving the media portrait of Congress, neither C-SPAN junkies nor Washington visitors see much that would create a positive image of the nation's legislature or instill any real understanding of its role in the American political system.

Congress may not be able to change the practices of the press, but it can alter its institutional image on C-SPAN, and it can alter the way it treats visitors who come to see the Capitol and the House and Senate in action. Start with C-SPAN. The problem, of course, is not the network itself. After fifteen years of exemplary service to the public and the process, C-SPAN has proven its worth over and over again. Besides its unbiased coverage of hearings and markups and its balanced call-in shows, C-SPAN does what it originally set out to do—present the action on the House and Senate floors, unvarnished and unedited.

To be sure, the legislative process in a democracy can never be smooth, orderly, and sharply focused. Still, neither the House nor the Senate has thought through how its floor procedures look in a C-SPAN era, much less how to change those procedures—without altering their basic character—to fit the times.

The need is obvious. A recent unpublished survey by Mark Mellman shows that regular C-SPAN viewers are *more* critical of Congress than nonviewers, and the difference is not explained by political orientation. To know Congress on C-SPAN is not to love it. Even to a veteran Congress watcher, activities on the floor of the House as captured by C-SPAN look confusing, erratic, and unfocused. Tuning in at random, viewers find it nearly impossible to understand what is going on. Floor debate, using the term loosely, is arcane, focused on obscure points about rules or narrow legalese about elements of proposed amendments or bills. And general debate, which is designed to have real give and take on the merits of a bill, is usually the perfunctory reading of boring statements by floor managers and their minority counterparts. It can sometimes take an hour or more of dedicated viewing to discover what bill or resolution is on the floor. Often, no one seems to be on the floor listening to what the speakers are saying (often, because no one *is* on the floor.)

Votes compound viewer confusion. For periods of fifteen minutes or more during a vote the sound is replaced with classical music while the picture shows members milling about aimlessly. The subject of the vote is superimposed on the scene, but the words are rarely helpful: if a viewer has not been watching every minute, it does not help much to know that the vote is on the Smith substitute to the Brown amendment to HR 10061.

In the Senate the voting takes much, much longer—sometimes hours while a quorum call drones on. Veterans of the legislative process know that the quorum calls are the legislative equivalents of timeouts, allowing leaders to work out the program or to work out compromises. But so what? To the C-SPAN viewer, it is pointless and boring—and that then shapes viewers' images of the institution.

Reforming special orders (under which speeches are given after the formal business on the floor has concluded), including stopping the camera's panning of the empty chamber, was one salutary step recently taken by the House. So, too, was the decision to try Oxford-style debates, which are independent of the formal consideration of legislation on the floor. With a few modest alterations in format to emphasize ideas and deemphasize boisterous conflict, they will become institutionalized and mark the House as a place for serious and intelligent debate on the big issues facing society. In addition, the House should work with educational and civic associations to distribute cassettes of the debates to schools and civic groups, along with supporting written materials, to spur discussion throughout the country. The Senate should also institute Oxford-style debates, unless it wants to yield the title of the world's greatest deliberative body to the House. Additional steps to take include the following.

—Transform general debate. Oxford-style debates would likely occur every three or four weeks, at least in the House. General debate on the specific direction and content of bills would occur much more regularly. Leaders in both parties need to put their heads together to make general debate matter for viewers and visitors. Restructuring general debate on legislation to make it more like traditional debate—opening statements by proponents and opponents, followed by brief rebuttals and some give-and-take—can be done without any changes in House rules if floor managers yield time in appropriate ways. Doing so would set the stage in a much better way for the ensuing debate on amendments in the Committee of the Whole.

—Let C-SPAN set up camera positions just off the House and Senate floors. With a table and an interviewer available near the chamber, C-SPAN could change the way it handles showing votes. Instead of classical music, viewers would hear members of both parties explaining what was going on and why. Instead of staring at members milling about or a clerk droning on calling the Senate roll, they would listen to lawmakers who are engaged in legislative combat or partisan maneuvering explain their strategies and approaches in the very midst of battle. Leaders have been fearful that doing this would mean giving free airtime to the extremists in both parties, encouraging bloody conflict and giving the public an unbalanced view of Congress. But that would not be C-SPAN's approach. If party leaders are unavailable because they are in the midst of negotiations, surely smart and articulate rank-and-file members could be recruited to serve in much the same way they do on C-SPAN call-in shows.

—Have the leaders do a joint weekly call-in show on C-SPAN. At the end of each week the Speaker and minority leader should do a joint call-in show to explain what has been done that week and to look ahead to the next week. The same, of course, should be done by Senate majority and minority leaders. The more party leaders can explain to audiences what has occurred and what to look for next, the better. C-SPAN viewers will be much better informed as they watch floor debates if they have the perspectives of the leaders to add to the picture.

Now consider the visitors. The Capitol is first and foremost a working institution. But it is also one of the most popular tourist attractions in the country. Millions of people get their first-hand impressions of the national legislature when they visit. But Congress does almost nothing to inform visitors about what it does, how it does it, and why. Here are suggestions for improving communication.

—Create a visitors center. The model Congress should follow is Colonial Williamsburg, a public institution that tries to orient visitors when they arrive as to its history, dynamics, and meaning. Of course, Congress must be able to get its work done, but as the working illustration of representative democracy, it has a responsibility to itself and to that public to provide not just access but appropriate information. A visitors center in the Capitol (the space exists and could easily be adapted) is a compelling possibility, but press commentary on the idea as another congressional perk (a notion encouraged by the demagoguery of some of the lawmakers themselves) and members' timidity have served so far to bury it. Congress should ignore the skeptics and appropriate the necessary funds (probably about $30 million,) or find a private sector donor, just as Colonial Williamsburg relied on the Rockefeller family.

—Implement a second Capitol tour, one explaining the legislative process. The tour of the Capitol is a staple for visitors. It is an excellent guide to the history, art, and architecture of the building, but tells visitors little about Congress. But the Capitol could inexpensively and easily create a second tour that would focus on what Congress is supposed to do, what it does, and how it does it. The tour could include a capsule constitutional history on what is behind Article I and a brief explanation of the legislative process. The tour could be created in conjunction with the U.S. Capitol Historical Society. It could and should mesh with a short film on how Congress works. The film could be newly produced or adapted from material that already exists. The excellent documentary, *HR 6161*, or one or more of the twenty-six programs in *Congress: We the People*, the series created in the mid-1980s by WETA-TV and the American Political Science Association, could easily be adapted without waiting for creation of a visitors center or a new film.

—Create user-friendly visitor materials on Congress. Visitors to the Capitol can buy good books on the building at the store opposite EF-100 run by the Capitol Historical Society. They can find a detailed pamphlet on how a bill becomes a law in their representatives' offices. But they cannot easily find lively and readable guides to the legislative process, especially at a level children can understand. It should be easy to commission a readable book about what Congress does and to create a pamphlet about the legislative process that will inform and entertain visitors and that they can take home with them. These introductory guides could be supplemented with a daily listing and explanation of the schedule of activities in committee and on the floor in the House and Senate.

—Change the gallery. When visitors enter the House or Senate galleries for their brief stays, they are given brochures that tell them little about what they are seeing other than explaining why many members are not on the floor at any given moment. They are told not to read and not to talk. Shuffled in and out with no sense of who is talking or about what, they cannot be learning much. Both chambers need to think through ways to make the experience more valuable. It should not be difficult to produce for visitors a page on what is being considered on the floor the day they are there. Even better, why not provide earphones in the seats, with either continuous commentary on who is speaking and about what, or with a taped explanation of what is going on? And why not give gallery visitors a more extensive pamphlet on the floor itself, and let them read it as they watch? A visit to the gallery should be an enlightening and upbeat experience, not an intimidating and confusing one.

For Congress to undertake these actions is not manipulative self-promotion; it is a public service to give civics-starved citizens who now get a distorted view of Congress an informed understanding of the principles and dynamics of their governmental system. Familiarity with Congress may never bring widespread enthusiasm, but it should breed at least understanding, not contempt.

Note

1. Elizabeth Theiss-Morse and John R. Hibbing, "Familiarity Breeds Contempt: Education, Political Knowledge, and Disapproval of Congress," paper prepared for the 1994 annual meeting of the Midwest Political Science Association.

2 Popular Support for Congress and Its Members

Herb Asher
Mike Barr

POPULAR SUPPORT for Congress as an institution and for the members themselves has often varied in response to presidential popularity, the state of the economy, congressional deeds and misdeeds, and other factors. But although Congress has endured significant public disapproval in years past, the 1990s have witnessed massive hostility toward the institution and surprisingly high levels of hostility toward the members. Reports about the abuse of House bank and House post office privileges, excessive congressional perks, skyrocketing campaign costs and the influence of PACs, and pre-1993 gridlock between Congress and the president have all fueled the anger expressed in public opinion polls.

This anger has been reflected in election outcomes and members' career decisions. In 1990, for example, the reelection margin of both Democratic and Republican incumbents decreased. In 1992 a post–World War II record nineteen House incumbents were defeated in primaries, and a record sixty-six voluntarily retired, undoubtedly for reasons including popular hostility toward Congress, the effects of redistricting, and the financial incentives for senior members to retire.[1] The widespread appeal and success of the movement to limit terms reflected voter antipathy toward legislators and legislatures at the national and state levels.

In this chapter we examine trends in popular support for Congress and its members. In particular, we investigate whether the current disdain for Congress is simply one of the periodic downturns in support for the institution or whether it constitutes a phenomenon fundamentally differ-

The data used in this analysis were made available (in part) by the Inter-University Consortium for Political and Social Research. The data for the American National Election Studies were originally collected by the Center for Political Studies of the Institute for Social Research at the University of Michigan. Neither the collector of the original data nor the consortium bear any responsibility for the analyses or interpretations presented here.

ent. To address this question, we examine patterns of support for Congress, focusing on whether the correlates of congressional approval and disapproval have remained stable. We also investigate evaluations of individual members. For many years scholars have noted that Americans love their congressmen but hate Congress. Indeed, many incumbents have successfully sought reelection by running against Congress. Has the low regard toward the institution spilled over into anger at the members themselves?

Support for Congress is an intrinsically interesting topic of political discussion that has received extensive news coverage and been a prominent topic of discussion among political elites. But there are more fundamental reasons for studying popular evaluations of Congress. Democratic institutions that lose popular support, many people believe, ultimately lose their viability as governing institutions. Their decisions may lose their legitimacy in the eyes of the public, and the stability of the political system itself may be at risk. Thus views of congressional performance become an indicator of how well the entire system is functioning.

Some observers argue that linking adverse views of congressional performance with political instability is too alarmist. Even as citizens dislike the members of Congress, they are not challenging the legitimacy of the institutions of representative government. Elizabeth Theiss-Morse and John R. Hibbing distinguished between the citizen's own member of Congress, the collection of legislators who comprise Congress, and the institution itself. Americans express antipathy toward the current members of Congress as a group, they concluded, but are highly supportive of the institution. The current unpopularity of Congress may thus not pose a serious threat to the viability of the institution.[2]

We believe this optimism is not fully warranted. First, it is not clear what citizens have in mind when they say they support the institution of Congress. Respondents are first asked, "How would you rate the current members of Congress?" They are then asked, "How would you rate the U.S. Congress as an institution?" Respondents are also asked questions about their approval or disapproval (the responses ranging from "strongly approve" to "strongly disapprove"): "What about the U.S. Congress, no matter who is in office?" and "What about the 535 members of Congress?"

The ordering of the first pair of questions cues the respondent to think of Congress apart from its members. The first item in the second pair of questions also cues citizens to think of Congress as different from its incumbents. It is therefore not surprising that Theiss-Morse and Hibbing find a sharp public differentiation between the institution and its incumbents. More important, one can reasonably speculate that if the members are discredited, their deliberations and decisions will readily come under attack by critics. When citizens, commentators, talk show hosts, and others routinely refer to the members as crooks and scoundrels, how legitimate and authoritative will congressional decisions on controversial issues be? At some point one must ask whether widespread disdain affects congressional performance, which could eventually undermine the effectiveness of Congress as an instrument of democratic governance.

Trends in Support

Three generalizations are apparent in support for Congress and its members. First, support for the members of Congress is consistently higher (50 to 75 percent approval) than is support for the institution itself (25 to 35 percent approval).[3]

Second, levels of support vary in response to short-term forces, including domestic and international events. For example, support for Congress as measured in CBS/*New York Times* polls reached a recent peak in January 1991 when 49 percent of respondents approved of Congress's performance and only 41 percent disapproved. This relatively high level of approval reflected the congressional debate on policy toward Iraq and the authorization to go to war if necessary.[4] Similarly, a Gallup poll conducted in August 1974 showed 48 percent of Americans approving the performance of Congress and only 35 percent disapproving. This poll was conducted when President Nixon resigned and many observers were asserting that our constitutional system had worked well during the Watergate crisis. Yet Gallup polls conducted four months before and six months after August 1974 showed only 30 and 32 percent, respectively, of Americans approving congressional performance.[5] Throughout the first half of 1992, support for Congress plummeted to less than 20 percent in reaction to scandals and perceptions of gridlock and unresponsiveness in government. In 1977 Glenn Parker estimated a general model of fluctuations in congressional popularity and found that increases in unpopularity were associated with deteriorating economic conditions, the absence of international crises, and the nature of the presidential administration.[6]

Third, support for the institution and for the members also covaries. We will say more about the question of causality between individual and institutional evaluations later.

Figure 3-3 in chapter 3 shows these three empirical generalizations from 1974 through 1992. As support for Congress dropped markedly in 1992, so did public approval of the members themselves. This suggests some limitation in the public's ability to keep judgments of the members separate from judgments of the institution. Extensive constituency casework, the skillful use of congressional perquisites, and running for reelection against Congress apparently go only so far in immunizing a member from harsh opinions about the institution.

Evaluations of Congress

As interesting as these trend lines are, it is important to ascertain whether they are similar across subgroups of Americans. One could certainly expect partisan differences in the evaluations of Congress and its members, depending on whether the partisanship of the respondent is congruent with which party controls Congress and which holds the congressional seat. There might also be demographic differences accompanying evaluations, depending on how Congress has treated issues of particular relevance for different age or racial groups and on how they perceive their stake in the political system. Of particular interest is how Americans' levels of education, political interest, and political information relate to their evaluations. If more educated and politically attentive citizens are more hostile, this would present a worrisome situation for long-term institutional support and viability.

We use two sources of information to trace correlates of congressional support over time. The first is the results of Gallup polls published in the *Gallup Poll Monthly*. These data have a number of advantages, including the relatively long time over which the polls have been conducted and the presentation of results in terms of various social subsets of Americans. Moreover, the Gallup polls are not all conducted immediately before or after a national election. One disadvantage of the published Gallup information, however, is that not all the relevant breakdowns of the sample are available.

The second source of information is the American National Election Studies surveys, which enable the investigator to perform more detailed analyses controlling for more variables than is permitted by the Gallup data. The ANES data also allow more in-depth analyses of evaluations of Congress and its members. One limitation of these data is that the surveys are conducted close to elections, when approval ratings of Congress and its members may be lower because of attacks on the institution by candidates, including incumbents. As we examine the relationships between various independent variables and support for Congress, the reader should keep in mind that patterns that hold in the bivariate situation may wash out when multivariate cases are considered.

The Gallup polls and the ANES data both permit examination of how educational attainment, political party loyalties, gender, and race affect responses. The patterns in both sources are similar, although some differences arise, particularly in the absolute levels of approval and disapproval of Congress. The differences may simply be the result of the surveys having been taken at different times.

In examining the relationship between education and evaluations of Congress, two points are important. There are small and inconsistent differences between Americans of high educational attainment and those of lesser attainment in assigning Congress a positive rating. However, highly educated Americans are more likely to express disapproval of congressional performance than their less educated counterparts. The real difference is that the less educated are more likely to offer no opinion; highly educated Americans are more likely to offer evaluations and more of these evaluations are unfavorable.

Figure 2-1 shows the positive and negative evaluations of Congress by Gallup poll respondents with various levels of education. For college-educated Americans the preponderance of negative ratings is particularly pronounced. Similar results are obtained using the ANES data. Because educational attainment and party identification are related—Republicans have somewhat higher levels of education overall—one would expect that more highly educated Americans who are relatively more Republican would indeed be somewhat more hostile to Congress, which throughout most of this period was controlled by the Democrats.

A brief methodological aside is in order. In popular discourse, including news coverage of the results of public opinion polls on support for political institutions, the typical story focuses on the percentage of Americans who approve of a particular institution. But the percentage approving may not tell the whole story, particularly because subsets of respondents may vary markedly in whether they offer an evaluation of the institution or simply provide a "don't know" or "no opinion" response. Space constraints do not permit analysis of other relationships that are as detailed as those provided for level of education, but we do present the information that best captures the underlying trends and relationships.

Figure 2-2 shows the difference between positive and negative ratings of Congress according to respondents' political party preferences. As one

Figure 2-1. Approval and Disapproval of Congress, by Poll Respondent Level of Education, 1974–91

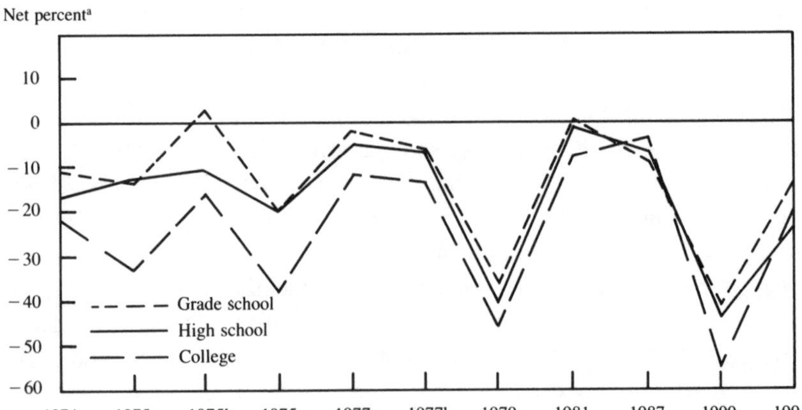

Sources: *Gallup Opinion Index*, no. 107 (May 1974), p. 10; no. 122 (August 1975), p. 13; no. 136 (October 1977), p. 5; and no. 144 (July 1979), p. 5. *Gallup Report*, no. 189 (June 1981), p. 15; and no. 264 (September 1987), p. 28. *Gallup Poll Monthly*, no. 301 (October 1990), p. 36; and no. 311 (August 1991), p. 46.

a. Percent approving minus percent disapproving.

Figure 2-2. Approval and Disapproval of Congress, by Poll Respondent Party Identification, 1974–91

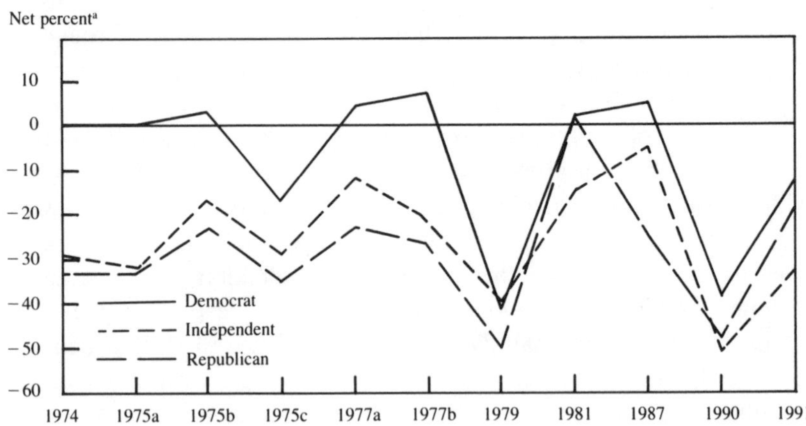

Sources: See figure 2-1.

a. Percent approving minus percent disapproving.

Figure 2-3. Approval and Disapproval of Congress, by Sum of Poll Respondent Campaign and Voting Activities, Election Years 1978–92

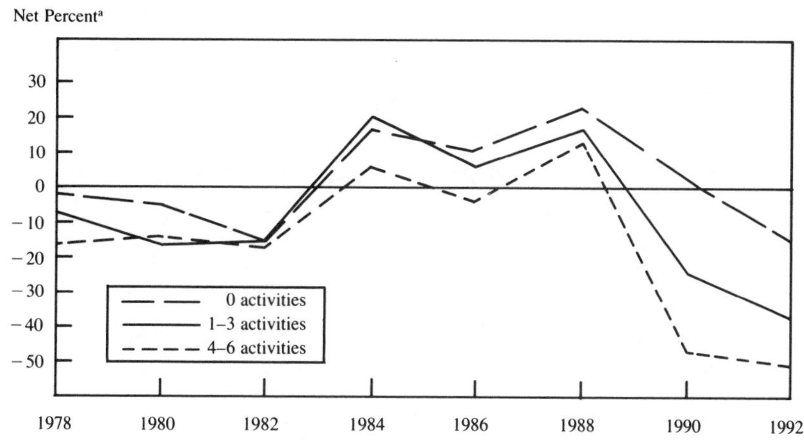

Source: *American National Election Study: Pre- and Post Election Surveys* (Ann Arbor, Mich.: Inter-University Consortium for Political and Social Research, biennial for election years).

a. Percent approving minus percent disapproving.

would expect, in years in which Democrats controlled both the House and the Senate, Americans who called themselves Democrats were more favorable to the institution. But even among Democrats, there were only a few instances in which more people expressed approval than expressed disapproval of Congress's performance, and only by a slight margin. Some years they expressed overwhelming disapproval of the Democratic Congress. In 1981, when control of Congress was split, slightly more Democrats and Republicans approved of it than disapproved; a substantial plurality of independents disapproved. The main point, however, is that for Democrats, Republicans, and independents, hostility was the typical reaction. Similar patterns emerge in the ANES data, although overall levels of support are higher, perhaps because of the different years in which the polls were conducted.

Men and whites were more hostile toward Congress than were women and blacks, but the evaluations from all groups were usually negative. There were no consistent differences of gender or race in support of Congress. The greater frequency of negative responses by men and whites simply reflects the fact that more respondents among these groups expressed an opinion and more opinions were unfavorable. As was the case with educational attainment, the greater the proportion of respondents offering a rating, the higher the proportion of those ratings that are negative. The ANES data yield similar results with respect to

Figure 2-4. Approval and Disapproval of Congress, by Poll Respondent Frequency of Following Government and Public Affairs, Election Years 1978–92

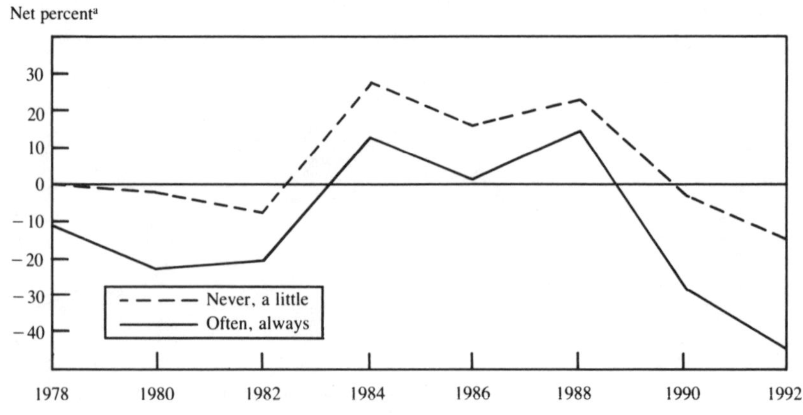

Source: See figure 2-3.
a. Percent approving minus percent disapproving.

gender, although the racial differences are weaker than those in the Gallup surveys.

The ANES data enable examination of the evaluations of Congress in light of citizens' level of political activity, information, and attentiveness. Here the news for Congress is very discouraging. Although overall ratings were low, they were even lower among the more politically active and attentive citizenry. Those involved in more campaign activities were markedly more likely to disapprove than were those who engaged in no campaign activities (figure 2-3). Citizens who paid a lot of attention to politics were more hostile than were their less attentive compatriots (figure 2-4). And those who were knowledgeable about control of the House were much more critical of Congress than were less informed respondents (figure 2-5). And the gap between the more politically involved and the less involved widened in the 1990 and 1992 surveys, certainly not good news for Congress.

Evaluations of Incumbents

More complex patterns emerge when evaluations of individual members as opposed to the institution are considered. The ANES data contain two measures of attitudes toward the incumbent House member—a thermometer rating and a standard approval-disapproval item. We examine both, controlling for a similar set of variables.

Figure 2-5. Approval and Disapproval of Congress, by Poll Respondent Knowledge of Party Control of the House, Election Years 1978–92

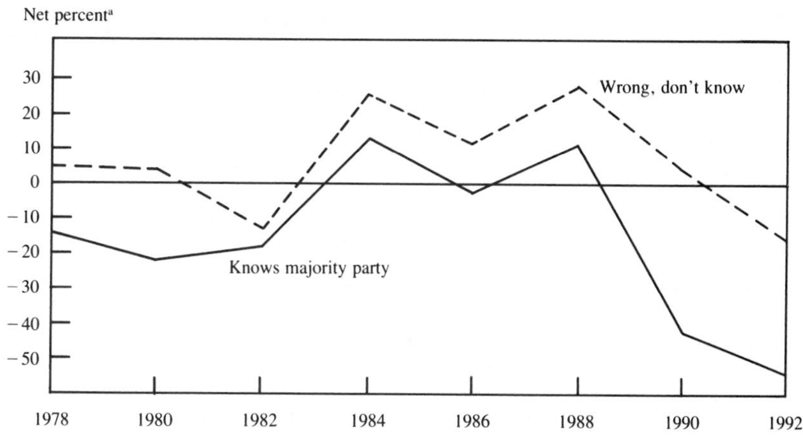

Source: See figure 2-3.
a. Percent approving minus percent disapproving.

More politically involved citizens tended to be more supportive of the individual member, even though these respondents were more hostile toward Congress as an institution. Figures 2-6, 2-7, and 2-8 show the net (approval minus disapproval) ratings of incumbents, considering respondent political activity, attentiveness to politics, and knowledge of which party controlled Congress. Although the differences are not striking, people who performed at least one campaign activity rated incumbents 20 percent more positively than people who engaged in no campaign activities (figure 2-6). Those who followed politics more regularly were more supportive of the incumbent than those who were uninterested (figure 2-7). With respect to knowledge of the majority party in the House, the differences are less pronounced (figure 2-8). But even here, in all years except 1992 those respondents who could name the majority party were more supportive of their incumbents than they were for Congress itself (figure 2-5). People who could not name the majority party were more supportive of Congress throughout the entire period.

The average thermometer ratings given to incumbents by different subgroups yield similar results. More politically attentive citizens and citizens who were more active in politics rated the incumbent more favorably than did less activist respondents. There were, however, no differences in assessments of the incumbent by whether respondents knew which party was in the majority.

Figure 2-6. Approval and Disapproval of House Incumbents, by Poll Respondent Campaign and Voting Activities, Election Years 1978–92

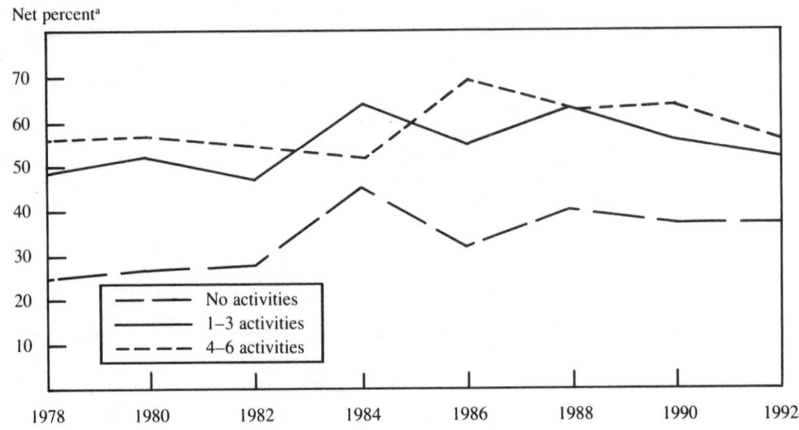

Source: See figure 2-3.
a. Percent approving minus percent disapproving.

Figure 2-7. Approval and Disapproval of House Incumbents, by Poll Respondent Frequency of Following Government and Public Affairs, Election Years 1978–92

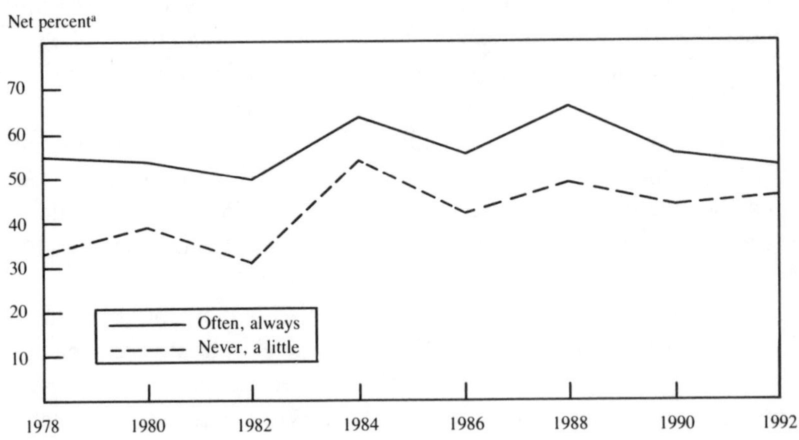

Source: See figure 2-3.
a. Percent approving minus percent disapproving.

Figure 2-8. Approval and Disapproval of House Incumbents, by Poll Respondent Knowledge of Party Control of the House, Election Years 1978–92

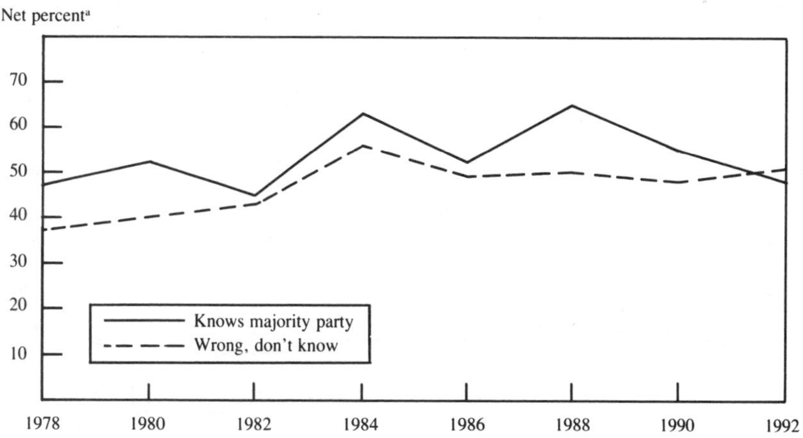

Source: See figure 2-3.
a. Percent approving minus percent disapproving.

Few systematic differences in incumbent evaluations were found when controlling for respondent background and demographic variables. Democratic and Republican evaluations of incumbents were very similar and very positive, with independents slightly less approving (though still strongly so). Differences in gender, race, and education of respondents had little effect and were inconsistent. The only consistent difference was a tendency for women to evaluate incumbents slightly more favorably than men did in both the thermometer scores and the difference in percent approval or disapproval.

Thus politically involved citizens are more supportive of incumbent members of Congress and less supportive of Congress itself. From the perspective of the representative seeking reelection, this is good news because the more politically involved citizens are more likely to be informed, participate in campaigns, and vote. But from an institutional perspective, the pattern is disturbing because strongest support comes from citizens who are less politically aware and involved.

The explanation for this pattern may be very simple. The more involved citizens are more knowledgeable about Congress and its members. And attitudes toward incumbents, particularly one's own representative, are much more likely to be favorable than are attitudes toward Congress as an institution. A great deal of research has examined why people evaluate Congress and its members as they do. Two decades ago, Richard Fenno pointed out that Americans apply different standards in their

Figure 2-9. Poll Respondents' Positive and Negative Comments about House Incumbents and Challengers, Election Years 1978–92

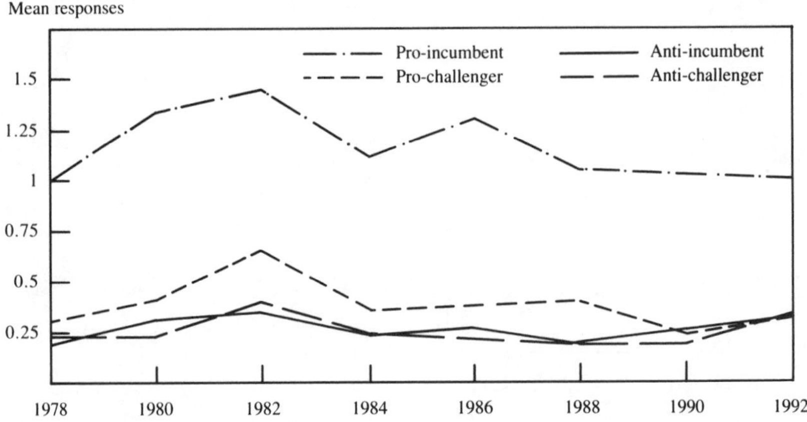

Source: American National Election Studies, 1978 and 1992; and the Cumulative ANES data set, 1952–90.

assessments of legislators and the institution. Evaluations of Congress are often based on the institution's ability to solve national problems; members are assessed more for their personal style and policy views.[7]

Glenn Parker and Roger Davidson have contended that Congress is increasingly judged unfavorably on its performance in domestic policy, how well it gets along with the president, and how well the legislative process is functioning.[8] Members are assessed more in terms of their work for constituents and their district as well as their personal styles. Timothy Cook has argued that support for Congress is related to support for national leaders and institutions, while the members themselves are seen more as state politicians whose popularity depends largely on their local activities.[9] The paradox arises because members are elected locally but serve nationally. To the extent that citizens know more about the local activities of their representatives, the members are better off. Indeed, running against the institution and against Washington makes a lot of sense given this local-national distinction.

Even though Cook wrote before 1980, his work may have even more relevance today. Between 1972 and 1992 the public's trust and confidence in national, state, and local government deteriorated, but the slide was steepest for the federal government (from 74 percent public confidence to 42 percent), less so for state government (67 percent to 51 percent), and least for local government (64 to 60 percent).[10] Thus members of Congress may have even more incentive to portray themselves as local politicians, as Washington outsiders, and as staunch critics of Congress.

Figure 2-10. Poll Respondents Reporting Contact with the House Incumbent and Challenger, Election Years 1978–92[a]

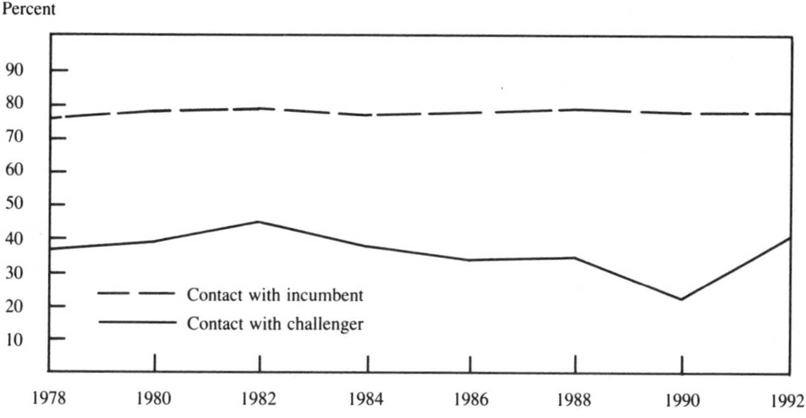

Source: See figure 2-3.
a. Challenger is the major party opponent.

Americans' responses to questions about their attitudes toward their representatives and candidates for Congress provide another perspective on popular support for incumbents. Figure 2-9 shows the average number of positive and negative comments offered by respondents about incumbents and challengers between 1978 and 1992. Americans are much more likely to make positive comments about the incumbent than about the challenger, even when there is little difference in the frequency of negative comments about each. The number of positive comments about incumbents has been gradually decreasing. This is especially noteworthy because until 1986, ANES coded up to a maximum of four comments and in 1988 and 1990 and 1992 increased that to five.

Figure 2-10 shows the percentage of Americans who reported having any of seven types of contact with the incumbent and the challenger from 1978 to 1992. Figure 2-11 shows the average number of contacts that citizens had with incumbents and challengers. As expected, contact with incumbents was far more common than with challengers. The percentage of Americans reporting any contact with the incumbent or challenger has remained very stable, averaging about 80 percent and 35 percent, respectively. The mean numbers of contacts with incumbents and challengers has also remained stable, but there was a slight upturn in contacts with challengers in 1992. These patterns reflect an interesting irony of contemporary congressional elections. Fewer and fewer seats remain uncontested, but in many contested districts the quality of the challenger's campaign is poor.

Table 2-1. Respondents Having Contact with Incumbents and Challengers, by Type of Contact, Election Years, 1978–92[a]

Percent

Year	*Any contact*	*Personal contact*	*Attend meeting*	*Met with staff*	*Received mail*	*Read about in paper*	*Heard on radio*	*Saw on TV*	*Through friends*
1978									
Incumbent	76	14	12	8	52	52	27	43	27
Challenger	37	3	2	2	13	23	11	20	6
1980									
Incumbent	78	12	10	8	52	48	24	44	26
Challenger	39	3	2	1	13	22	11	21	7
1982									
Incumbent	79	14	11	8	56	53	30	52	27
Challenger	45	7	4	3	19	29	15	29	10
1984									
Incumbent	77	15	13	11	62	57	26	49	26
Challenger	38	4	3	3	20	31	13	25	8
1986									
Incumbent	78	13	11	10	56	50	26	51	26
Challenger	34	3	2	1	12	21	8	19	7
1988									
Incumbent	79	12	10	7	57	51	23	47	22
Challenger	35	3	1	1	11	21	9	16	6
1990									
Incumbent	78	12	12	8	50	48	26	48	23
Challenger	23	1	2	1	7	13	6	13	4
1992									
Incumbent	67	10	7	6	37	39	19	43	17
Challenger	67	9	7	5	36	39	19	42	17

Source: American National Election Study: *Pre- and Post Election Surveys* (Ann Arbor, Mich.: Inter-University Consortium for Political and Social Research, biennial for election years).

a. Cell entries are percentage of respondents who reported each form of contact with the incumbent and challenger.

Figure 2-11. Poll Respondents' Contacts with Running House Incumbent and Major Party Challenger, Election Years 1978–92[a]

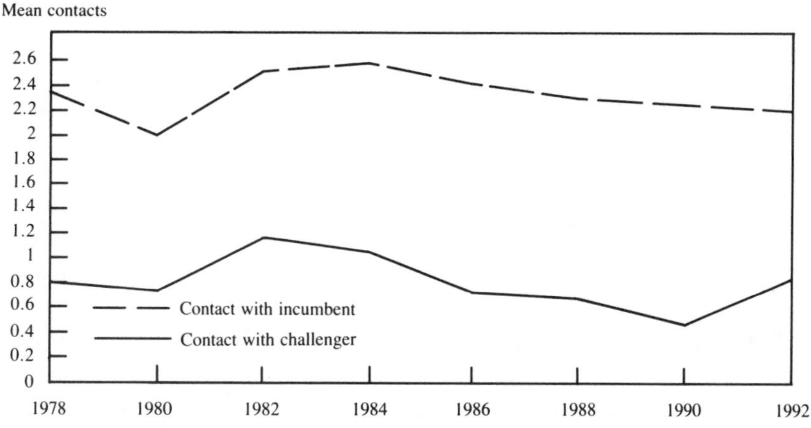

Source: See figure 2-3.
a. Maximum number of contacts is eight.

Table 2-1 shows the detailed information that underlies figures 2-10 and 2-11. Receipt of mail was the most common kind of contact with incumbents and the one for which the incumbent's advantage over the challenger was greatest. Television, newspaper, and radio were the next most common forms of contact, and again incumbents enjoyed a substantial advantage. This undoubtedly reflected the larger amounts of campaign funds available to incumbents and their stronger ability to garner free media coverage. One noteworthy pattern in table 2-1 is the decrease in media-based contacts with challengers between 1984 and 1990, a trend that was reversed in 1992. Certainly a typical challenger faces considerable difficulty in an election contest with an incumbent, although 1992 data suggest a stronger, more visible set of challengers has arisen. Perhaps the effects of redistricting and people's perceptions of greater incumbent vulnerability helped attract a stronger set of challengers in 1992.

In addition to evaluations of incumbents that respondents to polls make is the judgment that voters render on election day. Table 2-2 shows the average election margins (percentage of the vote for the incumbent minus the percentage for the major challenger) for three subsets of members of Congress. The results of the past three elections should probably cause some worry for incumbents. From 1976 to 1986 it was typical that if the average margin of one party's incumbents increased, the average margin of the other party's would decrease. But in 1990 the margins

Table 2-2. Average Incumbent Margin in Contested House Seats, 1976–92[a]

Subset	*1976*	*1978*	*1980*	*1982*	*1984*	*1986*	*1988*	*1990*	*1992*
Republicans	26.2	31.5	36.8	20.4	37.1	31.9	35.0	24.5	25.4
Northern Democrats	33.5	30.8	27.8	36.0	30.9	41.1	39.0	31.7	28.1
Southern Democrats	33.8	35.9	30.8	39.4	19.8	38.1	30.7	29.1	24.5

Source: Authors' calculations.

a. Average percentage difference between the share of the vote received by the incumbent and the share of the vote received by the major party challenger. House elections from Louisiana are omitted from the analysis.

of northern Democrats, southern Democrats, and Republicans all shrank. And while the margins for Republican incumbents remained practically stable between 1990 and 1992, the margins for Democrats again decreased.

Obviously, these are crude patterns, and much more analysis needs to be done, particularly a comparison of the identical set of incumbents over time. Likewise, many incumbents did not seek reelection in 1992. Nevertheless, the decreases in margins suggest a greater potential for attitudes toward incumbents to be influenced by attitudes toward Congress itself as well as by Americans' general dissatisfaction with the performance of their political system. Simply counting the number of incumbents who are defeated tells only part of the story. Shrinking margins, even if they do not result in defeats, may create a group of insecure incumbents. The consequences of this insecurity for public policy may be destructive to the political system, including Congress itself.

Multivariate Models of Evaluation

So far, we have examined how a set of independent variables is related to assessments of Congress and its members; most of the analyses examined bivariate relationships. Now we turn to multivariate models of support for Congress and for individual representatives.

Before examining the multivariate models, we must comment on the relationship between attitudes toward incumbents and Congress. After all, the stronger this relationship, the more the fortunes of Congress and its members would appear inextricably linked. And the weaker this link, the greater the protection the individual member has from hostile attitudes toward Congress. Certainly one might expect that attitudes toward Congress will spill over into opinions about its members. Likewise, people who like their incumbents might be expected to be more favorable to the institution itself.

Richard Born constructed a reciprocal (nonrecursive) model in which incumbent and institutional evaluations were treated as influencing one another. He estimated this model for each congressional election between 1978 and 1986 and found that in all years, attitudes toward Congress affected citizens' views about their individual House members, but only in 1980 did attitudes toward individual House members influence more general attitudes toward Congress. (He also examined senators, but still found that in three of the five elections he studied, the views did not affect institutional ratings). He concluded that a one-way causation was at work: attitudes toward the institution influenced those toward individual members.[11]

In examining the factors that affected the relationship between evaluations of the institution and the individuals, Born found that the assessments were more closely linked for people with less education. Thus although the fate of members of Congress was linked more than expected to the reputation of the institution, the fact that this link was more prominent for less well educated citizens raised normative questions about the prospects for accountability.

We conducted additional analyses of the relationship between attitudes toward individuals and Congress, controlling for the background and demographic variables on which we had previously focused. Although we will not report the full array of results, a few summary comments are in order. First, the correlations between member and institutional ratings are small—in the range of .1 to .2—but statistically significant. Second, with very few exceptions, the correlation coefficients for all years are positive: Congress and the incumbent are rated in the same direction. Third, controlling for other variables does not generate consistent differences in most instances. For example, in some years the correlation between assements of the institution and the incumbents is higher for college-educated Americans; in other years the correlation is higher for those with only a grade school education. Attitudes toward Congress and the individual representative are thus positively correlated, but the relationship is weak, although often statistically significant.

In constructing our multivariate models we relied on the work of various scholars and on our own ideas.[12] The scholars have established the importance of contact with the legislator, political knowledge and awareness, political efficacy, and other factors. Our strategy entailed the construction of different explanatory equations for incumbent and institutional evaluations and the estimation of these two equations for each election year between 1978 and 1992. For both equations, we included political attentiveness, campaign activity, ability to name the House majority, education, race, and gender. We also added age to both equations to see whether experience with the political system affected attitudes.

In the equation for Congress, we included party identification, the obvious hypothesis being that supporters of the political party that controlled Congress would have more favorable attitudes toward the institution. For the incumbent equation, however, we constructed a citizen-representative partisan congruence measure. We expected that respondents who were of the same party as the incumbent would be more supportive of him or her. In the Congress equation we also included measures of the broader political and economic environment within which Congress performs. These included a measure of trust in government (the obvious hypothesis being that more trusting citizens would be more supportive of Congress), two measures of citizens' financial situations (the hypothesis being that people who are more confident about their current and future economic position would have more positive attitudes about Congress), perceptions of national economic conditions, and a presidential popularity measure (even though some other studies have shown that this variable washes out when other factors are controlled). In the incumbent equation we included two variables indicating the respondent's contact with the incumbent and the challenger, the hypothesis being that the greater the contact with the incumbent, the more positive citizens would be toward him or her. The results are presented in appendix tables 2A-1, 2A-2, and 2A-3.

Attitudes toward Congress are measured by the standard approval or disapproval question. Assessments of the representative are measured in two ways, the standard question and a thermometer rating. Because responses to the approval or disapproval questions are dichotomous and because the distribution of these responses tends to be highly skewed, we employed logistic regression to assess the impact of the independent variables on approval ratings. But in the analysis of the determinants of incumbent thermometer ratings, we used ordinary regression procedures.

Table 2A-3 shows that consistently important variables (ones achieving statistical significance) in the explanation of attitudes toward congressional performance are trust in government and party identification, with approval of the president and age statistically significant in six of the eight years. Of the rest of the independent variables, only gender and following politics reach significance in at least four of the eight years.

People who trusted the government were more likely to view Congress favorably. Perhaps this indicates a more general confidence in the government and political institutions.

Older Americans were consistently less supportive of Congress. One wonders whether more extensive experience with the political system is associated with a less favorable evaluation of institutions. If so, this is certainly an indictment of their perceived performance. And when one adds that people who followed politics more regularly were also harsher evaluators of Congress, the standing of the institution among the American public drops lower. As expected, Democrats were more supportive of Congress, even though three of the surveys were conducted at a time of split party control of it. Finally, in all years, women were more supportive of Congress than men. This relationship achieved statistical significance in four of the elections in our data.

Table 2A-2 shows that the only variables consistently affecting incumbent ratings were the expected ones—citizens' political party congruence with the incumbent and contact with the incumbent and challenger. The other variables, including following politics, age, and gender, were not important in explaining approval of incumbents, even though they were relevant to approval of Congress. The greater the contact with the incumbent, the more likely he or she would be favorably evaluated. The greater the contact with the challenger, the more likely the incumbent would be unfavorably evaluated. One methodological point to keep in mind is that since most incumbents are rated positively, there is relatively little variance to account for in the first place.

Table 2A-3 also analyzes ratings of incumbents, but the dependent variable is the thermometer rating. The results are similar to those in table 2A-2, although a few more variables turn out to be significant in particular years, in part because the thermometer ratings generate greater variance. Party congruence and contact with incumbents and challengers were once again the most important predictors. Unlike their reactions toward Congress itself, the attitudes of older Americans were more favorable toward incumbents, the relationship being statistically significant in seven of the eight years. Measures of political activity and political interest were unimportant, but educational attainment and information did have an effect.

In all years the more educated citizens were more hostile to their incumbents; this relationship achieved statistical significance in five of the eight years (as opposed to only one of the eight years when the dependent variable was the dichotomous approval or disapproval rating).

Likewise, in all years people who knew which party controlled Congress were more hostile to incumbents than people who did not know, a statistically significant pattern in four of the eight years. That more educated and knowledgeable citizens were the ones more critical of their representatives is perhaps the only jarring note for incumbents concerned about electoral prospects.

Conclusion

One of the enduring patterns in American politics is the discrepancy between citizens' attitudes toward Congress and toward their own representatives. Despite the current disdain for Congress, individual representatives are still viewed very favorably by their constituents. What makes the continued popularity of the local incumbent even more noteworthy is that abundant polling data show Americans are not only hostile toward the institution of Congress but also the members themselves.

A recent review of contemporary and old public opinion data on Congress and its members showed much more negative contemporary opinion.[13] For example, 41 percent of Americans in 1990 agreed that "congressmen spend more time thinking of their own political futures than they do in passing wise legislation." Only 16 percent believed that way in 1937. In 1990 only 12 percent of Americans agreed that "congressmen pay a good deal of attention to people who elect them when deciding what to do in Congress"; 42 percent agreed in 1964. In 1989, 57 percent of Americans agreed that "most members of Congress make a lot of money by using public office improperly" and 76 percent agreed that "most members of Congress will tell lies if they feel the truth will hurt them politically."

These examples can be repeated many times, and yet Americans still seem to like their own members of Congress. These seeming contradictions can be easily resolved by noting that while most believe that members of Congress are seriously flawed, inept, and perhaps even corrupt, they believe that their own representatives are the exception and are indeed performing well and serving the district effectively. Thus members have not only done a good job separating judgments of themselves from judgments about the institution, but they have also been successful in separating themselves from their colleagues.

How much longer can incumbents keep up this protective barrier? The answer is unclear, depending on how scandals, the state of the economy, and other occurrences unfold. Americans are still some distance removed from a situation in which "throw the bums out" becomes translated into "throw my bum out." Nevertheless, incumbents should probably be nervous, particularly Democrats who will be called on to support an ambitious presidential agenda and may be facing angry voters in the 1994 midterm elections. But even Republicans must worry whether continuing perceptions of nonresponsiveness, gridlock, and a poorly performing economy might affect evaluations of all incumbents.

As to Congress as an institution, popular attitudes are solidly critical. And there is evidence that they are particularly so among Americans who are older and more likely to be attentive to politics and to vote. Attitudes toward Congress may also be part of broader attitudes toward American institutions and government, so that Congress may not be the master of its own fate when it comes to improving its ratings. Future evaluations will depend not only on how well it cleans up its own act but on how well the political system performs and on how opinion leaders portray it.

Finally, contemporary hostility toward Congress may be a qualitatively new phenomenon rather than simply another fluctuation in the ebb and flow of popular opinion. Although we cannot tell definitively (and indeed the answer will depend on unfolding events), there is ample evidence to argue that Congress must take its deteriorating reputation seriously. When the institution and its incumbents (except for one's own incumbent) are criticized so severely, when more politically attentive Americans are the most critical, when voters are approving the idea of term limits, when election margins seem to be shrinking, when news coverage of the institution is particularly brutal, and when citizens believe that Congress and its members are not performing with the interest of the country at heart, the time has come for the institution to engage in careful self-examination.

Certainly most of Congress's problems are of its own making. But responsibility for the problems and their solutions does not lie simply with the institution. The news media have been the sources of most of what Americans learn about Congress, and voters also bear some of the responsibility for current conditions. Congress bashing has become a media pastime. Indeed one might predict that a reformed Congress would still be the target of talk show hosts because it will never be a perfect institution. There will always be devastating anecdotes to tell about the foibles of the institution and the misdeeds of its members. Among the citizenry, cynicism toward institutions in general has become fashionable. This may be an appropriate response to what Americans have witnessed in recent years. But at some point one must wonder whether, perhaps because of frustration, they are simply responding to complex issues with a petulant trashing of individuals and institutions.

Still, the primary responsibility for improving the reputation of Congress rests with the members themselves. Unethical behavior, slow and confusing procedures, and poor legislative performance must be addressed successfully. The members must also think more creatively about how to present Congress to the public, and they must ask whether they themselves go too far in denigrating the institution to secure reelection and other political objectives. After all, if the members themselves are unwilling or unable to defend the institution, why should others take on the task? Journalists and other citizens also have contributions to make in the realms of accuracy, balance, and perspective. There is much at stake. A Congress discredited and disdained by the American people will lack the legitimacy and credibility to address the public policy challenges that confront the country.

Appendix A: Tables

Table 2A-1. Determinants of Approval of Congressional Job Performance, 1978–92[a]

Determinant	*1978[b]*	*1980*	*1982*	*1984*	*1986*	*1988*	*1990*	*1992*
Trust government to do right	.72* (2.05)	.62* (1.86)	.78* (2.19)	.81* (2.25)	.46* (1.58)	.85* (2.34)	.80* (2.23)	.94* (2.56)
Family economy past 12 months	.12* (1.13)	.01 (1.01)	−.09* (.92)	.06 (1.06)	.16* (1.17)	.03 (1.03)	0 (1.00)	.02 (1.02)
Family economy next 12 months	.08 (1.09)	.02 (1.02)	.04 (1.04)	.04 (1.04)	−.05 (.96)	−.07 (.94)	.11 (1.12)	.10 (1.11)
National economy past 12 months	.03[c] (1.03)	.06 (1.07)	.10 (1.11)	.03 (1.07)	.19* (1.21)	.12 (1.13)	.12 (1.13)	.07 (1.07)
Party identification	−.08* (.92)	−.08* (.92)	−.17* (.85)	−.13* (.88)	−.10* (.91)	−.20* (.82)	−.13* (.88)	−.18* (.84)
Approval of president	.15 (1.16)	.30* (1.35)	.41* (1.51)	.14* (1.15)	.16* (1.17)	.09 (1.10)	.28* (1.33)	.19* (1.21)
Follow politics	−.03 (.97)	−.14 (.87)	−.28* (.76)	−.22* (.80)	−.15 (.86)	−.17* (.84)	−.03 (.97)	−.28* (.75)
Age	−.01 (.99)	−.02* (.98)	−.01* (.99)	−.01* (.99)	−.01 (.99)	−.01* (.99)	−.01* (.99)	−.01* (.99)
Education	−.07* (.94)	−.04 (.96)	.03 (1.05)	−.05 (.95)	0 (1.00)	0 (1.00)	.05* (.95)	−.10* (.92)
Race (white)	−.08 (.92)	0 (1.00)	.04 (1.03)	.38* (1.46)	0 (1.00)	−.09 (.91)	−.27 (.76)	.08 (1.08)
Gender (men)	−.25 (.78)	−.31* (.74)	−.27* (.76)	−.37* (.69)	−.19 (.82)	−.43* (.65)	−.20 (.82)	−.07 (.93)
Political activities	−.02 (.98)	.02 (1.02)	.04 (1.04)	.05 (1.05)	−.09 (.91)	−.01 (.99)	−.10* (.91)	−.01 (.99)
Know House majority party	−.50* (.61)	−.19 (.82)	.06 (1.06)	−.16 (.85)	−.11 (.90)	−.19 (.83)	−.78* (.46)	−.41* (.66)
Intercept	−2.65	−.79	−2.65*	−.90	−1.06	−.72	−1.69*	−1.48*
Number	1,488	951	1,002	1,447	783	1,364	1,642	1,772
−2×LL	1,367	1,287	1,251	1,945	1,076	1,830	2,207	2,160
Improvement[d]	127*	117*	120*	149*	57*	152*	276*	260*

Source: See table 2-1.

* Significance is greater than .05 on a two-tailed test.

a. Numbers in parentheses indicate whether the odds of approving of congressional performance increase or decrease as the value of the independent variable increases. Numbers below 1.0 mean that the odds of approving decline when the value of the independent variable increases. Conversely, numbers greater than 1.0 indicate that the odds of approving of Congress's performance increase as the independent variable increases. Numbers close to 1.0 mean that a change in the independent variable does not affect the odds of approving or disapproving of congressional performance.

b. Except for 1978, the dependent variable is a measure of the approval of Congress's performance, where 1 = approve 0 = disapprove. In the 1978 survey the variable was recoded so that 1 = very good or good and 0 = fair, poor, or very poor.

c. Question referred to business conditions, not economic conditions.

d. Reflects the extent to which adding the independent variables to the equation improved the overall fit of the model.

Table 2A-2. Determinants of Approval of the Job Performance of House Incumbents, 1978–92[a]

Determinant	*1978[b]*	*1980*	*1982*	*1984*	*1986*	*1988*	*1990*	*1992*
Follow politics	.04 (1.05)	−.19 (.83)	.02 (1.02)	−.07 (.93)	0 (1.00)	−.10 (.91)	−.14 (.87)	−.16 (.85)
Know party in control	−.16 (.85)	.06 (1.06)	−.53 (.59)	.16 (1.18)	−.40 (.67)	−.17 (.85)	−.32 (.72)	−.47* (.62)
Same party as incumbent	.44* (1.56)	.58* (1.78)	1.09* (2.98)	.45* (1.56)	.71* (2.03)	.89* (2.45)	.51* (1.67)	.54* (1.71)
Age	.01* (1.01)	0 (1.00)	.01 (1.01)	.01 (1.01)	.01* (1.01)	0 (1.00)	.02* (1.02)	.01* (1.01)
Incumbent contacts	.44* (1.55)	.47* (1.60)	.35* (1.42)	.20* (1.22)	.31* (1.37)	.29* (1.34)	.23* (1.26)	.43* (1.52)
Challenger contacts	−.32 (.72)	−.44* (.64)	−.31* (.73)	−.27* (.76)	−.41* (.66)	−.21* (.81)	−.19* (.83)	−.56* (.57)
Race (white)	.27 (1.31)	.08 (1.08)	.29 (1.33)	.14 (1.15)	.44 (1.55)	.47 (1.60)	.05 (1.05)	−.44 (.64)
Gender (men)	−.23 (.80)	−.56* (.57)	.01 (1.01)	−.56* (.57)	−.34 (.71)	−.27 (.76)	−.32 (.73)	.34 (1.40)
Education	−.02 (.98)	−.05 (.96)	−.15* (.869)	−.06 (.94)	.01 (1.01)	0 (1.00)	0 (1.00)	0 (1.00)
Political activities	.12* (1.13)	−.13 (.88)	−.12 (.89)	−.21* (.81)	−.09 (.92)	−.16 (.86)	−.14 (.87)	.03 (1.03)
Intercept	−1.00*	2.55*	3.46*	2.94*	.92	2.38*	1.05	1.62*
Number	1,108	698	556	1,161	962	858	927	1,063
−2×LL	1,423	552	451	847	747	527	790	957
Improvement[c]	192*	83*	103*	73*	113*	66*	75*	154*

Source: See table 2-1.

* Significance is less than .05 on a two-tailed test.

a. Numbers in parentheses show how increases in the value of the independent variable affect the odds of approving of the incumbent's performance. Numbers below 1.0 mean that the odds of approving of incumbent performance decline when the value of the independent variable increases. Numbers greater than 1.0 indicate that the odds of approving of incumbent performance increase as the value of the independent variable increases. Numbers close to 1.0 mean that a change in the independent variable does not affect the odds of approving or disapproving of incumbent performance.

b. Except for 1978, the dependent variable is a measure of the approval of an incumbent's performance, where 1 = approve 0 = disapprove. In the 1978 survey the variable was recoded so that 1 = very good or good and 0 = fair, poor, or very poor.

c. Reflects the extent to which adding the independent variables to the equation improved the overall fit of the model.

Table 2A-3. Determinants of Approval of House Incumbents, Thermometer Ratings, 1978–92[a]

	1978	*1980*	*1982*	*1984*	*1986*	*1988*	*1990*	*1992*
Follow politics	.66 (.03)	.81 (.04)	.34 (.02)	.75 (.03)	.61 (.03)	.38 (.02)	.16 (.01)	−.78 (−.03)
Know party control	−4.97* (−.11)	−2.76 (−.06)	−3.15 (−.07)	−.71 (−.02)	−2.93* (−.06)	.95 (.02)	−2.18* (−.06)	−2.97* (−.07)
Same party as incumbent	3.30* (.14)	4.01* (.17)	6.15* (.26)	4.63* (.20)	4.80* (.19)	5.15* (.22)	4.70* (.19)	4.59* (.20)
Age	.08* (.07)	.16* (.14)	.06 (.05)	.14* (.12)	.15* (.12)	.10* (.08)	.11* (.09)	.18* (.15)
Incumbent contacts	4.67* (.43)	3.77* (.35)	3.99* (.37)	3.61* (.34)	4.16* (.38)	4.28* (.38)	3.96* (.35)	4.25* (.38)
Challenger contacts	−3.43* (−.21)	−2.78* (−.18)	−2.78* (−.21)	−2.18* (−.15)	−3.61* (−.21)	−2.88* (−.16)	−3.02* (−.15)	−4.84* (−.30)
Race (white)	−3.04 (−.04)	−4.70* (−.07)	−3.95 (−.06)	−1.05 (−.02)	−3.25* (−.05)	1.07 (.20)	−.90 (−.02)	−1.25 (−.02)
Gender (men)	−.90 (−.02)	−1.35 (−.03)	.15 (0)	−2.42* (−.06)	−1.85 (−.04)	−1.64 (−.04)	−1.25 (−.03)	−.41 (−.01)
Education	−.77* (−.10)	−.25 (−.04)	−1.05* (−.14)	−.45* (−.06)	−.54* (−.07)	−.56* (−.07)	−.68 (−.09)	.15 (.02)
Political activities	.31 (.02)	−.35 (−.02)	−.11 (−.01)	−.05 (0)	−.55 (−.03)	−.87 (−.05)	−.17 (−.01)	.80 (.05)
Constant	68.5*	58.2*	70.57*	53.53*	60.71*	57.61*	62.85*	47.78*
Minimum pairwise numbers	1,258	884	768	1,243	1,134	998	1,032	1,281
Adjusted R^2	.20	.18	.23	.17	.20	.19	.17	.23
SSE	19.64	19.23	19.42	19.69	20.23	19.36	20.43	18.85

Source: See table 2-1.

* Significance less than .05 on a two-tailed test.

a. Numbers not in parentheses are unstandardized regression coefficients. The numbers in parentheses are the standardized regression coefficients.

b. The dependent variable is a continuous measure of how warm or cold respondents feel about their respective incumbent in the House of Representatives. Ratings between 50 and 100 indicate warm or favorable feelings toward the incumbent; ratings from 0 to 50 indicate coolness or unfavorable feelings. A rating of 50 indicates the respondent has neither favorable nor unfavorable feelings about the incumbent.

Appendix B: Wording and Coding of Variables

The wording of questions and the response categories for the variables used in the analysis are shown below. The sources of the data are the American National Election Studies surveys conducted in midterm and presidential election years from 1978 to 1992.

Congressional approval, 1980–92. "Do you approve or disapprove of the way the U.S. Congress is handling its job?"

0. disapprove; 1. approve.

In the 1978 survey the question was "How would you rate the job that the U.S. Congress has been doing over the past two years—would you say Congress has been doing a very good job, good, fair, poor, or a very poor job?"

0. disapprove (fair, poor, and very poor); 1. approve (very good and good).

Incumbent approval, 1980–92. "In general, do you approve or disapprove of the way [running U.S. House incumbent] has been handling his/her job?"

0. disapprove; 1. approve.

In 1978 the question read "In general, how would you rate the job that your U.S. Representative has been doing—very good, good, fair, poor, or very poor?"

0. disapprove (fair, poor, and very poor); 1. approve (very good and good).

Following politics. "Some people seem to follow what's going on in government and public affairs most of the time, whether there's an election going on or not. Others aren't that interested. Would you say that you follow what's going on in government and public affairs most of the time, some of the time, only now and then, or hardly at all?"

1. hardly at all; 2. only now and then; 3. some of the time; 4. most of the time.

Know party majority. "Do you happen to know which party had the most members in the House of Representatives in Washington before the elections (this/last) month?"

0. don't know, or provided wrong answer; 1. correct answer.

Index of political activity. The sum of four campaign and two electoral activities. Respondents were asked if they had (1) attended a political rally or meeting, (2) worn a campaign button, (3) talked to people to get them to vote for a certain candidate, or (4) worked for a party or candidate. The other two items measured (5) whether the respondent was registered to vote, and (6) whether he or she did in fact vote in the recent election.

0. no campaign or electoral activities; 1. one activity . . . 6. all six activities.

Age. The actual age of the respondent was coded.

Education. The last grade or the number of years of school completed was coded.

Gender. 0. women; 1. men.

Race. 0. nonwhites; 1. whites.

Party identification. Variable summarizing the respondent's direction and strength of party identification.

−3. strong Democrat; −2. weak Democrat; −1. leaning Democrat; 0. independent; 1. leaning Republican; 2. weak Republican; 3. strong Republican.

Party congruence. If the incumbent and respondent had the same party identification, this variable was coded 1, otherwise 0. Independents were always coded as 0.

Presidential approval, 1980–92. "Do you approve or disapprove of the way that [President______] is doing his job? How strong or not strongly?"

1. Disapprove strongly; 2. disapprove, not strongly; 3. approve, not strongly; 4. approve, strongly.

In 1978 the question was "In general, how would you rate the job that President Carter has been doing over the past two years—would you say that he has been doing a very good job, good, fair, poor, or a very poor job?"

1. very poor; 2. poor; 3. fair; 4. good; 5. very good.

Incumbent and challenger contact. An index of the number of contacts the respondent had with the incumbent candidate and the major party challenger in the congressional election. Types of contacts included personal contact, contact with a staff person, or seeing the candidates at a campaign meeting. Contact through the mail, media, and acquaintances were also measured: receiving mail from the candidates, reading about them in the newspaper, hearing about them on the radio, learning something about them on TV, and knowing someone who had contact with one of the candidates.

0. no contact . . . 7. seven contacts.

Trust government to do right. "How much of the time do you think you can trust the government to do what is right—just about always, most of the time, or only some of the time?"

1. none of the time (a volunteered response); 2. some of the time; 3. most of the time; 4. just about always.

Family finances over the past year. "We are interested in how people are getting along financially these days. Would you say that you and your family living here are better off or worse off financially than you were a year ago?"

1978–82: 1. worse; 3. same; 5. better.

1984–92: 1. much worse, 2. somewhat worse; 3. same; 4. somewhat better; 5. much better.

Family finances in the coming year. "Now, looking ahead—do you think that a year from now you and your family living here will be better off financially or worse off, or just about the same as now?"

1978–84: 1. worse; 3. same; 5. better.

1986–92: 1. much worse; 2. somewhat worse; 3. same; 4. somewhat better; 5. much better.

Economic conditions over the past year, 1980–92. "How about the economy as a whole. Would you say that over the past year the nation's economy has gotten better, stayed about the same, or gotten worse?"

1980–92: 1. much worse; 2. somewhat worse; 3. same; 4. somewhat better; 5. much better.

The same question was not asked in 1978, so a different question had to be used to assess respondent's evaluations of the national economy. It read, "Would you say that at the present time business conditions are better or worse than they were a year ago?"

1. worse; 3. same; 5. better.

Notes

1. Norman J. Ornstein, Thomas E. Mann, and Michael J. Malbin, *Vital Statistics on Congress, 1993–1994* (Washington: Congresssional Quarterly, 1994), pp. 58–59.

2. Elizabeth Theiss-Morse and John R. Hibbing, "Public Enemy: People's Perceptions of Congress," paper prepared for the 1993 annual meeting of the American Political Science Association.

3. Kelly D. Patterson and David B. Magleby, "Public Support for Congress," *Public Opinion Quarterly*, vol. 56 (Winter 1992), pp. 539–40.

4. David E. Rosenbaum, "Public Calls Lawmakers Corrupt and Pampered," *New York Times*, October 10, 1991, p. B17.

5. Patterson and Magleby, "Public Support," pp. 543–44.

6. Glenn R. Parker, "Some Themes in Congressional Unpopularity," *American Journal of Political Science*, vol. 21 (February 1977), pp. 93–109.

7. Richard F. Fenno, Jr., "If, as Ralph Nader Says, Congress Is 'The Broken Branch,' How Come We Love Our Congressmen So Much?" in Norman J. Ornstein, ed., *Congress in Change: Evolution and Reform* (Praeger, 1975), pp. 277–87.

8. Glenn R. Parker and Roger H. Davidson, "Why Do Americans Love Their Congressmen So Much More Than Their Congress?" *Legislative Studies Quarterly*, vol. 4 (February 1979), pp. 53–61.

9. Timothy E. Cook, "Legislature vs. Legislator: A Note on the Paradox of Congressional Support," *Legislative Studies Quarterly*, vol. 4 (February 1979), pp. 43–52.

10. Timothy J. Conlan, "Federal, State, or Local? Trends in the Public's Judgment," *Public Perspective*, vol. 7 (January–February 1993), pp. 3–5.

11. Richard Born, "The Shared Fortunes of Congress and Congressmen: Members May Run from Congress, But They Can't Hide," *Journal of Politics*, vol. 52 (November 1990), pp. 1223–41.

12. Born, "Shared Fortunes"; Roger H. Davidson and Glenn R. Parker, "Positive Support for Political Institutions: The Case of Congress," *Western Political Quarterly*, vol. 25 (December 1972), pp. 600–12; Samuel C. Patterson and Gregory A. Caldeira, "Standing Up for Congress: Variations in Public Esteem since the 1960s," *Legislative Studies Quarterly*, vol. 15 (February 1990), pp. 25–47; Samuel C. Patterson, Randall B. Ripley, and Stephen V. Quinlan, "Citizens' Orientations toward Legislatures: Congress and the State Legislature," *Western Political Quarterly*, vol. 45 (June 1992), pp. 315–38; and Randall B. Ripley and others, "Constituents' Evaluations of U.S. House Members," *American Politics Quarterly*, vol. 20 (October 1992), pp. 442–56.

13. "Public Opinion and Demographic Report," *American Enterprise* (November–December 1992), pp. 80–104.

3 Public Opinion toward Congress: A Historical Look

Karlyn Bowman
Everett Carll Ladd

IT HAS BECOME a cliché to say that voters dislike everything about Congress except their own members, although as Herb Asher and Mike Barr note in chapter 2, the reality is not quite as simple as that. If it is indeed true that voters are deeply skeptical about Congress's efficiency and generally desire to sweep the Capitol clean, some things remain unclear. Are current opinions about Congress different in kind or intensity from those in the past? And do the opinions reflect a general indictment of large powerful institutions in an antipolitics age or are they focused on Congress? These questions are particularly important as Congress begins another effort to rebuild public confidence in the institution and make it more effective and responsive to the needs of the American people.

Polls can be helpful in answering such questions. Of course, they have limitations. Many polling questions about Congress have been asked during the past fifty years, but researchers who seek identically worded questions asked over long periods to draw precise conclusions about attitudes will be disappointed. There are significant gaps in the data. The Gallup Organization, for example, inaugurated the first genuine time series of Congress ratings in 1946 but discontinued it a decade later. The Roper Organization asked Americans to rate the institution in 1946, but did not ask the identical question again until 1975. Louis Harris and Associates in the early 1960s and Gallup in the mid-1970s launched more regular soundings of attitudes toward Congress, but even these data have gaps (figures 3-1, 3-2, and 3-3).

Here we look at some early questions asked about Congress and then move into a fuller discussion of contemporary opinion, bringing in comparisons from earlier surveys where they can be made.

Public Attentiveness to Congress

Polls suggest that most of the public did not think much about Congress as an institution until recently. In April 1944, for example,

Figure 3-1. Approval Ratings of Congress, Periodic Gallup Surveys, 1946–58[a]

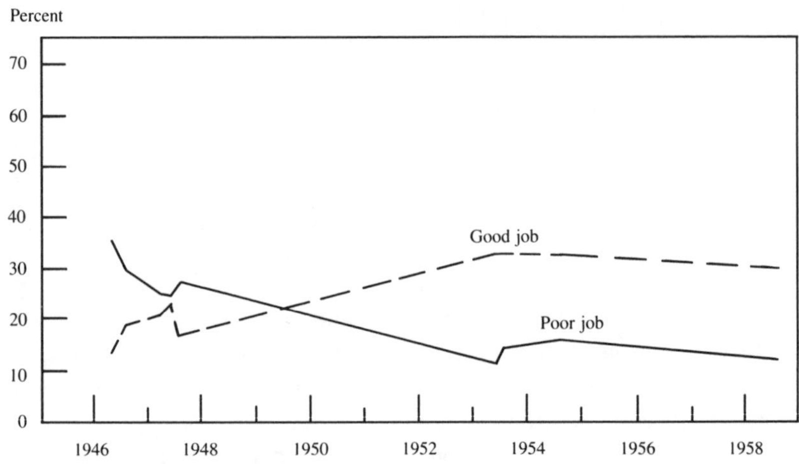

Sources: Periodic surveys by the Gallup Organization April 1946–August 1958.
a. Question: In general, do you think the present Congress has done a good job or a poor job? (1946–1947). In general, do you think that the new Congress that took office in January 1953 has done a good job or a poor job up to now? (May 1953). In general, do you think the present Congress in Washington has done a good job or a poor job to date? (July 1953–58).

Figure 3-2. Approval Ratings of Congress and Representatives, Periodic Louis Harris Surveys, 1963–90[a]

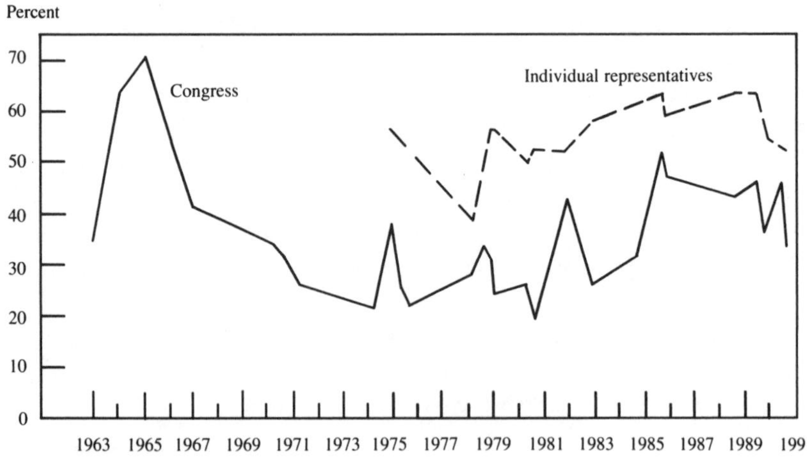

Sources: Periodic surveys by Louis Harris and Associates, December 1963–July 1990.
a. Question: Is Congress/congressman doing an excellent or pretty good job?

Figure 3-3. Approval Ratings of Congress and Representatives, Composite of Four Periodic Surveys, 1974–94

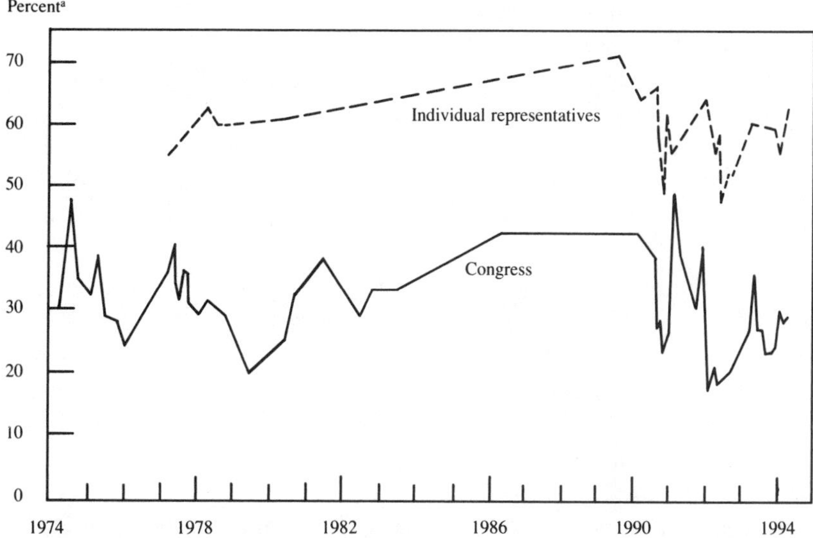

Sources: Periodic surveys by the Gallup Organization (April 1974–March 1994), CBS/*New York Times* (July 1977–October 1991), ABC/*Washington Post* (June 1985–February 1992), and NBC/*Wall Street Journal* (November 1989–March 1994).

a. Percent of respondents approving of the way Congress and their representatives are handling their jobs.

44 percent of Americans told Roper Organization interviewers that they had not paid any attention to the job their congressman was doing. Of those who had, 24 percent said he was doing a good job and 6 percent a poor one.[1] In 1965, when leaders again saw the need for substantial reform of Congress, much of the public did not express either praise or blame for the institution. In an October Gallup poll, 47 percent of respondents could not give a grade to their current representative in Congress, although the question did not provide a "can't grade" response. Of those who did rate their congressman, 35 percent gave him or her an A or B, 13 percent a C, and 5 percent a D or F.[2] Once again, those who had opinions were more approving than disapproving. On this question, even a third of those with a college education chose not to grade their representative.

Things are different now. A question asked in January 1994 about "names of some people in the news today" by Yankelovich Partners for *Time* and CNN found only 30 percent of respondents saying that they were not familiar enough with the U.S. representative who represented their district in Congress to say "one way or another."[3] This category was offered to them; they did not have to volunteer it. In recent years, when asked simply to give a judgment about their representatives, Americans have had little hesitancy. In 1978 CBS News asked Americans for the first time whether they approved or disapproved of the job their representative in Congress was doing, and the poll has repeated the question a dozen times since then.[4] In only one instance has the proportion not responding been greater than 20 percent. ABC News and the *Washington Post* asked a variant of the question for the first time in 1989, and they have repeated it regularly. In a dozen iterations of the question, the "don't know" or "no answer" responses have never been more than 14 percent of those surveyed.[5] The picture is roughly the same for the Gallup Organization, which has asked a handful of approve or disapprove questions about individual representatives since 1990. In only one instance has the proportion of those not willing to offer an opinion been greater than 20 percent.[6] Louis Harris and Associates has a four-part "excellent," "pretty good," "only fair," or "poor" rating for individual representatives. In ten iterations of that question between 1980 and 1990, the response "not sure" has never represented more than 7 percent of those surveyed.[7] To say that Americans are ready to offer an opinion does not mean, of course, that they are well informed about Congress. It could be that the institution is simply far more visible now in an age of television and that people do not resist making judgments about institutions.

It is possible that the way Congress and other political institutions such as the presidency are performing has become much more an issue to the public than it used to be. This conjecture is admittedly one of tea-leaf reading: poll questions do not deal with the matter conclusively. But pollsters are asking more questions about Congress and the presidency than they used to. Of course, they are asking more questions about almost everything, but Congress's share has expanded greatly. The Roper Center archive at the University of Connecticut contains 1,303 questions on Congress for the period from 1986 to 1989. For 1990 to 1993 it contains 2,252 questions about it. The entire data base contains 42,513 questions asked in 1986–89 and 49,450 questions in 1990–93. Thus the increase for Congress was 73 percent, while that for all national poll questions was 16 percent. If one goes back further, the same progression appears. Polling organizations are giving increasing relative representation to questions about Congress.

Effectiveness and Honesty

From 1946 to 1958, opinion about Congress as a whole in Gallup's time series improved. In April 1946, for example, 14 percent of Americans rated the job Congress was doing as good, 42 percent fair, and 35 percent poor. When Gallup stopped asking the question in 1958, the number of Americans who had a good opinion had doubled, to 30 percent; only 12 percent had a poor opinion. Attitudes toward the institution in Harris polling fluctuated wildly in the 1960s, but since the 1970s, people have more often expressed disapproval.[8] In sixty-eight separate questions rating Congress that were posed by different survey organizations from 1990 through early May 1994, approval of the institution has outweighed disapproval only twice.[9]

One question of a different sort does span fifty years and it points clearly to increased dissatisfaction. In 1937 the Roper Organization, polling for *Fortune*, inquired about attitudes toward the "present" Congress as a whole. It repeated the question verbatim in 1990. In 1937 44 percent of Americans said that Congress is "about as good a representative body as it is possible for a large nation to have"; in 1990 only 17 percent gave that response. Sixteen percent in 1937 and 41 percent in 1990 responded, "Congressmen spend more time thinking of their own political futures than they do in passing legislation." Thirteen percent in 1937 and 21 percent in 1990 said that Congress had "wasted many months this session doing nothing but talking."[10] Although there is certainly some hyperbole in the present critique of Congress, in both 1992 and 1994 in response to a question posed by ABC News/*Washington Post* interviewers, six in ten Americans disagreed with the statement, "Congress is not so bad as it's made out to be." Thirty-six and 38 percent respectively agreed that malperformance was overrated.[11]

To this result one must add concerns about Congress's honesty and ethical standards. There are no questions that have been asked across the entire span of polling history, but one posed by the Opinion Research Corporation in 1952 has a rough counterpart in more current polling. In the late spring that year, ORC asked which groups needed to improve honesty and integrity the most. Senators and congressmen ranked fourth (at 27 percent), receiving fewer mentions than labor unions (31 percent), state and local government officials (36 percent) and far fewer mentions than federal government officials (65 percent).[12] By way of rough comparison, Gallup has asked the public nine times since 1976 to rate the honesty and ethical standards of people in different fields. Eleven groups were rated in 1976 when the question was first asked. Senators were rated very high or high on honesty and ethics by 19 percent and representatives by 14 percent (table 3-1) of respondents. In 1993 the query extended to twenty-six groups. Pharmacists topped the list, with 65 percent of re-

Table 3-1. Poll Rankings of Honesty and Ethical Standards as Very High or High, by Profession, 1976, 1993[a]
Percent

Profession or job	*1976*	*1993*
Druggists and pharmacists	n.a.	65
Clergy	n.a.	53
College teachers	49	52
Medical doctors	56	51
Policemen	n.a.	50
Dentists	n.a.	50
Engineers	49	49
Funeral directors	n.a.	34
TV reporters and commentators	n.a.	28
Bankers	n.a.	28
Journalists	33	26
Newspaper reporters	n.a.	22
Business executives	20	20
Building contractors	23	20
Local officeholders	n.a.	19
U.S. senators	19	18
Lawyers	25	16
TV talk show hosts	n.a.	16
Real estate agents	n.a.	15
Labor union leaders	12	14
U.S. congressmen	14	14
State officeholders	n.a.	14
Stockbrokers	n.a.	13
Insurance salesmen	n.a.	10
Advertising practitioners	11	8
Car salesmen	n.a.	6

Source: Surveys by the Gallup Organization, June 11–14, 1976, and July 19–21, 1993.
n.a. Not available.
a. The question was "How would you rate the honesty and ethical standards of people in these different fields—very high, high, average, low, or very low?"

spondents rating their honesty and ethical standards highly, followed by the clergy (53 percent), college teachers (52 percent), and physicians (51 percent). Representatives ranked near the bottom with only 14 percent rating their honesty and integrity as very high or high, followed by stockbrokers, insurance salesmen, advertising practitioners, and car salesmen; senators were rated highly by only 18 percent of those surveyed. In January 1994, in a question asked by Yankelovich Partners for which there is no earlier counterpart or comparative measure, 26 percent of respondents said that Congress was doing a good job maintaining high ethical standards among its members, but 64 percent said it was doing a poor job.[13]

It would be a mistake to assume, of course, that Americans thought highly of Congress in earlier times and only soured on the institution recently. From the time of our early humorists to today's late night talk show hosts, Congress has been an inviting target. Although on questions of ethics and honesty the institution has ranked low compared to other institutions and professions for the eighteen-year period for which we cite comparable data, an August 1993 ABC News/*Washington Post* question found that 65 percent of Americans believed that members of Congress were about the same as most people in terms of honesty, while 2 percent believed members were more honest than most people. Still, 33 percent of those surveyed said members were more dishonest than most.[14]

Low Ratings

A host of recent data underscore both the relative and absolute disaffection of contemporary public opinion about Congress. A question asked in 1964 by the University of Michigan Survey Research Center and repeated in 1990 by CBS News and the *New York Times* captures the extent to which Americans feel the institution does not pay attention to them. In 1964, 42 percent of Americans felt that their representatives paid a good deal of attention to people who elect them in deciding what to do in Congress; by 1990, only 12 percent said that. Thirty percent in 1990 but only 15 percent in 1964 said that Congress did not pay much attention to the people who elected them.[15] In September 1978 CBS News asked Americans whether they agreed or disagreed with this proposition: "Generally speaking, those we elect to Congress in Washington lose touch with the people pretty quickly." Seventy percent agreed and 23 percent disagreed. Gallup repeated the question in 1984 and found 65 percent agreed and 29 percent disagreed. ABC News and the *Washington Post* reiterated it in 1991, 1992, and most recently in March of 1994. Negative sentiment has increased about 10 percentage points over the sixteen-year period.[16] In March 1994, 80 percent agreed with the statement, and 18 percent disagreed. Three times during the 1980s, ABC News/*Washington Post* pollsters asked whether most members of Congress care more about keeping power than they do about the best interests of the nation, and on each occasion, more than 60 percent said most care more about keeping power. Slightly more than 70 percent told the same polling organization in 1985 and 1989 that "to win elections most candidates for Congress make promises they have no intention of fulfilling."[17]

What may be more damaging to the institution's credibility in the long run is the public's belief that the kind of scandals that have beset

Congress in the 1990s are "business as usual" in Washington. In 1992, 72 percent of respondents viewed the House bank scandal that way. Twenty-two percent were willing to say that this was an "isolated exception to the rule in Congress." About 70 percent believed that Congressmen wrote bad checks "because they knew they could get away with it."[18] With that scandal past, ABC News and the *Washington Post* asked a similar question in August 1993 about two members of Congress who allegedly took cash from the House Post Office instead of the stamps they were entitled to receive; 68 percent affirmed that this was "business as usual," and 29 percent said it was an isolated incident.[19]

Congress is not alone in getting poor ratings. Americans have also expressed unhappiness with the performance of business, labor, and government generally in the past two decades. In a January 1994 poll by Yankelovich Partners for *Time* and CNN, 55 percent expressed only some or no confidence at all in the people running labor unions, 48 percent in the people running Congress, 48 percent in those running major corporations, and 46 percent in those running the executive branch. Other organizations in this poll that are perceived as big and powerful fared poorly too, including hospitals and health care providers and organized religion.[20]

A long-standing distrust of large powerful institutions hurts Congress, but there are other causes of distrust more specific to the legislative branch. In a generally critical climate, long-standing irritants such as congressional pay raises do nothing to improve public impressions and may contribute to the belief that the institution is out of touch with the lives of ordinary Americans. The Roper Organization has asked Americans five times since 1987 how much income per year they and their families would need "to live in reasonable comfort," "just to get by," and finally, "to fulfill all [their] dreams." The responses have been remarkably constant and modest. In 1993 the median answer to live in reasonable comfort was $35,500, just to get by, $23,700, and fulfill all dreams, $100,300.[21] The fact that members of Congress are paid so much more than most Americans reinforces the impression of an institution far removed from them. Americans have long felt that institutions closer to them have their interests more at heart. This continues to be true today. In a 1994 question asked by Yankelovich Partners for *Time* and CNN, 64 percent of Americans said that their state legislatures cared more about them than Congress did (only 16 percent believed Congress cared more), 52 percent believed that their state legislature got more done than Congress does (30 percent said Congress does) and 56 percent said their state legislature was more efficient in its use of taxpayers' money (17 percent said Congress was).[22]

A review of the data shows that Congress consistently gets more blame for the country's problems than do other institutions or the president. This may be because people perceive Congress as a more powerful institution, and it may be because it is easier to blame an institution than an individual president. Whatever the reasons, Congress is the target of overwhelmingly negative opinion.

Confidence in Key Institutions

For more than two decades, Gallup, the National Opinion Research Center, and Louis Harris and Associates have asked Americans how much confidence they have in important institutions. The various wordings of the question produce differing results, but the esteem in which people hold Congress and its leaders has clearly declined sharply.

In 1973 when Gallup first asked Americans how much confidence they had in seven institutions, Congress ranked fourth; 42 percent of respondents expressed a "great deal" or "quite a lot" of confidence in it. It followed the church and organized religion (66 percent), public schools (58 percent), and the Supreme Court (44 percent). In 1994, of those same seven institutions, Congress ranked last; only 18 percent of Americans expressed a great deal of confidence or quite a lot in it. In the twenty-two year period, Congress and the public schools dropped 24 percentage points, but the schools started from a base of higher confidence. The church and organized religion suffered a smaller drop (12 percentage points), as did the Supreme Court (2 points). There was no erosion in confidence in big business, but the institution had started much lower (26 percent) in public esteem than Congress did (table 3-2).

The National Opinion Research Center has tracked the public's confidence in the people running various institutions since 1973. The categories differ from those selected by Gallup, but both organizations show that Congress is now the lowest ranked institution. Confidence in the people running it dropped from 24 percent in 1973 to 7 percent in 1993. Confidence in the executive branch suffered an identical decline, and education and medicine suffered a 15 point drop. The military and the scientific community rose in public esteem. The Supreme Court stayed even (table 3-2). Neither Gallup nor NORC included banks in their earliest rankings. NORC added the category in 1975 and Gallup in 1979. Both organizations show that the drop in confidence in banks has been

Table 3-2. Survey Respondents Expressing a Great Deal of Confidence in Large Institutions, by Institution, 1973, 1993, 1994
Percent

National Opinion Research Center survey[a]			*Gallup Organization survey*[b]		
Institution	*1973*	*1993*	*Institution*	*1973*	*1994*
Military	32	42	Military	58[c]	64
Medicine	54	39	Church or organized religion	66	54
Scientific community	37	38	Supreme Court	44	42
Supreme Court	31	31	Public schools	58	34
Organized religion	35	23	Banks	60[d]	35
Education	37	22	Newspapers	39	29
Major companies	29	21	Organized labor	30	26
Banks and financial institutions	32[c]	15	Big business	26	26
Television	19	12	Congress	42	18
Executive branch	29	12			
Press	23	11			
Organized labor	16	8			
Congress	24	7			

Sources: Surveys by the National Opinion Research Center, February–April 1973 and 1993; and the Gallup Organization, May 4–7, 1973, and 1994.

a. Question: I am going to name some institutions in this country. As far as the people running these institutions are concerned, would you say you have a great deal of confidence, only some confidence, or hardly any confidence at all in them?

b. Question: Now I am going to read you a list of institutions in American society. Please tell me how much confidence you, yourself, have in each one—a great deal, quite a lot, some, or very little?

c. 1975.

d. 1979.

equivalent to the drop in confidence for Congress. In both polls, the military is the most highly regarded institution today, a position that represents an improvement from its standing at the end of the Vietnam War.

Decreasing Support across All Subgroups

Most institutions, even relatively unpopular ones, have partisans. Congress does not. It gets low marks overall and low marks from every group. Consider, for example, the CBS News/*New York Times* polls of 1978 and 1992, each asking respondents whether they approve or disapprove of the way Congress is handling its job. Overall, the proportion expressing approval was 20 percent in 1992 as opposed to 31 percent in 1978. For those with less than a high school education, the fall-off was 12 points, while for college graduates it was 11. For easterners, the decline was 10 points, for southerners 15, westerners and midwesterners, 10. The drop-off was 16 points among Republican identifiers, to a level of just 17 percent approval in the 1992 question; among Democrats the decline was 11 points, to 24 percent approval.[23]

Term Limits and Reelection

The public knows things are not working well in its national legislature, and it is now prepared to do some things to express its discontent. The support that term limits have received when they have been put on the ballot in various states is the most important evidence. Fifteen states have enacted term limits for federal representatives. The depth of support for the idea is shown by the results of a poll conducted during November 1993 and January 1994 by the Americans Talk Issues project. The organization found that 73 percent of Americans favored term limits even after four strong arguments were presented against them.[24] These arguments included the belief that term limits would increase the power of unelected career staff people, bureaucrats, and lobbyists because they would have more experience than elected representatives; that limits would penalize the representatives doing a good job and the people they represent; that limits would take away voters' fundamental right to elect anyone they want as their representative; and that limits would prevent great lawmakers from developing in the institution.

Polls show that respondents with some college or more, who probably are the part of the public most aware of what is happening in Congress, are now the educational groups most supportive of term limits. In a 1992 Gallup question, 56 percent of those with less than a high school education, 63 percent of high school graduates, 75 percent of those with some college, and 73 percent of college graduates supported the idea. In the 1960s and earlier, college graduates gave the idea the least backing. Forty-eight percent of those with less than a high school education and 39 percent of college graduates supported the idea in a Gallup question from 1964.[25] Informed opinion has thus moved on the need to make changes.

Still, many voters do not see a way out of their dissatisfaction with Congress's performance. From February through October 1992, in five surveys, majorities ranging from 52 to 62 percent told NBC News/*Wall Street Journal* interviewers that they thought it was time to give a new person a chance. In the same period the number saying that their representative deserved to be reelected ranged between 27 and 37 percent (table 3-3). But on November 3, 1992, 88 percent of House incumbents

Table 3-3. Public Attitudes toward Reelection of Current U.S. Representatives, Selected Months, November 1989–May 1994[a]
Percent

Month	*Feel your representative deserves to be reelected*	*It is time to give a new person a chance*	*Not sure*
November 1989[b]	41	36	23
October 1990[b]	39	48	13
October 1991[b]	40	48	12
December 1991[a]	35	52	13
January 1992[b]	42	48	10
February 1992[b]	37	52	11
April 1992[b]	33	57	10
July 1992[b]	27	62	11
September 1992[b]	31	56	13
October 1992[b]	31	56	13
July 1993	30	55	15
September 1993	37	47	16
October 1993	34	52	14
January 1994	35	47	18
May 1994	34	50	16

Source: Surveys by NBC News/*Wall Street Journal*.
a. Question: Looking ahead to this year's election for U.S. Congress, do you feel your representative deserves to be reelected, or do you think it is time to give a new person a chance?
b. Asked of registered voters; all other surveys asked of all adults.

on the ballot were reelected. NBC News and the *Wall Street Journal* have repeated this question five times since 1992, and majorities or strong pluralities continue to endorse the idea of giving a new person a chance. ABC News and the *Washington Post* tap the same sentiment by posing the question in a different way. They ask Americans whether they are inclined right now to reelect their representatives or whether they are inclined to look for someone else. In ten iterations of this question since 1990, majorities or pluralities have told the surveyors they were inclined to look for someone new.[26]

Although many give symbolic expression to their dissatisfaction, they either do not understand how to proceed or they are not prepared to take the only step that would give them a chance to regain control of their national assembly: kicking out incumbents and then promptly kicking out the new crowd if performance does not improve. Even though incumbents have financial and other advantages, there is no structural impediment to the public's regaining control of Congress through this kind of action. But most of the public is not prepared to do so. In response to a question posed in December 1993 by the bipartisan polling team of Mellman-Lazarus-Lake and the Tarrance Group, 53 percent of

Americans disagreed that "it is time to send a message to Washington that the American people are unhappy with the way things are being run by voting against every single incumbent up for reelection in 1994." Still, 41 percent agreed that the message should be sent, and of those, 24 percent agreed strongly.[27]

Is there any prospect that attitudes about Congress will become more favorable in the immediate future? Early in 1993 optimists thought that they saw some recovery in Congress's ratings. And in spring 1994 attitudes toward the institution were slightly more favorable than they were in 1992 in the Gallup, CBS News/*New York Times*, NBC News/*Wall Street Journal*, and ABC News/*Washington Post* polls.[28] The fact that Congress went a few months without any notable institutional scandal may have produced a modest rebound in public backing. But there is no evidence this improvement is building. Response to a question posed by NBC News/*Wall Street Journal* interviewers in July 1993 gives one pause. Americans were asked: "As you may know, one hundred ten new members were elected to the House of Representatives last November. Do you feel that Congress has heard and understood the messages of reform and ending gridlock, or do you feel Congress has not heard and understood these messages?" Sixty-seven percent said Congress had not understood the message; just 23 percent said it had.[29]

Nothing fundamental seems to have changed in the public's assessment of Congress. Its dissatisfaction has increased but remains unfocused. To answer the question we posed at the beginning of this chapter, opinions about Congress are more unfavorable now than they have been in other periods for which polling data are available—the 1930s through the 1960s. Polls do not sustain a definite answer to whether the institution is more prominent in the public mind than in the past, although the evidence points in that direction. Still, in a generally adversarial media climate, Congress must take the recent erosion of its reputation seriously.

Notes

1. Roper Center for Public Opinion Research, Public Opinion Location Library (POLL) Database.
2. Ibid.
3. Yankelovich Partners, news release, Claremont, Calif., January 17–18, 1994, p. 5.
4. POLL Database.
5. Ibid.
6. Ibid.

7. Ibid.
8. Ibid.
9. Ibid.
10. Ibid.
11. Ibid.
12. Ibid.
13. Yankelovich Partners, news release, January 17–18, 1994, p. 20.
14. ABC News/*Washington Post*, news release, August 6–8, 1993, p. 17.
15. POLL Database.
16. ABC News/*Washington Post*, news release, March 25–27, 1994, p. 16. For 1978, 1984, 1991, and 1992 data see *American Enterprise*, November–December 1992, p. 83.
17. POLL Database.
18. Ibid.
19. Ibid.
20. Yankelovich Partners, news release, January 17–18, 1994, p. 18.
21. Roper Organization, *Roper Reports 93-5* (April 17–24, 1993), pp. 47, 49.
22. Yankelovich Partners, news release, January 17–18, 1994, p. 22.
23. POLL Database.
24. Alan F. Kay and others, "Steps for Democracy: The Many Versus the Few," survey 24, Americans Talk Issues Foundation, Washington, March 25, 1994, p. 61.
25. POLL Database.
26. ABC News/*Washington Post*, news release, March 25–27, 1994, p. 18.
27. Mellman-Lazarus-Lake and Tarrance Group, "Battleground 1994," news release, Washington, D.C. and Alexandria, Va., December 6–8, 1993, p. 10.
28. POLL Database.
29. NBC News/*Wall Street Journal*, news release, July 24–27, 1993, p. 17.

4 Press Coverage of Congress, 1946–92

Mark J. Rozell

CONGRESS HAS ALWAYS been a favorite target for critics and comedians. Stereotypes of legislators who use public office for private gain and subvert the national interest have been a press staple since the earliest Congresses. Indeed, skepticism about the motives and activities of the nation's leaders has been considered a necessary, and even healthful, element of representative government. But healthy skepticism toward Congress has now largely been replaced with a debilitating cynicism that potentially undermines the foundation of representative government. Recent coverage of Congress, even by the most prestigious news organizations, smells of tabloid sensationalism. The emphasis on petty scandal and conflict reinforces the worst stereotypes of dishonest, lazy, and vindictive legislators and perpetuates widespread public belief that corruption and malfeasance permeate life on Capitol Hill.

My analysis of the coverage of Congress is based on a comprehensive review of press commentary from three news weeklies, *Newsweek*, *U.S. News and World Report*, and *Time*, and three dailies, the *New York Times*, *Wall Street Journal*, and *Washington Post*, during ten important periods since World War II. The periods are the Legislative Reorganization Act (1946), the Great Society (1965), enactment of the House and Senate Ethics Code (1968), the Legislative Reorganization Act (1970), Watergate (1973–74), the prospects for party governance (1977), enactment of President Reagan's economic program (1981), the Iran-contra investigations (1986–87), the Middle East crisis (1990–91), and Congress under siege (1991–92).[1]

After reading every news analysis, editorial, and op-ed column (by regularly featured columnists) about Congress during these periods, I have summarized and analyzed the major themes in congressional coverage.[2] As George C. Edwards explained, journalists "frame the news in themes" as a way to simplify complex events and then reinforce these themes through repetition. Thus images or stereotypes are built up that people perceive as reality.[3] Content analysis of the major themes in congressional coverage helps illuminate press perceptions of Congress, the kinds of legislative activities that generate favorable and unfavorable coverage, and changes in the nature of congressional coverage.

The Legislative Reorganization Act (1946)

Because of the enormous expansion of executive branch powers during Franklin D. Roosevelt's administration, many members of Congress recognized a need for reform of the legislative branch.[4] Scholars too urged changes to strengthen Congress. As a 1945 report by the American Political Science Association stated,

> Congress must modernize its machinery and methods to fit modern conditions if it is to keep pace with a greatly enlarged and active Executive branch. This is a better approach than that which seeks to meet the problem by reducing and hamstringing the Executive. A strong and more representative legislature, in closer touch with and better informed about the Administration, is the antidote to bureaucracy.[5]

In 1945 the House and Senate established a Joint Committee on the Organization of Congress to include six members from each chamber (divided equally by party). Senator Robert M. La Follette, Jr., of Wisconsin was named committee chairman and Representative A. S. Mike Monroney of Oklahoma vice chairman. The committee considered many reform proposals. Among those left out of the final report were that seniority not be the basis for selecting committee chairmen, that some of the powers of the House Committee on Rules be curtailed, and that debate in the Senate could more easily be limited. President Harry S. Truman signed the Legislative Reorganization Act of 1946 on August 2, and even though it left out the three proposals, it did include substantial reforms.

> *Committees*. The law reduced the number of standing committees from 33 to 15 in the Senate and from 48 to 19 in the House, dropping inactive committees and merging others with related functions.
>
> All standing committees (except Appropriations) were directed to fix regular days for meeting, keep complete records of committee

action including votes, and open all hearings to the public except executive sessions for marking up the bills or for voting, or where the committee by a majority vote orders an executive session.

Legislative Budget. The act directed the House Ways and Means, the Senate Finance, and the Appropriations Committees of both Houses, acting as a Joint Budget Committee, to prepare each year a legislative budget, including estimates of total receipts and expenditures.

Workload. The act prohibited the introduction of private bills for the payment of pensions or tort claims, the construction of bridges, or the correction of military records—categories of legislation that at one time consumed much time.

Staff. The act authorized each standing committee to appoint four professional and six clerical staff members, although no limit was placed on the number that could be hired by the Appropriations Committee. It also made the Legislative Reference Service . . . a separate department of the Library of Congress.

Salaries. The act increased the salaries of senators and representatives from $10,000 to $12,500, effective in 1947, and retained an existing $2,500 non-taxable expense allowance for all members. The salaries of the Vice President and the Speaker were raised to $20,000.

The Legislative Reorganization Act also included, as Title III, the Federal Regulation of Lobbying Act which for the first time required lobbyists to register with and report their expenditures to the clerk of the House.[6]

The Act also strengthened congressional oversight and investigative authority by stating the intention to have investigations carried out primarily by standing committees rather than by specially created ones. And it called for continuous oversight of programs rather than occasional hearings.

As the Reorganization Act was being debated, *Newsweek* columnist Raymond Moley offered a common postwar criticism of Congress. "Its organization and methods of operation do not correspond to the vital interests of the nation." He continued, "there are committees which are pure anachronisms," and "there are other committees whose duties are so heterogeneous that their names no longer have meaning. And the seniority system has placed utter misfits in many chairmanships. There are, in fact, too many committees in both houses. . . . We cannot," he concluded, "expect Congress to regain its lost influence until it modernizes itself."[7]

The rest of the press agreed on the necessity of congressional reform, the reasons for that necessity, and extolled the virtues of the changes that Congress enacted. The *New York Times* praised the reform proposals of the La Follette-Monroney committee and believed that there should be little opposition "on Capitol Hill or off it" because of the "harassing clutter of detail" that members of Congress had to sift through to do their jobs. The members needed staff assistance and more efficient organization to perform their duties. The editorial only criticized the committee for not changing the seniority system responsible for chairmanships of standing committees.[8]

After Congress adopted the reforms, the *Times* again praised the effort and approved of the pay raise. Indeed, it emphasized the responsibilities of serving in Congress and the need for "the kind of men and women we want to attract." Although the bill was not perfect, "it is a beginning and a good one. Congress members should now be able to do their job more creditably, and, having less anxiety over their personal pocketbooks, can confine their attention more fully to the essential business of making the nation's laws."[9]

The *Washington Post* reacted similarly to the committee proposals:

> "We are not inclined to carp about its failure to bring in a plan to abolish the seniority rule or clip the wings of the arbitrary Rules Committee in the House. . . . The public interest can best be served by concentrating full attention upon the progressive and intelligent reforms it has proposed by almost unanimous agreement, and forget for the time being about any inevitable sins of omission.[10]

The *Post* also later praised the increase in member salaries as well deserved—"they are underpaid in terms of their responsibilities and commitments"—and noted that the streamlining of legislative procedure was most welcome given Congress's dilatory performance before and during the war in providing credit to Britain and enacting a new Office of Price Administration.

> All through the war Congress refused to follow the lead of the country and undergo reconversion in the interest of efficient operation. . . . With the valiant generalship of Senator La Follette and Representative Monroney, they have helped to make the Seventy-

> ninth Congress memorable, and in future there should be fewer of those snarls in Congress which have recently been productive of jeremiads about the imminence of a constitutional crisis.[11]

The *Wall Street Journal* particularly congratulated Congress for adopting such important reform measures "without executive inspiration or executive pressure."[12] Like most of the press corps, Marquis Childs of the *Post* criticized Congress for not addressing the seniority system—one of the "defects" of the democratic process—but applauded the recommendation to provide a pension system to its members.[13]

After Senate passage of the bill, Raymond Moley of *Newsweek* urged readers to pressure House members also to pass the reforms, summing up the bill as the "most constructive measure to improve the efficiency of the national legislature that has appeared in a hundred years." He, too, emphasized the necessity of the pay raise to attract the most able people to Congress.[14]

Despite their groundbreaking nature, the congressional reforms of 1946 received relatively little press coverage, even though the leading newspapers and newsmagazines certainly did not ignore the effort. The lack of coverage or analysis lends credibility to the belief that the press does not adequately cover stories concerning process and institutional development. As Raymond Moley wrote, "public interest goes to the sensational and bizarre in Congress."[15]

What coverage there was, however, was positive.[16] Reports favored the congressional pay raise and pension plan. Journalists portrayed work in Congress as an honorable form of public service, often less than glamorous, and deserving of the kinds of financial rewards that would attract the best qualified representatives. The press also strongly endorsed the modernization of the committee structure. What criticism there was focused on the failure to reform the seniority system. The more extensive reform agenda would have to wait.

The Great Society (1965)

The first session of the 89th Congress is widely regarded as one of the most remarkable legislative periods in congressional history. Massive legislative output gave substance to President Lyndon Johnson's Great Society. A civil rights bill was enacted, as was a general education bill, medicare, rent subsidies, and a constitutional amendment on presidential succession—all unsuccessfully proposed in previous administrations.

The policy activism of the session was encouraged by Johnson's landslide victory, his renowned legislative leadership, and large Democratic majorities in both chambers (295-140 in the House, 62-37 and 1 independent in the Senate). In addition, large numbers of freshman Democratic legislators (72 in the House) had been elected, many of whom owed their victories to Johnson's strength at the polls and were committed to liberal reforms and quick action on problems. Also helpful were the earlier reforms of the Rules Committee that, until reconfigured and enlarged from twelve to fifteen members, had blocked many progressive proposals.

The press covered this extraordinary session extensively. President Johnson's role in engineering the Great Society programs received most of the attention and credit, but considerable coverage also focused on Congress.

If any Congress since World War II could be presented as a reporter's model of the ideal, the 1965 legislative session has to be it. The *New York Times* referred to the 89th Congress as "the best Congress since World War II"; the *Washington Post* pointed to "a great record of achievement," and others grasped at laudatory observations—"miracle," "revolution," "worldwide significance," "outstanding record," "massive," "distinguished," "extraordinary," "historic significance," and "matchless in our time."[17]

Some criticized Congress for not going further, for not enacting home rule for the District of Columbia or repealing the federal code that permits states to enact right-to-work laws. A few also complained that Congress had not aggressively pursued legislative reform—particularly of the seniority system. The *Wall Street Journal* expressed reservations about the Great Society programs being enacted at such a frenetic pace. But the *Journal* was one of the few voices raised against the fast pace. Other press criticisms emphasized the need for Congress to do more than it had—hardly criticisms at all.

At the opening of the 89th Congress, the *New York Times* speculated that the first legislative session would be very productive. Given the resounding vote of confidence the public gave to the Democrats in 1964, the president and Congress had a rare opportunity to work together. Among the actions the *Times* called for were medicare, tax reform, education reform, employment programs, antipoverty programs, housing and urban renewal, funding for mass transit and passenger railroads, pollution control, conservation, consumer protection laws, and an overhaul of Congress's rules and customs. "The voters have left the president and his party on Capitol Hill with no excuses," the *Times* concluded.

"The time has come to make good on yesterday's brave promises and the bold statements of the ideal."[18]

The *Times* praised the president's aggressive efforts to move his Great Society agenda forward as well as his strategy of concealing his proposals and then presenting them dramatically in the State of the Union address to avoid allowing an opposition movement to build. The key, it said, was to make the legislative process operate more efficiently.[19]

After the administration's first hundred days, the *Washington Post* marveled at the congressional activism.

> In sharp contrast to its recent predecessors, this Congress has been working as an industrious and responsible body alert to the needs of the Nation. If it keeps up the good work of the first 100 days, it will rank high among the most responsive Congresses of the present century.
>
> This Congress has responded well to President Johnson's leadership, but it has not enacted undigested executive bills with the recklessness that marked the first spurt of recovery legislation [during Roosevelt's first hundred days]. Despite the powerful influence of President Johnson on Capitol Hill, there is far more give and take in the present executive-legislative relationship. To its great credit, the present Congress is legislating without resort to either the rubber stamp or blind obstructionism. It is giving the country . . . a fine example of representative government action.[20]

Tom Wicker of the *Times* agreed and observed that by the traditional Easter break "most sessions of Congress have done little more than organize committees and hold hearings on a few bills," but the 89th Congress already had acted on far-reaching education, medicare, voting rights, poverty aid, and presidential succession measures. "The education and medicare bills alone would make most congressional sessions historic."[21]

Arthur Krock of the *Times* attributed the success of the one-hundred days to Johnson's leadership acumen and changes in Congress that led to a turnover in personnel and some key committee positions. Krock made clear that the legislative process worked best under the leadership of a strong president.[22] A *Times* editorial added, "Now that Congress has begun to act as a creative partner with the executive branch in the legislative enterprise, rather than merely a critic, obstructionist and irritant, there are few discernible limits to what it can achieve for the common good."[23]

Later in the year, when journalists reflected on the accomplishments of the session, enthusiasm had not subsided. James Reston wrote that Johnson was "getting everything through the Congress but the abolition of the Republican Party, and he hasn't tried that yet." Reston credited him with breaking "the consolidating spirit of the Eisenhower era" and also congratulated the new Congress composed of freshman members committed to progressive reforms.[24]

Tom Wicker, along with others, called the work of the 89th Congress "the most extensive record of legislative accomplishment since F.D.R.'s Hundred Days" and noted that although "the Presidency is still the paramount force in the American Government, the Congress is neither an obstructionist anachronism nor a rubber stamp." Nonetheless, Congress had not "developed the sort of active, sustained and intelligent influence on national policy that ought to be its true role in the 20th century."[25]

A *New York Times* editorial suggested that the president should continue to take advantage of the opportunity because much more needed to be done and Congress "has its own tempo and tends to work in spurts." The editorial concluded that "the 89th Congress is of that rare breed: it moves to a presidential tempo."[26] William S. White marveled at the "unexampled scope of the legislation that has moved so sedately and surely through the Senate and House." He added, "What Congress under Mr. Johnson's spur is doing in all fields of social legislation is in depth and total meaning beyond what any Congress has ever done for any President in any like period."[27]

When Congress adjourned in October, Marquis Childs wrote that the new legislation meant "advances in every field from the arts to medical care to highway beautification." Drew Pearson attributed much of this success to the reform-minded Democratic legislators who "put new verve into the tired old seniors who had been around so long that their idealism was tarnished, their ambition jaded."[28] Tom Wicker added, "Congress proved itself neither a rubber stamp nor a balky mule. Mr. Johnson showed himself a shrewd, powerful leader rather than a magician, and those who had begun to regard Congress as a dragging anchor on the executive were given a fresh perspective on its potentiality."[29]

The *Washington Post* commented that Congress had acted to fulfill "the two profound impulses" of the Enlightenment. "One of these was the concept of the equality of man—and this session of Congress has done as much as any session since the Civil War to reaffirm that principle and to give it practical effect. The other was the notion that well doing is not the province of individual behavior alone but a purpose of government itself." The *Post* offered a salute:

> The President and the Congress together have written a great record of achievement without any departures from the principles of the Constitution, without any deviation from the appropriate separation of powers, without any corruption by patronage or impropriety.[30]

The *New York Times* exulted, "At last the decks have been cleared of numerous old problems and old quarrels. At last the nation has had the benefit of the work of a modern-minded Congress that addressed itself to the needs of a complicated industrial society entering the last third of the twentieth century."[31]

Despite these praises, press commentaries noted the failure of Congress to enact other far-reaching programs. It rejected the president's proposals for rent subsidies, a national teacher corps, home rule for the District of Columbia, repeal of section 14(b) of the Taft-Hartley Act authorizing right-to-work laws, and strict ethics codes. The *Times* stated that the activist 89th Congress was praiseworthy, but an even more activist Congress would have been better.[32] And the *Wall Street Journal* did not concur at all with "the deluge of praise." Congress, it warned, had embarked upon a "flood of thoughtless, inflation-threatening legislation." Recalling the *New York Times* characterization of the 89th Congress as "the best since World War II," the *Journal* demured.

> That's lavish acclaim indeed for an institution which, in the not too distant past, was being roundly condemned for its lethargy, its unresponsiveness to the needs of the nation. How has Congress accomplished the transition from brickbats to bouquets? Certainly the lawmakers have passed lots of legislation . . . [and] laid out lots of the taxpayers' money. . . . It's not at all clear, however, that all of the laws and all of the spending will help meet the country's real requirements.[33]

Raymond Moley of *Newsweek* also expressed reservations about the pace of the legislative process. "Very few members of Congress had the slightest idea how these beneficial gestures were going to be realized. They merely voted for the bills and dumped the job of management upon already overburden bureaucracy. . . . Good intentions alone will never create a great society."[34]

The enormous legislative activity overwhelmed other events in Congress that otherwise would have received more coverage. The session opened with important reforms that paved the way for policy activism. These included changing a rule to allow a majority of the House to vote to dislodge bills that had been waiting for clearance by the Rules Committee for at least twenty-one days; a change to allow the House by majority vote to send a bill to conference with the Senate, ending the practice of permitting the objection of a single member to send a bill back to the Rules Committee; and elimination of a rule that allowed a single member to block a vote for a day by requesting a printed copy of the legislation. *The Washington Post* praised these as "a splendid start" but noted the need for further reforms to "strike at the blind workings of the seniority system." In iteration of its stance twenty years before, it called for "an overall study of the rules of Congress, along the lines of the La Follette-Monroney study in 1946. Such a study could well ask why it is that Congress is the only democratic legislature in the world that hews solely to seniority in naming powerful committee chairmen."[35]

To the extent that the press noticed congressional reform in 1965, coverage emphasized the need for more reforms to make the legislative process efficient. Nonetheless, the hectic pace of legislation had somewhat "stilled the clamor for congressional reform."[36] Congress received high press marks for its performance. Journalists applauded its policy activism and reform; they held slow decisionmaking and tradition in low esteem. Congress's performance in 1965 may represent the press's ideal of how the legislative branch should operate. Although Congress is not geared toward efficient operation, journalists believed that it needed to improve its efficiency. To the extent that the press, with the exception of the *Wall Street Journal* and Raymond Moley, criticized the 89th Congress, it did so for not moving more aggressively in domestic policy and for not enacting sweeping internal reforms.

House and Senate Ethics Codes (1968)

In 1968, when Congress took up the problem of member violations of ethical conduct, concern inside and outside the institution had long been building over such matters as the sources and uses of campaign funds and conflicts of interest.[37] Some members had been able to make substantial incomes from private business interests and law practices while serving in Congress. Some even had financial holdings in industries regulated by the government. But although members had been disciplined from time to time for unethical or dishonest behavior, it was not until scandals dramatized breaches of ethical conduct that matters of behavior began to come under sustained scrutiny and the reform of ethics codes was pushed to the fore of the legislative agenda.

The instigation occurred in 1963, when Bobby Baker, secretary of the Senate majority, was charged with using his position to promote private financial interests. In 1964 the Senate established the bipartisan six-member Select Committee on Standards and Conduct. It was granted the authority to investigate Senate members and staff charged with improper behavior. The committee's first investigation resulted in the 1967 Senate censure of Senator Thomas J. Dodd of Connecticut for improper use of campaign contributions.

In the House, investigations into numerous improprieties on the part of Representative Adam Clayton Powell of New York also publicized the need for stronger oversight of members' ethical conduct. In 1967 the House established its bipartisan twelve-member Committee on Standards of Official Conduct. In 1968 the House and Senate committees proposed a number of reforms for the codes of ethics of their respective chambers.

On March 22, 1968, by a 67-1 vote, the Senate adopted the recommendations of the Senate committee to limit the outside employment of Senate employees, provide disclosure of gifts of more than $50 and honoraria more than $300, and require all senators, their employees, and senatorial candidates earning $15,000 a year or more to file sealed financial reports with the U.S. comptroller general. The Senate rejected a proposal for full public disclosure of member finances. The House also adopted ethics rules, including rule 43, which limited honoraria, prohibited personal use of campaign funds, and prohibited the use of official position to receive compensation and acceptance of gifts from people with an interest in pending legislation. The House also adopted rule 44, requiring members and certain staff to file reports on their financial interests with the House Committee on Standards and Official Conduct.

Press coverage of the ethics reform efforts was generally unfavorable. Although the House and Senate had taken important steps to strengthen their codes of conduct, editorialists emphasized what they did not do. The *Washington Post* described the Senate committee's recommendations as "a net gain, but a narrow and disappointing one" and found the somewhat broader House committee recommendations merely "a useful beginning." The editorial particularly criticized the Senate's failure to require full public disclosure of members' financial interests: "reports held in confidential files can be of little value in policing day-to-day conflicts of interest." A week later another editorial described the Senate as "very eager indeed to improve its image," but not serious enough to have made more than a "first feeble effort." Still, it added, "the courageous advocates of a stricter code should find it easier to patch up the holes in the new framework than to start from scratch."[38]

The *New York Times* stated, "since Congress has been notoriously and deliberately obtuse on the subject of ethical standards, the reports submitted to both houses last week have to be considered progress. But the report to the House is less than ideal, and the Senate committee's 'important beginning' is hopelessly inadequate." The *Times* deplored the failures to require full financial disclosure and to eliminate testimonial dinners. A second editorial called the Senate code "pretentious in aim and pathetic in fulfillment . . . the kind of ethical code that a corrupt man could easily live by—presuming he had intelligence and a little tact."[39] After Senate adoption of the committee rules, the *Times* managed to offer faint praise—"some ethics are better than no ethics"—but it still deplored the failure to accept full public disclosure of business interests and earnings.[40]

The *Wall Street Journal* declared of the Senate's 67-1 vote to adopt the committee proposals that "only Senator George Aiken had the courage to label the code as 'the farce of the year.'" In an op-ed column, *Journal* writer Jerry Landauer summed up the mood: "Congress, quick to pounce on indiscretions elsewhere and more scarred by scandal than the other two branches of Government, is most reluctant to accept similar restrictions."[41]

A *Time* magazine news story joined the chorus, calling the Senate effort

> a pale cautionary code unlikely to infringe on the rules of the club or invade any Senator's privacy. . . . Behind a thicket of perquisites and protocol, the U.S. Senate has long guarded its majesty from the vulgar eye. It forbids cameras in the visitors' galleries, permits a member to edit gaucheries and gaffes out of his speeches before they appear in the *Congressional Record*, grants Senators a unique immunity from legal action for what they say in committee or on the floor.[42]

Like legislative reorganization, however, ethics reforms received little press attention. Although coverage of the controversies surrounding Baker, Dodd, and Powell had been heavy, institutional efforts to prevent recurrences lacked the immediate human appeal. This disjuncture lends credibility to the belief widely held among media scholars that the press gives much greater emphasis to Congress stories involving personal controversy, rivalry, and scandal than it does to ones dealing with complex policy issues and institutional processes.

Legislative Reorganization Act (1970)

The Legislative Reorganization Act of 1970 (P.L. 91-510) was the first such law for reforming Congress since 1946 and the first in a series of major reforms of Congress adopted in the 1970s.[43] The reforms have profoundly influenced the nature of the legislative process. Although the 1970 act had its origins in a 1966 reorganization bill that failed to pass the House Rules Committee in 1968, the act did not go as far as the defeated proposal. It did not fully address the problems of the seniority system, nor did it attempt to limit the power of the House Rules Committee and the Senate cloture rule. The law did, however, open Congress to closer public scrutiny. Committee roll call votes now had to be made public. The House practice of voting in anonymity by unrecorded teller votes was abolished. The act also decreed that committees must have written rules, a reaction against the arbitrary power of some committee chairmen.

Certain rules affected only the Senate. For example, minority party members of a committee could now call witnesses at hearings. A majority of committee members could call meetings in spite of a chairman's refusal to do so. A senator was limited to membership on two major committees and one minor, select, or joint committee. No member could serve on more than one of the more powerful committees—Armed Services, Appropriations, Finance, or Foreign Relations. And no member could chair more than one full committee and one subcommittee of a major committee.

As with the 1968 ethics reforms, the press considered the 1970 act as at best a useful first step. *New York Times* editorial board member Robert Bendiner, who castigated Congress's "organization, its division into feudal baronies, [and] its veneration of procedures which are neither democratic nor efficient," harshly criticized the institutional failure to reform the seniority system. He concluded that members must have been satisfied with "the whole cozy arrangement because it guarantees them, if they are cooperative, the power to favor their constituents."[44]

Most of the press, however, welcomed even limited efforts to reform legislative rules and seniority. In response to a Democratic caucus decision in March 1970 to allow the Democratic Study Group to examine the seniority system, the *New York Times* commented, "revolutions in the House of Representatives are so rare that even the limited concession won by Democrats opposed to the seniority system must be considered an important advance." But the *Times* was disappointed that Congress failed to move boldly and quickly to rid the institution of "this sixty-year old blight."[45]

In July *Times* reporter William V. Shannon wrote,

> The House of Representatives, which is supposed to be the part of the Federal Government closest to the people, has long hidden many of its significant operations behind a bewildering set of procedures. Most members preferred it that way and the public did not seem to care. It was therefore a major shift in the House's sense of itself when it decided last week to abandon the most important of these procedures, the unrecorded teller vote. . . . The abolition of teller votes still left the House of Representatives far short of becoming a completely open and fully accountable body.

Shannon also lamented the failure of the House to reform the seniority system and to open committee meetings to full public view.[46]

The *Washington Post* also praised the decision to end unrecorded teller voting and also described the reforms as inadequate.

> Congress should not be allowed to forget that the major sources of its inefficiency and loss of public confidence remain untouched. Nothing in the bill would alter the elevation of misfits into key positions through the seniority system. Nor did the House take advantage of the occasion to give its leadership power to make and carry out an agenda. . . . So the great tasks of congressional reform still lie ahead.[47]

After the November midterm elections, the *New York Times* observed that the House would hardly be changed at all by a turnover of only fifty members and, more important, the entrenched seniority system guaranteed the system of power would remain sluggish.

> It is the rigid observance of seniority that stultifies and obstructs the work of the House. It is seniority that makes the House a graveyard of talent and drives able, younger members to run for other office. . . . The legislative branch of the Government cannot be responsive to the public unless the majority party assumes the responsibility to act. The seniority system defeats responsible government because it gives excessive scope to special-interest groups, parochial pressures and personal aggrandizement.[48]

The editor of *U.S. News and World Report*, David Lawrence, also blamed the seniority system, as well as the system of staggered elections, that "discourages any sense of responsibility."[49] And finally, *Newsweek* examined the "inefficient, undemocratic and largely unfunctioning parliamentary machinery" that inspired the calls for reform. It identified nine committee chairmen, all older than age seventy, who held enormous power. The report labeled four of them as "fighting," "traveling," "ailing," and "forgetting," whereas the other five were "not necessarily the best, but simply the longest-lived." The article concluded that "despite all the reformist oratory, the Nine Old Men seem as snug in their chairmanships as Abraham Lincoln's statue does in its marble mausoleum down by the Potomac."[50]

Press commentary on the 1970 legislative reform efforts was thus strikingly uniform. Congress was a bastion of outdated traditions that impeded change, openness, procedural democracy, and even realization of the values of the young. None of the editorials, op-eds, or news commentaries defended seniority. They applauded efforts to improve openness and procedural democracy. For the press, the more sweeping the reform proposal, the better. The major criticism was that Congress did not enact the most fundamental reforms proposed by liberal activists.

Watergate (1973–74)

As the Watergate scandal unfolded over nearly two years, Congress took the lead in exposing the various crimes and improprieties committed in the Nixon White House. At no other time in history had Congress so dramatically and effectively exercised its duty as the "grand inquest of the nation." As the Senate Select Committee on Watergate, chaired by Senator Sam Ervin of North Carolina, and the House Judiciary Committee, chaired by Representative Peter Rodino of New Jersey, conducted public hearings on the coverup, Congress came under the watchful eyes of the nation. Reporters carefully evaluated its performance, and their commentaries tell much about the qualities they found praiseworthy in the nation's legislature and those they deplored.

Not surprisingly, Watergate press coverage focused on the revelations of executive branch wrongdoing and on the drama that resulted in the downfall of the Nixon presidency. But when the press did focus on Congress, its portrait was generally flattering, the portrait of an institution that dispatched enormous responsibilities effectively during a constitutional crisis.

January 1973–June 1973

Although some partisans criticized Congress early in the investigations for disrupting the nation's policy agenda, the press encouraged the legislature to assume the responsibilities of the nation's grand inquest. The *Washington Post* called the Ervin committee hearings "an undertaking of enormous importance to the mechanisms by which we try to maintain our freedom." It added that a congressional inquiry, not a criminal trial, offered the best opportunity to achieve that end. The *New York Times* noted that Congress had the duty to help find the truth, assess the damage, and pass laws to correct the weaknesses of the governing system. It called on Congress to enact campaign finance reforms to end the "corrupting flow of money."[51]

Many commentators extolled the benefits from a newly resurgent Congress. Vermont Royster of the *Wall Street Journal* wrote that despite all the criticism of its lack of independence from the presidency, credit belonged to Congress for preventing the Watergate affair "from being buried." James M. Naughton of the *New York Times* added that Congress, "long a slumbering giant," had awakened to challenge the president's authority.[52] And the *New York Times* observed,

> While the Executive slips into deeper disarray, a rejuvenated Congress has begun to move with remarkable determination and unity of purpose to restore the balance of power that the Founding Fathers had perceptively prescribed to check excesses of any branch of the Federal Government. . . . The revival of the constitutional system of checks and balances through an awakened Congress offers hope for ultimate restoration of the nation's damaged political health.[53]

The *Times* subsequently offered editorials that praised the investigation. The newspaper extolled the "educative function" of the Ervin committee. Despite administration claims that the inquiries diverted congressional attention from urgent national issues, it declared that "no other item of public business is more important. . . . No other forum is more appropriate—indeed, no other forum is available—for this inquest."[54]

Nonetheless, press comments were not wholly laudatory. The *Times* expressed concern that Watergate had diverted congressional attention from "disastrous cuts" in administration spending on social programs and regretted that Congress lacked the internal machinery required to assess national budgetary needs. It advised Congress to adopt reforms to challenge administration budget analyses. The *Washington Post* criticized Congress for allowing the president to impound funds for programs enacted by the legislature. Constitutional processes would be subverted, it said, if Congress failed to assert its power over federal spending.[55] Other press commentaries also emphasized the need for the legislature to become more aggressive in asserting its prerogatives.[56]

During the early stages of the hearings, the Nixon White House complained that the Ervin committee was taking too long and not accomplishing much. Press commentaries replied that the hearings were too crucial to be hurried along.[57] When Special Prosecutor Archibald Cox expressed concern that the hearings could prejudice the legal process, the *Washington Post* responded that the Senate had to continue the hearings to help the nation get through the crisis.[58] Even the *Wall Street Journal*, which had been critical of the effects of the hearings on the presidency, declared that the Ervin committee "may be the last best hope for restoring public confidence in American political processes." In a later editorial the *Journal* hinted at the need for reforms to strengthen Congress's policymaking roll in the event of a post-Watergate weakened presidency. It cited the familiar criticisms of Congress as generally being incapable of decisive decisionmaking and concluded, "it will not be easy for Congress, as it is now organized, to assume a greater leadership role even if the presidency looses some of its influence."[59]

July 1973–December 1973

In attempting to sway public opinion against continued Watergate hearings, President Nixon persisted that Congress was "wallowing in Watergate" while the nation's business went unattended. Nixon's defenders warned that the public hearings weakened the country's stature abroad.

The press defended Congress and continued to urge it to persist. "Watergate, far from slowing the Congress down," the *Washington Post* commented, "has actually spurred it to great activity and independence. This may be little comfort to the President, but it should be welcome news for a nation which—*before* Watergate—probably had more reason to worry about weakness and inertia on Capitol Hill."[60]

The *New York Times* referred to pressures to end the hearings quickly as "partisan and self-serving." The hearings constituted "as grave a duty to discharge as any congressional committee in the history of the Republic," and besides, the record showed that "as many bills have been considered and voted upon as in the past sessions." The *Times* later emphasized the imperative of the inquiries because "the judicial process alone cannot present to the nation a cohesive picture of the policies which came dangerously close to subverting free government." Furthermore, Congress had the responsibility to "transmit to the American people the knowledge that is essential to the reaffirmation of democratic rule."[61] Finally, it said the Senate Watergate committee had

> acted in the public interest by resisting political pressure to call off its hearings, or to close them to coverage by press and television. . . . Full public scrutiny of grievous violations of the public trust is reassuring to those, here and abroad, who cling to belief in the continued validity of government by the people.[62]

After the notorious Saturday Night Massacre the *Times* implored Congress to continue the investigations and "to enable the courts and the grand jury to reconstitute the abolished office of special prosecutor." Congress, it said, had the highest duty to take action to ensure the independence of the special prosecutor.[63]

Newsweek replied to President Nixon's accusations by summarizing the accomplishments of the 93d Congress with high praise:

> As Congress closed its first session . . . its members had put in nearly 2,000 hours in debate, racked up a new record for roll-call votes—and enacted a staggering total of more than 200 new laws. . . . In foreign affairs, the Congress reaffirmed its policymaking role by forcing an end to U.S. bombing in Cambodia and by putting sharp new limits on the President's war-making powers. . . . The legislators moved to streamline their own budgeting procedures, and the House took a major step toward internal reform by limiting the role seniority plays in the choice of committee chairmen.[64]

Press coverage generally emphasized the need for Congress to reform the legislative process and curb presidential powers, and the press criticized Congress when it appeared not to be moving aggressively enough to enact reforms. A *New York Times* editorial chided the Senate Rules Committee for having tried to weaken campaign finance reporting laws at a time when the Watergate scandal had "transformed the political scene." The *Times* also proposed legislation to establish a truly independent and powerful office of special prosecutor.[65] But at the conclusion of the 1973 legislative session the paper praised congressional challenges to presidential authority: "The initiative [has] passed from the White House to Capitol Hill. Historians may some day mark the decline of what one of them has called 'the Imperial Presidency' from Nov. 7, 1973, when Congress enacted the War Powers bill into law over Mr. Nixon's veto."[66]

James Reston also called for legislative reforms and extolled the need for "corrective legislation" to create "a more equal and corruption-proof system of paying for political campaigns." He regretted that campaign finance reforms, although of enormous importance, rarely received news media coverage.[67] The *Wall Street Journal*, although at times defending Nixon against Watergate charges, agreed that reforms were needed to curb presidential powers: "liberals and conservatives alike agree that they have an obligation to curb presidential power and restore checks-and-balances."[68]

In October 1973 the House commenced a formal impeachment inquiry by the Committee on the Judiciary, chaired by Peter W. Rodino. The *New York Times* applauded the move. "In a way, it is a sign of constitutional health that the overlay of awe and fear covering the process of impeachment has been swept aside. . . . The Congress and its leaders would be no more justified in backing away from this provision of the Constitution than the President is in ignoring and defying other sections of the fundamental law of the Republic."[69]

Many journalists initially doubted whether Congress could carry out this extraordinary duty. Anthony Lewis wondered if Congress had determination enough to pursue impeachment or whether it would "go back to its usual ways of indecision and nest-feathering." William Raspberry charged that, "Congress hasn't the guts to do its job" and that there was "no leadership in the House of Representatives." Members "only respond to polls and constituent pressures and generally do not carry out their constitutional responsibilities with distinction."[70] The *Wall Street Journal* also expressed a skeptical view. "Congress has assumed the duty of assuring the public that justice is done in the Watergate affair. It is a heavy burden for a body that shows all the weaknesses of any other committee of 535 souls. . . . It is the habit of Congress, as of other committees, to avoid difficult decisions whenever possible."[71]

George Will maintained that after months of indecisiveness, "the intellectual seriousness of Mr. Nixon's construing of the Constitution deserves the definitive ruling that only the Congress can provide."[72] The *New York Times* again insisted that Congress enact legislation to ensure an independent special prosecutor and criticized the Rodino committee for failing to act.[73]

David Broder wrote one of the most critical commentaries on Congress's failure to move quickly on impeachment. Despite the weight of evidence, Congress's hesitation proved that "an opposition-controlled legislature is peculiarly ineffective in remedying or rectifying a serious abuse of power by the executive, even after it has occurred." Broder believed that members of Congress prolonged the controversy because they benefited politically. He criticized Congress for not enacting more stringent curbs on presidential powers.[74]

January 1974–June 1974

From January to June 1974 the press continued to praise Congress for undertaking the Watergate inquiries and for attempting to restore balance to the executive-legislative relationship. The *New York Times* commented, "the nation owes a debt of gratitude to Senator Ervin and his colleagues for the delicate work they performed so tirelessly, for the impact and the impetus which they provided toward the task of awakening the national conscience." David E. Rosenbaum agreed that, "the committee's most lasting achievements were the civics lesson that it taught the American people and the detailed documentary record that it developed and passed on to the prosecutors and the impeachment inquiry." Another benefit was that "it almost certainly paved the way for more use of the investigative powers of Congress."[75] After the House voted 410 to 4 to support an impeachment inquiry, the *New York Times* beamed that "the clear-cut action by the House . . . signals an end to temporizing." The paper later praised the Rodino committee for its "commendable and scrupulous concern for the integrity of the process to impeach President Nixon."[76]

Despite this praise, public esteem for Congress remained low. A February 1973 Harris poll had shown that despite the efforts to resolve the national crisis, Congress had an even lower public approval rating than President Nixon (21 percent for Congress, 30 percent for Nixon).

William S. White expressed surprise at these results because Congress had nothing to do with instigating Watergate and noted the irony that public anger was "directed primarily toward the Senate, which until lately has been the only active congressional show in town on Watergate, and specifically at the Senate Watergate committee."[77]

The press continued to applaud efforts to strengthen the legislature and weaken presidential powers. *Time* commended the "reappraisal of what the proper constitutional balance between the Executive and Legislative branches of Government should be." Tom Wicker wrote that Congress needed to scrutinize the powers of the presidency and to enact limitations on such powers, including the exercise of executive privilege. The *New York Times* editorialized that "with the Watergate scandals ravaging public confidence in the nation's political system, it would be reckless for the leadership of either party to frustrate the demand for reform." *Newsweek* declared that Congress's post-Watergate task was "restoring the balance of power between [it] and the executive branch," consequently displaying the will to assert itself. Finally Russell Baker criticized Congress for not having "considered itself in the imperial weight class with Presidents." He characterized it as satisfied with conferring vast powers on the presidency while focusing its own energies on constituent service activities. Baker preferred an activist Congress willing to challenge presidential powers.[78]

By mid-1974, the press began once again to criticize Congress for not having moved quickly enough on impeachment. *Newsweek* called the Rodino committee "the tortoise on the Hill" and the *Washington Post* implored it to stop prolonging the inquiries in the hope that perhaps it could "avoid the burden of judgment."[79] Joseph Kraft wrote, "how many times does the President have to streak before the Congress says he has no clothes?" And Joseph Alsop warned that the "entire U.S. government" would become paralyzed by "Watergate-mania."[80]

July 1974–December 1974

As the Watergate crisis spiraled toward its conclusion, the press reflected favorably on the role Congress had played. The Rodino committee in particular was congratulated for its fairness in handling the impeachment inquiry, an assignment that, the *New York Times* said, "had few modern precedents or guidelines. . . . The country can rightly feel that a thorough, conscientious and nonpartisan job has been done."[81] A later editorial elaborated:

> Members of the House Judiciary Committee have been eloquent in conveying their sense of agony and awe at the decisions which chance has called upon them to make this summer of 1974. Less evident, but equally justified, is the sense of confidence among legislators and the observing public alike over the way this solemn and fateful political process is operating within the democratic structure.[82]

Times reporter William V. Shannon wrote that the Rodino committee hearings had refuted claims that the inquiries would tear apart the country. Instead, "Americans are gaining some encouragement by watching their elected representatives at work."

> The debate is spirited but free of rancor, informed by intelligence, shaped by self-discipline and occasionally graced by eloquence. On both sides of the impeachment question, members are acting with dignity and responsibility. They are not selling their votes to the highest bidder, they are not trying to shout one another down, they are not throwing inkwells at one another, and no one is hammering the desk with his shoe. In short, in response to the threat of illegitimate power, a recurrent threat in human history, they are proving once again that the highly civilized and always difficult practice of self-government is possible.[83]

And Anthony Lewis concluded that the Watergate hearings had restored "belief in our political process, and especially in the legislative branch of government."[84]

The *Washington Post* summarized the significance of the proceedings.

> The Committee's debate has served to illuminate for the whole country the nature of political responsibility as Americans have traditionally understood it. The Committee has concentrated on the most important charges, and it has drawn them up in terms that ground them directly on the Constitution. In the Committee's debates, the opposition to impeachment has been carried on at a considerably higher level than any defense that the White House has ever provided for itself over these past two years. . . . The idea that all of American politics had fallen into decay has been demonstrated to be manifestly wrong. One element of our government

went grievously astray, and now Congress is carefully proceeding to correct these errors.[85]

After Nixon's resignation, Congress turned to the reforms that had been called for. By the end of the legislative session it had produced the War Powers Act, campaign finance reform, creation of a joint congressional budget committee, a budget control law, energy legislation, education aid, and pension fund standards. *Time* applauded the "monumental reform in the financing of Presidential campaigns" and emphasized the importance of broad-based reforms of the legislative process.[86] *Time* had earlier concluded that the reformists in Congress had broken the "restraints of tradition" and "the results were astonishing. For the House, that glacially sluggish institution, it amounted to a revolution."[87] *U.S. News* agreed that the 93d Congress would "go down in history for its action on Watergate" and that its "record has been a surprise to many who had expected the Watergate affair to crowd legislation off the agenda this year."[88]

Press coverage of Congress's role in investigating the Watergate scandal indicates what journalists expected from the legislative branch. They believed that Congress was at its best when investigating the executive branch, exposing corruption, and taking forthright action to remedy defects in the governing process—an activist, reformist Congress that is willing to assert and even strengthen its own powers. When Congress appeared to be moving too slowly in the Watergate investigations or not aggressively enough to enact institutional reforms, journalists implored the members for action.

During Watergate, press coverage emphasized that Congress had displayed its capacity for leadership in a crisis, conducted its constitutional duties with a minimum of partisanship and petty politicking, performed a vital democratic function by educating the public about government corruption and threats to the constitutional system, and acted strongly to restore balance to the separation of powers.

The Prospects for Party Governance (1977)

After the tumultuous Nixon years, the unprecedented reforms of Congress, and the 1976 election of Jimmy Carter to the White House, the country appeared poised for a new era in presidential-congressional relations.[89] A *New York Times* editorial expressed a common view: "For the first time in eight years, the Presidency and Congress are under the control of the same party, providing hope that legislative stalemate and government-by-veto may be finished."[90] Tom Wicker wrote that "Jimmy Carter may be coming into the White House in January with the best prospects for achieving a legislative program since the Johnson administration took over in 1965. With that one exception, in fact, Mr. Carter's legislative outlook probably is the best for any new President since 1948." Wicker noted that the Democrats held nearly as many seats in the House as they did in 1965, that they also held a 62-38 Senate majority, and that large Democratic majorities had undercut the old House coalition of Republicans and southern Democrats. Finally, reformed congressional procedures made it "easier for legislation to be properly considered and brought to the floor for action."[91] *U.S. News* predicted that large Democratic majorities and the erosion of power of committee chairmen in Congress would facilitate party governance.[92] A few weeks later its optimism overflowed.

> For the first time since the mid-1960s, a large degree of harmony between Congress and the White House is in the cards for the new year. The heavy atmosphere of stalemate that has hung over Washington since 1969 is lifting, now that Democrats once again are to be in command at both ends of Pennsylvania Avenue. . . . A new spirit of cooperation seems guaranteed.[93]

To the extent that observers discounted the inevitability of efficient party governance in 1977, they mostly did so because of reservations about Carter's leadership.[94] But by the end of 1977 it had become evident that the expectations for presidential-congressional cooperation were not going to be fulfilled. Conflicts had erupted over presidential appointments, energy policy, tax policy, pork-barrel projects, and even interbranch protocol. Press coverage of Congress's role in the failure of party governance followed the curve of disintegrating harmony.

By the end of 1977 *U.S. News and World Report* noted Congress's "degree of independence from the White House that defies the predictions of amity voiced early in the year." The article expressed surprise at congressional demonstrations of unpredictability and independence and attributed those characteristics to the postreform institutional "habit" of challenging presidential power. A few weeks later *U.S. News* concluded that "Congress's Democratic majorities proved in 1977 that they are not about to be led by the nose by any Chief Executive, Democrat or not, especially when the issues at stake have mobilized powerful special interests with clout in lawmakers' home districts."[95]

What is most striking about the press coverage of legislative-executive conflict in 1977 is the near uniformity of opinion that Carter deserved most of the blame. Journalists thought of Congress as an institution that must be led effectively by the president in order to get anything done. Without presidential leadership, there would be stalemate.[96] The press did not look to Congress for leadership.

Most journalists believed that Congress's contribution to the legislative stalemate stemmed from the congressional reforms of the 1970s. Despite earlier assessments that the reforms created an environment for presidential-congressional cooperation, the changes seemed to have harmed the chances of realizing a policy agenda. Furthermore, the press contended, the reformers had felt little deference to anyone, including the president. *Wall Street Journal* congressional correspondent Albert R. Hunt wrote in early 1977 that despite the eagerness for legislative-executive harmony, "habits change slowly and many legislators have grown accustomed to their more assertive roles." He later noted "the growing determination of Congress in recent years to insist that it not be taken for granted by an 'imperial' presidency."[97] *New York Times* deputy Washington bureau chief John Herbers observed that "John F. Kennedy could get Congressional consent by appealing to a few leaders who controlled the institution. Now Congressional power is fragmented, and members have become more independent."[98]

In April *U.S. News* assessed the troubled relationship. There was a general perception of ineffective presidential leadership, but there was also a more independent spirit on the part of Congress.

> The leadership in Congress . . . is new and eager to assert itself. In addition, the growing independence of younger members often is stronger than party loyalties. Carter also took office at a time when members of Congress had tasted success in wresting back powers that they had let slip to the White House in recent years. Most members are fearful of returning to a subservient role—even under a Democratic President.[99]

In May *U.S. News* Senior Editor Gerald Parshall wrote that although the president's "special brand of leadership" had much to do with interbranch conflict, changes in Congress had contributed to Carter's difficulties with the legislature. The Vietnam War and Watergate had touched off a desire in Congress to recapture powers that had been gradually surrendered to the executive branch in decades past. It is a trend that is still running strong, despite the return of the White House to Democratic hands. Two thirds of the Democrats in the House have never served under a Democratic President. They are used to going their own way, and the habit is proving hard to break.[100]

Lou Cannon observed that the many new Democrats elected to Congress had "no intention of approving legislation merely because it carries a presidential stamp or the imprimatur of the leadership." Consequently, "the House is now in many respects the 'open institution' that the reformers of a few years ago wanted to make it. Committees operate with a high degree of independence, the younger members are allowed to talk as well as be seen, and amendments even from the minority are frequently considered on their substantive merits." Although Cannon, too, focused on congressional concerns with Carter's governing style, he noted that the independence asserted by the new House members made it very difficult for legislative leaders to overcome policy stalemate.[101] Throughout the summer, a great many journalists echoed Cannon's analysis.[102]

In September the chief of the *U.S. News* congressional reporting staff, Thomas J. Foley, also emphasized the mixed blessings of the 1970s congressional reforms.

> The unhorsing of autocratic committee chairmen and general dispersion of power . . . have come at a price. Instead of consulting a handful of senior legislators, the norm only a few years ago, leaders now must cope with an often mercurial throng of 535 lawmakers. The result sometimes is delay and deadlock. It makes Congress look to many Americans like a headless and erratic force thrashing about wildly while national problems fester.[103]

At the end of the first session of the 95th Congress, *U.S. News* reanalyzed why the earlier predictions of interbranch cooperation under one-party rule had proven wrong.

> Part of the answer lies in the changing makeup of Congress. Its newer members have only weak ties to their party. They were elected as individuals committed to putting local interests above partisan considerations. . . . As for older lawmakers, a great many

> became convinced during the Vietnam and Watergate years that Congress had yielded too much power to the White House. . . . Even with a Democrat once again heading the executive branch, the habit of putting a congressional imprint on national policies is proving impossible to break.[104]

The press criticized Congress in 1977 for more than its failure to work with the president. Meg Greenfield wrote that the Senate in particular did not work effectively because of its outmoded folkways and rules as well as its "peculiar spirit—its haughtiness, sensitivity to slight and rather grand sense of self." She referred to the Senate as the Club and criticized its "preoccupation with the entitlements and independence and importance of the institution (never mind that it doesn't always look so hot to the public)." Joseph Kraft blamed the Senate's ineffectiveness on its failure to adopt reforms as broad-based as those adopted by the House.[105]

Congress also received close coverage of scandals. Thomas J. Foley wrote that "this Congress is proving as adept as any in memory at giving itself one black eye after another."

> First came the pay raise. It was handled in a way that won lawmakers blame both for taking the raise and for initially refusing to vote on it. Then came the disclosure that for years the House and Senate have been drastically understating the costs of overseas junkets, which have long been a sore point with taxpayers. Next was the blowup over the South Korean bribery scandal, which has filled the air with charges of cover-up and foot dragging. . . . [I]t is no wonder that opinion polls continue to show public confidence in Congress hovering near an all-time low. Many Americans clearly believe that their national legislature is worthy of ridicule and disdain.

But, Foley concluded, because of reforms in leadership structure and ethics guidelines, the institution did deserve some praise for being less secretive, more democratic, and less wedded to the seniority system.[106]

The congressional pay raise (from $44,600 a year to $57,500) generated press criticism for how members handled the matter, even though a number of editorials endorsed the decision. Most criticism focused on what Marvin Stone of *U.S. News* called "the shameless conniving and cowardice that Congress displayed in arranging to raise its pay without having to vote."[107] As the *Wall Street Journal* intoned, "the hypocrisy of the process is becoming a bit tiresome. While Congressmen obviously feel down deep in their hearts that they are entitled to more money . . . they do not feel equally strongly that anyone should know their views on the subject."[108]

Press coverage of Congress in 1977 reinforced the public's conviction that the institution does not work effectively without strong presidential leadership. Journalists identified the congressional reforms of the 1970s as among the sources of problems in presidential-legislative relations. According to the prevailing interpretation, the legislature had become an undisciplined institution incapable of advancing a coherent policy agenda.

As for the pay raise Congress awarded itself without publicly voting on it, reporters did not, as they had in 1946, defend the need to pay legislators a decent salary that befits their responsibilities, nor did they emphasize the need to offer the kind of salary that would attract quality people to public service.

Enactment of the Reagan Economic Program (1981)

To Ronald Reagan's partisans the 1980 Republican presidential landslide gave the new administration a mandate to enact sweeping changes in government policy, including strong reductions in spending on domestic programs, strong increases in defense spending, and deep tax cuts. The unexpected election of a Republican Senate, the able leadership of Senate Majority Leader Howard Baker of Tennessee, and the president's skills at public persuasion and building legislative coalitions in the House combined to make possible the smooth passage of the administration's economic programs in 1981.

During the administrations of Presidents Gerald Ford and Jimmy Carter, many political analysts had written about the imperiled presidency and the ungovernability of the nation. But with the startling legislative victories in 1981, Reagan's presidency appeared to have refuted the prophecies of endless gridlock. Indeed, journalists now referred to Reagan's successes as a revolution in American politics.

Reagan's 1981 triumph on Capitol Hill comprised five main victories.

1. Passage of the Economic Recovery Tax Act, a multiyear package that projected a reduction of nearly $750 billion.
2. Enactment of a budget reconciliation resolution designed to reduce domestic spending by over $35 billion.

> 3. Approval of a defense plan of nearly $200 billion for 1982, less than the President wanted originally, but more than President Carter had proposed.
>
> 4. Significant reductions in the Aid to Families with Dependent Children (AFDC) benefits, food stamps, certain antipoverty programs, and other minor welfare benefits.
>
> 5. Savings in Medicaid and Medicare programs, but postponement of an overhauling of the social security retirement system.[109]

As usual, Washington reporting of these events focused much more on the presidency than on Congress. Still, a good many press reports and analyses examined Congress's performance in 1981.

For its role in approving the Reagan economic program, Congress received press criticism for failing to be an assertive opponent to the president and failing to act responsibly as the government's budget-making institution.

Early in the year, in response to Reagan's aggressive efforts to advance his proposals for budget cuts, the *New York Times* asked, "where are the Democrats?" The House, led by the opposition party, did not know how to "perform as a coherent opposition." House members were more interested "in protecting one ox or another" than in fighting for causes or even defining which values they stood for.[110] A month later the *Times* was troubled that Reagan's economic program was moving through Congress so unchallenged.

> In its eagerness not to test the new President's popularity, the legislators seem to have abandoned altogether their proper role in the making of economic policy. Congress alone can provide an independent, skilled and detailed evaluation of the President's economic program. Until it does, the public loses. . . . Congressional scrutiny need not mean partisan warfare with the White House. . . . It is one thing for Congress to accept the direction and dimension of his program, quite another to abandon its role in determining the detail of policy.

The paper hoped for "more courage" from Congress in challenging the president's economic leadership.[111]

A June editorial in the *Times* recalled that legislators intended the 1974 budget reforms "to give Congress more say over economic policy and more discipline over its own fragmented spending. But the reform was born a colt with shaky legs. Inflation continued to push the budget above the levels that Congress set for itself, and old spending habits were hard to change." The editorial expressed reservations about the budget reconciliation bill and asked "why has Congress gone along so limply? Because the President is thought to be hugely popular and few politicians want to cross him." The editorial compared the sweeping changes of 1981 to those that led to the Great Society programs. It concluded that perhaps the only way to move programs at such a pace was to have an enormously popular president and "a compliant Congress."[112]

A *Wall Street Journal* editorial also looked back at the 1974 budget reforms and concluded that "despite all of its procedural finery, the process has not worked before this year." The *Journal* identified common abuses—stopgap funding measures, phony budget cuts—and concluded that the process outlined by the 1974 reforms could only work "given the right amount of leadership" from the president. The editorial made clear the view that Congress could not exercise responsible budgetary leadership otherwise.[113] A subsequent *Journal* editorial attributed the lack of sound budgetary policy to "a Congress-bureaucrat-lobbyist complex grown increasingly contemptuous of the broad public interest and popular will." The editorial referred to congressional efforts in the 1974 Budget Act to enforce budgetary discipline as a "fraud" and again said that controlling the process required a reassertion of presidential authority.[114]

David Broder also believed that, despite the 1974 reforms, Congress remained unprepared and unable to exercise leadership.

> Congress has not, in the eight years since it rebelled against Nixon's dictatorship, systematically addressed the conditions that would allow it to fill that leadership gap, either on its own or in tandem with the president. The crucial questions still remain on Congress' own agenda: policy integration vs. jurisdictional fragmentation; party loyalty vs. individual autonomy; national perspective vs. parochial representation.[115]

Congressional Democrats were often singled out for not being aggressive opponents of Reagan's programs. "The Democrats," Hobart Rowen wrote, "have thrown in the towel. Reagan is an authentic American hero, and the Democrats don't have the stomach for fighting him." Haynes Johnson, reacting to the common label of Reagan as "King of Congress," said "So he is, for the moment. The Democrats, if not exactly his loyal subjects, are his serfs. They are his to command. The president has his way on all he wishes. He shatters the ranks of his opponents, and leaves them in the position of political supplicants." And George F. Will gloated that "the Democrats' ideas are the crumbs of Republican ideas." Rather than propose substantially different economic policies, they merely tried to modify Reagan's programs.[116] At the end of the year, when it became clear that the nation had to prepare for a sharp economic downturn and unprecedented budget deficits in 1982, the *Washington Post* concluded that "Congress must accept some blame for the present dilemma. It swallowed the administration's economic program nearly whole last summer—and then threw in some extra tax cuts for good measure."[117]

It is clear that in looking for leadership from the federal government, journalists look instinctively to the White House. They look to Congress as a collection of individuals dedicated to parochial interests and self-serving causes. As Steven V. Roberts explained, "Capitol Hill is a maze of vested interests and power centers, each with its own motives, and priorities." Legislators favor budget cutting in theory, but "they all howl when their own programs get axed."[118] Journalists criticized Congress for ignoring national needs. The *Wall Street Journal* editorialized, "sure, we know that Congress people have to think about their next election. But we expect them to think about the general weal, too."[119]

The most critical review came from a *Wall Street* editorial, "The Treason of Congress," that charged Congress "has let spending run out of hand, relied on unlegislated tax increases and phony bookkeeping for any semblance of budget balance, driven the nation's largest trust fund to the verge of bankruptcy, and, when confronted with a national mandate to change its ways, thrown up its hands at the 'political difficulty' of reform." The *Journal* then summarized the litany of press criticisms that Congress was privileged, out-of-touch and incompetent.

> Congress lives in an isolated, self-indulgent universe, oblivious to the way its rhetoric translates into the real world. . . . For members of Congress, Social Security remains an abstract problem interesting only for its short-term politics, since they pay no Social Security taxes and don't have to worry whether any of this considerable bite on the payroll will be around for their retirement in the next century.
>
> Congress is one of the main victims of the elephantiasis that infects the federal government. . . . Pampered, privileged, surrounded by aides who regard him with servile contempt, your Congressman has become adept at confusing the public good with his

> own interest and interests. Campaign reforms become a means for protecting incumbents. Budget outlays become a mutual aid arrangement with budget constituencies. The duty to the folks back home becomes a matter of winning them federal goodies, to the point that it is a question whether the Congressman is serving his electors or corrupting them. . . . Congress has sold us out.[120]

In 1981, then, to the extent that the press applauded the federal government for advancing an aggressive domestic agenda, credit accrued to the Reagan administration. To the extent that journalists reported Congress's performance on domestic matters, they blamed it for failing to challenge the president or for obstructing his leadership. Press reviews reinforced the common perception that the nation's legislature was incapable of leadership, primarily in business for itself, and not attuned to national interests and needs.

The Iran-Contra Investigations (1986–87)

In November 1986 the nation learned that, with President Reagan's approval, the United States had sold weapons to Iran.[121] Some of the proceeds had been diverted to the Nicaraguan contra movement in violation of the Boland Amendment, which prohibited the use of federal funds to aid the contras. The president insisted that he neither approved nor even knew about the diversion carried out by his administration.

Congress established House and Senate Select Committees to investigate the controversy. Televised hearings lasted forty-one days in the summer of 1987. Congress called thirty-two witnesses, the most important of whom were National Security Council Adviser John Poindexter and Lieutenant Colonel Oliver North. The hearings were the most publicly visible displays of Congress's investigatory powers since Watergate.

The image of the congressional investigation created by the press was not the image of the courageous legislature restoring the constitutional balance of power during Watergate. Throughout the controversy liberal voices in the press complained that the legislators were not challenging the executive vigorously enough. Conservative journalists charged them with eroding the president's authority to conduct foreign policy.

Early in the controversy, Congress received some encouragement to get involved in the investigations. The *Washington Post* called for a "broad inquiry" because the office of the independent counsel could not do the job alone. The *Post* recommended that special congressional committees hold public hearings "into questions of public policy, foreign relations and ethics that are at the heart of the matter and beyond the jurisdiction of an independent counsel."[122] Tom Wicker added that Congress had "to inquire into the real extent of Mr. Reagan's dereliction. . . . All that's needed is a tough and relentless investigation." A few weeks earlier, however, Wicker had been uncertain whether Congress was tough enough to challenge presidential authority. If precedent was a guide, Congress would avoid the serious issues and defer to presidential national security powers.[123]

New York Times reporter Linda Greenhouse considered the inquiries as an opportunity and a challenge for Congress to unravel the controversy and strengthen its foreign policy power.[124] Steven V. Roberts identified another challenge—and potential pitfall: "By investigating and evaluating a major element of the Administration's foreign policy, the committees represent an important assertion of Congressional influence over the executive branch and threaten to tip the balance of power in Washington toward Capitol Hill."[125]

A number of conservative columnists had strong reservations about Congress's role in the investigations. Norman Podhoretz believed that the balance of power had already been tipped in Congress's favor. Congress had been "handed, and happily seized, an opportunity to mount an assault on the presidency. . . . An Imperial Congress [was] attempting to make [foreign] policy instead of consenting to or opposing presidential initiatives." He warned that "a body as large and diverse as Congress can never run an activist foreign policy: mostly it can obstruct and delay."[126] James Kilpatrick speculated that the congressional investigations would "manifest the inefficiency that infects [Congress] as a whole. Why two separate committees? Why not one joint committee. The answer, gentle reader, is that two committees require twice the staff and generate twice the publicity than would be true of one committee." Summing up his opinion of Congress, Kilpatrick growled, "the inefficiency is appalling; the rules are archaic; the waste of time is incredible."[127]

Wall Street Journal columnist Suzanne Garment believed that the impetus to investigate Iran-contra derived from a mindless pattern of responding to every crisis as though it were the next Watergate. She feared that Congress might enact more rules restricting presidential policymaking in foreign affairs. And George F. Will cited the familiar criticism that Congress was unable to keep secrets. He believed that it needed to grant immunity to North and Poindexter to ensure that the full story would be told unless, of course, "it is television rather than truth that Congress craves."[128]

The *Wall Street Journal* persistently criticized Congress for meddling where it did not belong. An editorial in February 1987 stated,

> the core of this country's difficulties in foreign policy is that many members of the Washington community have adopted the quite radical position that Congress not only has powers to debate and fund foreign policy but is entitled to engage itself directly in policy execution. That is a prescription for paralysis. The Founding Fathers . . . vested primary responsibility for foreign affairs in the president.

A week later the paper iterated the view.

> Put bluntly, much of the blame for this fiasco goes to dangerous and perhaps unconstitutional attempts by Congress to regulate how the executive branch conducts foreign policy. Time and again, the 248-page [Tower commission report] traces the root source of the mistakes in the Iran-contra affair to congressional interference with normal executive branch activities. The president made mistakes, but partly because his advisers felt constrained by congressional legislation from advising him.[129]

On May 5, 1987, the first day of the televised congressional hearings, the *Journal* declared the Boland Amendments "patently unconstitutional" and added that "much of the problem of Iranian policy results from the contortions of trying to run a policy in the face of congressional restrictions of dubious constitutionality." And a week later it stated that "these months of hearings will be worth the effort if congressmen are forced to take their fair share of the blame." Therefore, members of the Iran-contra committees framed the issues on legalistic rather than policy terms so that they would not "have to accept some of the blame for policies gone awry."[130]

As Congress proceeded with the hearings, press criticism persisted. Charles Krauthammer asserted that "the air of moral superiority of some congressional inquisitors is hard to take. Contra policy has not exactly been Congress' finest hour. In fact, there is not one congressional contra policy but five." He further criticized Congress's performance in the controversy.

> If Congress were a person, it should be recalled for such conduct—subject perhaps to its version of the 25th amendment, which allows for relief from duty owing to demonstrated mental incapacity. But Congress isn't a person. It is a shifting coalition of interests and factions. Precisely for this reason it ought to be circumspect about conducting foreign policy, particularly regarding an issue on which it has shown itself to be incapable of defining a minimally coherent policy. There is a reason why the Constitution assigns primary responsibility for the conduct of foreign policy to the president and not to Congress. The Boland saga is a case study.[131]

Linda Greenhouse reported that because of North's skillful testimony, the televised hearings had become "the scourge of Congress." Rather than appearing statesmanlike, members of the investigating committees "appeared off stride, scrambling to regain momentum and public credibility."[132]

Although much of the press criticism of Congress's handling of the investigations came from conservative political observers, more liberal journalists also found its performance unimpressive. *Washington Post* columnist Mary McGrory lambasted Congress for not acting more decisively to prevent the controversy.

> You listen to Congress' record on the contra war—no, yes, maybe—and you wonder, what were [the Founding Fathers] thinking of to confer the power of the purse on foreign policy on such a collection? . . . Congress eventually, in spite of itself, got wind of it all. What did the great, slow-moving, cowardly beast do? Well, nothing, actually. . . . The membership of the select committee is sewn with closet monarchists who long for trumpets and ermine and royal edicts. They think the Founders were dead wrong to give people like themselves the right to rein in a giant such as Ronald Reagan.[133]

In another column McGrory declared that "Congress is hanging on to relevancy in the conduct of foreign policy by a thread." When it comes to serious policy matters, she commented, Congress is more interested in grandstanding than in genuine accomplishment. "It holds hearings, summons witnesses, pontificates, marks up, postures through long debates, haggles with the White House, temporizes, compromises and, if it passes the tattered shreds of what it had in mind, pats itself on the back."[134]

The *Post*'s David Ignatius believed that Congress appeared weak and unable to assert its authority in the wake of North's testimony. Committee members "rush[ed] to the network interview booths to say what a persuasive witness North had been" after he admitted he had lied to Congress and shredded government documents. Ignatius speculated that the Iran-contra committees would issue a "blistering final report criticizing the president" and that Congress would pass a new statute to try to control covert activities. "But none of these steps will go to the heart of the matter—which is to deter abuse of presidential power." Ignatius predicted the "acquiescence of a bootless Congress" to the view that some intelligence operations are beyond the realm of law.[135]

Meg Greenfield acknowledged that if North charmed the public by playing to the television cameras, "so in large measure was the committee playacting. I think viewers knew this, sensed at once that there is something *not quite jake* about the committee procedure as advertised, and so they were disposed to favor the witness who seemed to beat the interrogators at their own game."[136]

Newsweek described the various problems created when Congress tried to assert its authority to make foreign policy.

> Congress can rarely initiate foreign policy; much more often it reacts—and all too often overreacts, as it may have done in 1976 when it imposed a blanket ban on U.S. aid to rebels in Angola. In other cases Congress hedges with vaguely worded legislation—like the Boland amendment restricting U.S. aid to the contras—registering its disapproval but avoiding a clear "no." In still other instances oversight becomes "micromanagement": the House has voted to dictate what kind of wine to serve at embassy receptions and interfered with decisions about closing consulates. . . . The Iran-contra revelations point sharply to the need for congressional review. Legislators can also help the president build public support for policies that may be dimly understood. The problem is that congressional review often shades into congressional direction.[137]

Few journalists praised Congress's efforts in the Iran-contra hearings. Haynes Johnson did report that "not since the Vietnam war has there been so serious a debate about the respective constitutional roles and responsibilities of the legislative and executive branches of government." The hearings, he said, had at least provided "a wealth of new information." In another column Johnson applauded the committee members who, on the fifth day of North's testimony, made appeals for a stronger public understanding of the constitutional issues at stake in the controversy.

> The result was an outpouring of expressions of democratic values. This was no "cave-of-the-winds" kind of political rhetoric common in the hot air of Congress. . . . This was serious exposition of greater public purposes and of the proper workings of the constitutional system, expressed memorably and movingly. . . . Whatever else lies ahead, the Iran-contra hearings have accomplished their central purpose. They have provided what cynics said could not happen: a public forum, held in the most visible arena, in which a genuine debate about basic democratic principles and values has taken place.[138]

At the end of the hearings in August, however, Johnson offered a less affirmative interpretation. "Despite fascinating hearings that produced extraordinary information. . . . in the end, the hearings were as untidy and as inconclusive—if also as essential—as the democratic process itself. Some of the questioning was sloppy, and many leads were never pursued. By allowing North to dictate the terms of his appearance, the panels opened themselves to second-guessing that will undoubtedly continue for years."[139]

Of all the press reviews of Congress's performance, none was more favorable than a *New York Times* editorial.

> The investigating committees—indeed, the whole process that began with the Senate Intelligence Committee, the Tower Commission and continues with the special prosecutor—affirm American democracy. The process proves the political system's strength, not its fragility. It counters abuse of power, and holds those who abused trust accountable. It deters future leaders who might be tempted to transform their election or appointment into limitless mandates for unlawful action. . . . Congress, proceeding with abundant fairness, had many of its finest hours upholding the Constitution's integrity. Failure to have done that would have invited future zealots and

> liars, self-assured that they alone know the national interest, to transform American democracy into dictatorship.[140]

But the *Wall Street Journal* continued to offer blistering criticism. It characterized the majority report of the Iran-contra committees as "masterful political advocacy."

> The congressmen faced the daunting task of somehow beating up on President Reagan after clearing him of lying or lawbreaking. The congressmen didn't flinch. They stared hypocrisy straight in the face and didn't blink once in their report's 427 pages. . . . The most baldfaced hypocrisy is the idea that Congress wants President Reagan to be more aggressive in enforcing the laws.[141]

The *Journal* had written what was perhaps its most blistering barrage, however, in the middle of the hearings, when it referred to the committees' members as "the commander in chief pretenders of Congress" and scorned the "overbearing congressional meddling in [presidential] foreign affairs powers." Finally, it summed up, "the unconstitutional usurpation by Congress of the executive's foreign-policy powers is necessary to explain the Iran-contra 'scandal.'"[142]

Before the hearings had begun, *U.S. News* described Congress as "increasingly intrusive in foreign affairs." After their conclusion it expressed disappointment that, in effect, Congress had not been intrusive enough.

> What emerged from the weeks of televised hearings was not a complete or fully coherent narrative but, rather, a jumbled puzzle with many of its pieces missing. In many instances, witnesses' assertions went unchallenged, contradictions were not cleared up and key questions were not answered; as to the money from the arms sales, which so intrigued investigators at the outset, some still couldn't be found.[143]

U.S. News Editor in Chief Mortimer B. Zuckerman had earlier summed up what needed to be done: In light of the Iran-contra hearings, Congress had to reexamine its role in two respects. First, it needed a small joint oversight committee to remove any excuse for executive branch secrecy. Second,

> Congress has to recognize that its role in foreign policy requires consistency and candor. Members have a deplorable tendency to pass legislation that gives them protection on both sides of difficult issues. For example, the requirement that the President notify Congress of covert actions "in a timely fashion" is a deliberate ambiguity. Congress should make the time limit precise.[144]

Thus despite having taken the initiative in investigating the Iran-contra affair, Congress received generally unfavorable press commentary for its efforts to expose executive branch wrongdoing and restore balance to interbranch relations in foreign policymaking. At times during the hearings the press portrayed Congress as feeble in its efforts to hold the perpetrators of the controversy accountable and at times as intrusive and grandstanding. Commentaries focused on familiar criticisms of Congress: lack of leadership, failure to act vigorously and efficiently, inability to conduct a coherent and consistent foreign policy, holding public hearings merely to get publicity, and using hearings for partisan purposes to embarrass the president and weaken his presidency.

The Middle East Crisis (1990–91)

After Iraq's invasion of Kuwait on August 2, 1990, President George Bush put together an international coalition to back U.N. resolution 678 authorizing economic sanctions against Iraq and resolutions supporting the use of force in the Persian Gulf if Iraq failed to leave Kuwait. Although the president showed considerable diplomatic skill in building the international coalition, he experienced difficulty developing a bipartisan congressional coalition to support potential U.S. actions against Iraq. For weeks before his ultimatum to Iraq to remove its forces from Kuwait by January 15, 1991, Congress appeared mired in uncertainty over whether to debate U.S. policy in the Persian Gulf, to oppose military action and support only diplomatic efforts and economic sanctions, to fully support the president's actions, or to issue a formal declaration of war.

The president was reluctant to seek congressional approval for the authority to take military action against Iraq. He was concerned that a vote against granting the authority could undermine both constitutionally and politically his authority to act. And Congress, despite having agonized over the appropriate course of action, debated the issue of further sanctions versus granting war powers until just before the January 15 deadline. On January 12 it granted the president—by votes of 52-47 in the Senate and 250 to 183 in the House—the authority to wage war against Iraq to expel its military from Kuwait.[145]

Press coverage of Congress during these months was concentrated in the weeks leading up to the House and Senate debates and the days immediately after the vote on January 12, 1991.

Before the debates the press criticized Congress for not asserting its authority to help make foreign policy. There was a strong consensus that Congress had a legitimate and necessary role in the decision of whether to go to war. "Congress should share the responsibility of a decision as grave as this one," Anthony Lewis wrote, and he later implored Congress not to abdicate its constitutional authority to declare war.[146]

George F. Will agreed: "now that there soon may be 400,000 U.S. personnel in the Persian Gulf region, it is time to involve 535 other Americans." The conservative columnist warned about the danger of "a war begun with unclear goals and uncertain domestic support. Congress should be convened to listen, watch, learn, clarify and legitimize." Later he argued that the potential political damage to the president of a weak majority vote in Congress was unimportant. The larger issue was one of "due deliberation" and "constitutional propriety." Congress, therefore, must debate and decide.[147] Nor was the involvement in decisionmaking constitutionally ambiguous. The day before the vote was taken, Will asserted,

> Constitutionally, Congress must authorize any launching, from a standing start, of one of the largest military operations in American history. Authorization does not mean after-the-fact ratification. Authorization must be formal and explicit, not merely inferred from legislative silence or statements by individual legislators or collateral legislative activity. Congress must do this even though many members are eager to flee from responsibility. It is a duty, not a perquisite.[148]

Charles Krauthammer had earlier written much the same, but with less rhetorical balance. Because Congress, he said, was shirking its responsibility by not deciding either to support or oppose the president's actions, "the president should call Congress back into session immediately, present it with a resolution authorizing the use of force and make the gutless wonders choose."[149] He noted elsewhere that the president's actions in the Middle East, including the massive military buildup in

Saudi Arabia, were tantamount to "an executive declaration of war. In America, however, the legislature is supposed to declare war."

> The issue is not just constitutional. It is political. War cannot be waged successfully without popular support. If Congress is not consulted, it will simply criticize, fatally compromising any military action that runs into the slightest difficulty or delay. . . . The worst thing Congress can do is simply to debate the issue without resolving it—i.e., without coming to a vote on the use of force.[150]

Congressional irresolution drew out a spectrum of press commentary that reflected the themes sounded by Will and Krauthammer. "For Congress the issue now seems to have become one of whether the wimp mantle has been passed from George Bush to Capitol Hill," Nathaniel C. Nash wrote, and was echoed by Mary McGrory in a column titled "The Hill's Own Wimp Factor," which outlined options available to Congress to play a more substantive role in Persian Gulf policymaking.[151] Although in another column McGrory had criticized Bush for failing to make a clear, consistent, convincing case for the war, she added, "it is not necessary to be eloquent, or even consistent, about war aims as long as the opposition is represented by a Congress that deep down agrees with Bush and Baker that foreign policy is really none of its business."[152]

The editorial pages of the *Washington Post* and the *New York Times* led the charge for more congressional involvement. The *Post* reasoned that "congressional involvement alone could produce the kind of intensely sifted judgment suitable to a momentous national undertaking."[153] The *Times* acknowledged that the president has substantial war-making authority, "but it is astonishing to claim that all Congress can do is go along. Congress has more authority than that, if only it will reclaim it." As January began, the newspaper became more shrill. Congress had "shirked its constitutional duty to debate a declaration of war." Further delay on a vote would be "unconscionable. While hundreds of thousands of young Americans gird for battle in the deserts of Arabia, their elected representatives can't summon up the courage to confront their responsibilities at home. . . . Debate over the wisdom of war is raging everywhere in America except where it's supposed to—in Congress."[154] Finally, the *Times* turned to mockery. Congressional leaders, it explained, had adopted the "Calhoun strategy."

> That refers not to John C. Calhoun of states' rights fame, but to the hard-running fullback on an otherwise hapless football team whose exploits Lyndon Johnson used to recount when he was Senate majority leader.
>
> In one lopsided contest, Calhoun's team was unable to gain any ground. Yet, unaccountably, Calhoun didn't carry the ball once. The coach began yelling, "Give the ball to Calhoun!" To no avail. Time and again his orders went unheeded; time and again his team was thrown for a loss. Exasperated, he called time out. "Why don't you give the ball to Calhoun?" he demanded of his quarterback.
>
> " 'Cause Calhoun says he don't want it, Coach."[155]

The *Wall Street Journal* registered reactions that mirrored those in the *Washington Post* and *New York Times*. Paul A. Gigot, for example, wrote that "Congress wants to be 'consulted,' as long as it never has to accept any responsibility," and he implored it to stop "niggling" and declare itself by presenting "an up or down vote."[156]

Once Congress debated and voted, press coverage changed. The institution now received high praise for squarely confronting the crisis and taking a position. Robin Toner explained,

> These have not been glory years for Congress. Ethical storms, budget squabbling and the chronic appearance of political deadlock have all left their mark on the image of this proud institution. But over the last few days, as the House and Senate debated whether to authorize the President to go to war in the Persian Gulf, the lawmakers have struggled to step up to what the framers of the Constitution had in mind. One by one, congressmen and senators took the floor and reached for the legacy of history, for Kennedy and Roosevelt and Churchill. They spoke, too, of their children, and the children of their constituents, and of past wars and the lessons they taught. Throughout the debate was the wrenching, sobering consciousness of their own responsibility.[157]

The *New York Times* stated that the "debate over going to war showed how conscientiously Congress can address momentous questions." And Anthony Lewis wrote, "the congressional debate on war in the Persian Gulf paid belated respect to the constitutional system for deciding when America goes to war. It was an impressive debate."[158] E. J. Dionne, Jr., of the *Washington Post* offered,

> After many years in which American politics has been derided for game-playing, sound-bite mongering, narrow partisanship and just plain foolishness, the Persian Gulf debate in the Capitol has proven something surprising: The country's politicians are still capable of carrying out a serious debate on a serious subject with touches of eloquence and all the gravity that the topic of war demands. . . .
>
> After many hours of talking, it was clear that just about everyone had tried to come to grips with the others' arguments, that each side was willing to engage the other with civility and a minimum of name-calling. . . . The course America is about to take may represent genius or folly, but no one will be able to say Congress failed to air the alternatives and debate them with sobriety and conviction.[159]

The most congratulatory review came from David Broder.

> One thing on which everyone could agree in the tense hours leading up to the deadline for war in the Persian Gulf was that Congress—that familiar whipping boy—had dealt with the issue of authorizing the use of force in a manner befitting the gravity of the subject. The weekend debate was civil and somber, always serious and often eloquent. Senators and representatives dealt respectfully with each other's arguments and showed compassion for the anguish even their opponents felt. The debate served superbly well the requirements of representative government, informing the public and reflecting the electorate's divided views.

Broder identified the conditions "that permitted and encouraged Congress to behave so responsibly," and implied that these should always be present. First, Congress moved quickly and, despite separation of powers and divided government, placed the president's priority at the top of its agenda. Second, Congress framed the debate clearly so that there would be no doubt about the institution's position. Third, debate time was limited and occurred simultaneously in both legislative chambers. Fourth, legislators, not staffers, wrote the speeches, which were unusually eloquent and heartfelt. Finally, interest groups stayed out of the way, allowing "genuine two-way communication between lawmakers and constituents to take place."[160]

Thus press commentary on Congress before and after the debates was dramatically different. When Congress appeared to recoil from debate over Persian Gulf policy, the press criticized it for failing to assert its constitutional powers in a crisis. After debate the press praised the legislators for their leadership. For the press, a Congress that defers to the president in a crisis and appears to avoid adopting a politically difficult position is not fulfilling its constitutional role.

Congress under Siege (1991–92)

Congress bashing appears to have become a national pastime.[161] An October 1991 *New York Times*/CBS News poll showed that only 27 percent of the public approved of the job Congress was doing, 57 percent disapproved. An overwhelming 83 percent said that members of the House of Representatives overdrew their House bank accounts "because they knew they could get away with it." Only 9 percent said that the members had overdrawn by mistake. And 58 percent said that the perquisites of office given to members of Congress are "unjustifiable."[162] A March 1992 *Washington Post*/ABC News poll found that 63 percent of respondents believed that members who had overdrawn House accounts had acted illegally, and 84 percent said they had behaved unethically. Finally, 79 percent said they were less likely to vote for a representative who had overdrawn his House bank account.[163]

Given the press coverage of Congress in 1991–92, it is no wonder the public holds its national legislature in such low esteem. In a column conspicuous because it argues for more balanced coverage of Congress, David Broder laid responsibility for the prevailing public contempt at the feet of the media. Many journalists, he wrote, had practiced a form of prejudice "that makes it impossible for people even to recognize individual differences within the reviled group." He identified some "hard-working, principled and effective" members of Congress and concluded,

> Somehow, their efforts go largely uncelebrated in the press. It's easy to get on the best-seller list by writing of Congress as the "Parliament of Whores" or to jump aboard the term limits bandwagon, feeding popular prejudice in the process. It takes more courage and independence to challenge the notion that everyone in Congress is crooked or incompetent or both. . . . Where is the journalism that reminds people that it's just as wrong to say that politicians are all crooks as to pretend they are all saints?[164]

Sensational news stories about transgressions of varying degrees of seriousness contributed to the disparaging coverage of Congress. One subject was the so-called Keating Five, senators accused of pressuring federal banking regulators on behalf of campaign contributor Charles Keating, head of the former Lincoln Savings and Loan. Another topic was abuse of perquisites. Rubbergate involved the revelation that members of the House of Representatives had frequently overdrawn their accounts at the House bank, and Lunchgate the revelation that members of Congress had run up large unpaid bills at the Capitol dining room. Other reports focused on free parking, franked mail, free medical care, and cut-rate barber shops. Reports also pointed out that Congress exempts itself from various laws that it imposes on others, including title VII of the Civil Rights Acts, the Americans for Disabilities Act, and the minimum wage. Finally, the Clarence Thomas confirmation hearings brought a barrage of stories criticizing the Senate confirmation process.

The editorial pages of the prestige newspapers led much of the criticism. The *Wall Street Journal* suggested a movie about the Keating Five directed either by Martin Scorsese or Francis Ford Coppola because "both have a fine feel for depicting little groups of men who decide they'll live by their own rules. They'd catch the elaborate traditions of deference, the mystical loyalties built on common behavior, and the system's real rewards." The *Journal* maintained that during its investigations Congress vilifies people who break laws but that for its own members it tolerates "all but the most crass kinds of influence-peddling and interference with regulators" as "'constituent service.'"[165] Another *Journal* editorial decried Congress's "abuse of constituent service" and "lap-dog Ethics committees." It called for, and offered, "a deeper re-evaluation of what the modern Congress has become."

> There *is* a cancer eating away at the health of Congress. It is the stupendous expansion of government itself. The incentives to corruption are inevitable in any system where huge sums of money in endless categories are controlled and distributed by politicians and bureaucrats. A quarter of the nation's wealth—$1.2 trillion—is now siphoned off to Washington. It is a utopia for middlemen, dealmakers and arrangers. . . . Congress has become less of a deliberative body and more like a special-interest vending machine.[166]

The *Journal* also picked up the hue and cry on the House bank controversy, which it described as "Congress's BCCI, the Bank for Check-

Kiting Congressional Incumbents." Another editorial commented with some sarcasm, "this is of course the same House of Representatives whose Members have been howling for a regulatory jihad against the real banking industry. . . . Curiously, the only Americans to have such banking privileges are the same ones who consistently fail to balance the nation's checkbook."[167]

The *New York Times* also denounced Congress for alleged breaches of ethics. "Representatives have given new meaning to the expression 'on the House,' bouncing checks in the House bank, ignoring bills from the House restaurant, getting House officials to fix their parking tickets. All over the country voters have been smelling self-indulgence." But another editorial pointed to something more unsavory than self-indulgence.

> For an angry public, the twin embarrassments of the bouncing bank and the delinquent diners are fresh reminders of the need to transform Congress's attitude toward ethical behavior. It's the same smug attitude that, among other things, perpetuates a discredited campaign finance system and permits lawmakers to accept free trips from powerful lobbies.[168]

Six months later the *Times* was still tearing at the subject (in March 1992 alone there were four editorials on the House bank controversy). "Congress's problems go far beyond self-indulgent perks and shoddy housekeeping. Both houses stagger through self-imposed obstacle courses that interrupt and paralyze their capacity to legislate. The larger task before Congress is to change the way it does business."[169] Among the changes that the *Times* suggested were reforms of campaign finance and the franking privilege.[170]

The *Times* also attacked the Senate for the Keating Five scandal. It suggested that members of the Senate Ethics Committee be dubbed "the Senate Six" for not taking strong action against the members accused of influence peddling. "That has made the committee a laughingstock even in Washington, awash in scandals over private piggy banks and other Congressional perks." A subsequent editorial referred to the Senate as "The Keating One Hundred."

> The mixed conclusion to the scandal brought to 100—the full Senate membership—the number of senators tainted by the exposure of wretched ethical standards and subservience to big money. The

Senate's refusal to reform campaign financing haunted the disciplinary proceedings from the first. . . . Now the remaining senators can address the larger sin: a system of moneyed politics of which the Keating episode is merely the most recent scandal.[171]

In one of its several editorials denouncing the House bank, the *Washington Post* appealed to a populist disposition among readers.

How would you like to be able to go to your bank and draw a no-fee, interest-free loan on a no-questions-asked basis whenever you're in the mood? Suppose you could get your hands on the money without agreeing to a repayment date? Well, no federal- or state-regulated bank in America would let you get away with that. Not even family or close friends are likely to indulge that fantasy. The one exception is the House of Representatives. Membership there means treating yourself as if you are every inch a king.[172]

Inexorably the focus broadened to include attacks on political privilege and scandal in general. An October 1991 *Time* news story declared Washington, D.C., "perk city." In bold black letters the article screamed, "wonder why Congress is so arrogant about bounced checks? Perhaps because its members are so used to the freebie life." "Freebies" included three-dollar car washes, five-dollar haircuts, free picture framing, free prescription drugs, special parking privileges, a House gym with a masseuse, and subsidized eating establishments, "ranging from simple cafeterias to opulent dining rooms with crystal chandeliers and black-tie waiters" serving filet mignon for less than eight dollars. The list was by no means exhausted.

What could be a better invitation to civil-disobedience revolt than watching lawmakers who earn $125,100 travel around the world for free, have massages in the House gym for free, have their cars parked for free and have their tickets fixed, refusing to pay for the few perks that are not granted outright.

Time went on to point up a meaning that transcended the perquisites:

When uninsured workers live in fear that one illness could wipe out their life savings, it is enraging to hear of the House pharmacy dispensing free prescription drugs. . . . When families who know

> how to squeeze a dollar until the eagle screams still cannot find the money for a haircut, the House barber takes on a special symbolic weight. When young families cannot get a mortgage on a house, the idea of free loans to lawmakers is bound to rankle.[173]

The following issue of *Time* decried Senate members as "pampered denizens of a virtually all-male bastion" and accused the upper chamber of institutionalized sexism.

> When the Senate is not operating like a men's club, it behaves like a family—a patriarchal, dysfunctional family. Not only does the Senate have all the institutionalized forms of sexism common in the corporate suite, but by dint of its privileges and power it is one of the few places where acting like a cross between a rock star and the dictator of a banana republic is tolerated.

Furthermore, the Senate operates by arcane rules, "often unwritten, [that] demand a lifetime of male bonding to understand."[174]

Such word pictures were complemented by a resort to cartoons. A *Newsweek* story on the bank overdrafts and unpaid restaurant bills carried a drawing of startled congressmen sitting down to eat in a Capitol Hill restaurant and being served stacks of unpaid bills by the waiters. A *U.S. News* report carried a drawing of rats, clothes stuffed with cash, bouncing rubber checks off the Capitol. The report declared that "the bank mess simply confirmed the institutional arrogance that makes all members politically suspect." In another cartoon accompanying a *U.S. News* story a woman proclaims, "I just saw our Congressman on T.V." "Not another campaign ad," her husband complains. "No. 'America's Most Wanted,'" the woman answers. A disapproving child fires his slingshot at the television screen.[175]

The nation's best known columnists also contributed to the poor image of Congress. David Gergen, then *U.S. News* editor-at-large, acknowledged that "there are far fewer drunks, crooks and scalawags roaming the halls" of Congress than there were twenty years ago. But he asked,

> How can Congress justify having its own pharmacy that dispenses free medicine, an ambulance service for members only and a system that tears up parking tickets? How does it explain a congressional retirement plan that pays out two to three times as much as most private pensions? . . . The arrogance of Congress is most vividly

> on display when it passes major legislation, proclaiming on television that it is saving the country from some horrid practice, but quietly exempts itself from the law's operation.[176]

George F. Will has been one of the most vocal advocates of term limits for members of Congress. Calling limits "an auxiliary precaution against the perennial lust for power," Will characterized Congress as overly solicitous of pressure groups, trying to do too much for them while failing to do its important duties. In another column Will referred to term limits as "antitrust policy in politics," or an attempt to "regulate competition in order to intensify it." The "seasoned professionals" in Congress had created huge deficits, were mired in scandal, and had failed to deal effectively with the nation's policy problems. "Do you think 'amateurs' would do worse?"[177] And *Time* columnist Michael Kramer observed, "Attempts to level the playing field—for example, by instituting campaign finance reform laws that would even the odds of a challenger's unseating an incumbent—have been regularly gutted. If real reform is beyond the capacity of Congress to fashion, the only option left is to kick the members out."[178]

In its 1992 "Man of the Year" issue, *Time* featured a harsh critique by Stanley Cloud. "Like fish in a barrel," he opened, "Congress has always been too good a target to miss. From the very beginning, the tendency of the nation's lawmakers to posture or steal or make damn fools of themselves has been an inspiration to reformers and parodists alike."

> What's to be said in defense of an institution that prates endlessly about equal opportunity, fair employment, and freedom of information, then excludes itself from most of the laws that would help achieve those goals? How can there be anything but contempt for politicians who decry the projected $365 billion federal deficit even as they pour more and more dollars into their pet programs? Is there a case for the Keating Five and the way those purblind Senators opened their doors to convicted savings and loan rip-off artist Charles Keating—not to mention the purblind way in which the Senate ethics committee investigated the offense?
>
> Only a chronic rubber-check artist, after all, is likely to applaud the sweetheart deal Congress cut for itself with its own private bank. And only sophists are likely to go along with the argument that accepting bundles of money from political-action committees

> is not tantamount to taking bribes. Congress's refusal to consider real reform of its campaign-finance system makes sense only to other professional politicians, for many of whom retention of power is the paramount goal.[179]

Tom Kenworthy, who covered Congress for five years for the *Washington Post*, declared, "there's no shortage of buffoons, charlatans, blowhards and intellectually dishonest people on Capitol Hill." But with all of the criticism of the national legislature, "perhaps a little Congress-defending is in order. Not much, mind you, but if [mass murderer] Jeffrey Dahmer deserves a defense, then Congress does too."

> Sure, Congress as an institution seems hopelessly paralyzed, unable to do anything meaningful about health care, the economy or anything else. Sure, Congress is so hog-tied by the campaign finance system and so terrified of 30-second commercials that many lawmakers are incapable of casting a tough vote. Sure, lots of members of Congress spend so much time with guys wearing $1,200 suits that they start thinking like them. Sure, Congress is so gutless about the elderly and other powerful voting blocs that they've spent the country into what seems like permanent bankruptcy. But all of that has very little, if anything, to do with parking spaces or the House gym or free allergy medication at the office of the attending physician. Or kiting checks.[180]

Finally, the darkest reading of Congress's transgressions came from Mary McGrory, who contended that Congress could not effectively challenge the power of the president. Because of the "proliferating lists of sinners," she wrote, the legislature was "incapacitated," unable to confront serious national problems. Suddenly, a good many congressmen decided to call it quits. "People who were at least in a position to do something about the staggering problems that face us have thrown up their hands. What are the rest of us, who have no power, supposed to do? Is it any wonder the turnout in the [presidential] primaries is so low? What good is government anyway?"[181]

The criticism of Congress in 1991–92 was unrelenting. The press left the overwhelming impression of the institution as self-indulgent, scandal ridden, incompetent, and corrupt. It is no surprise that the public held Congress in such extraordinarily low esteem when influential editorialists and columnists had nothing positive to say about the institution.[182] The coverage and consequent public anger led many members to retire from public service. One of them, Mathew McHugh of New York, said that he had become tired of having to defend himself merely because he was a congressman. By March 1992 a *New York Times*/CBS News poll showed that only 14 percent of registered voters approved of Congress's performance. As late as July 1992 the approval rating stood at only 18 percent.[183]

Conclusion

Since World War II, the press has generally held Congress in low esteem. Deliberative, unexciting, usually uneventful, and often riddled with conflict, Congress is easily either ignored or criticized by the press. Negative and superficial congressional coverage is nothing new. But in recent years the extent and tone have become more severe, more disturbing. The most recent accounts focus on allegations of unethical and possibly illegal conduct by members of Congress. Many reports resort to humiliating caricature.

This study supports the findings of many other accounts of how the media cover Congress. Charles Tidmarch and John Pitney analyzed all items on Congress in ten news dailies during one month in 1978 and found that journalists focused on "conflict, malfeasance and breach of public trust." On the whole, they concluded, the press "has little good to report about Congress and its membership." Such coverage has tended to "harden the image of Congress as a defective institution."[184] A major study of the impact of newspaper coverage on public confidence in institutions, also focusing on the late 1970s, found that coverage of Congress was much more unfavorable than was coverage of either the presidency or the Supreme Court. Furthermore, Michael Robinson and Kevin Appel's analysis of network news coverage of Congress during a five-week period in 1976 found that all news stories that presented a point of view about the institution were critical of it. Even the first post-Watergate Congress failed to receive a single favorable assessment.[185] More recently, Robert Gilbert concluded that congressional coverage during the spring of 1989 emphasized scandal and further contributed to the legislature's weak reputation.[186] And Norman Ornstein's study of network news reporting on Congress in 1989 concluded that two-thirds of the coverage "concerned . . . three episodes of turmoil and scandal that had little to do with the constitutionally mandated duties of Congress."[187]

Over the years press coverage of Congress has moved from healthy skepticism to outright cynicism. When Congress enacted a 25 percent pay increase for its members in 1946, for example, both the *New York Times* and *Washington Post* commented that the increase was needed to attract top-quality people to public service and contended that political leaders must be paid a salary commensurate with the responsibilities of pubic service. The few criticisms of the raise emphasized either the principle of public service as its own reward or the need for an even larger pay increase. More recently, however, the story has been far different. The press has skewered Congress for enacting pay increases. To believe the modern reporter or editor, legislators are egregiously overpaid, indulged, and indifferent to the problems of constituents who lack six-figure incomes and fantastic job perquisites. The press portrays the nation's legislators as self-interested, self-indulgent politicians who exploit the legislative process for personal gain.

Sources of Negative Coverage

To answer the question of how Congress can try to set the record straight, one must first explain why press coverage of Congress is so harsh. As I have shown, press coverage of Congress focuses on scandal, partisan rivalry, and interbranch conflict rather than the more complex subjects such as policy, process, and institutional concerns. The recent emphasis on such controversies as Rubbergate and Lunchgate underscores this.

Many studies have speculated about the reasons for the intense interest in scandal, rivalry, and conflict. A partial explanation is the emergence of a more aggressive, scandal-conscious news media after Watergate. Thomas Dye and Harmon Zeigler pointed to "a post-Watergate code of ethics" in which journalists seek out scandal and delve into the personal lives of public figures and other areas once considered off limits. Norman Ornstein also noted a new generation of investigative reporters, inspired by Watergate sleuths Bob Woodward and Carl Bernstein, that had "accentuated and refocused the media coverage of Congress" toward "scandal and sloth."[188]

Scandal, rivalry, and conflict may also be emphasized because the legislative process is tedious—"the very driest form of human endeavor," as Senator Alan Simpson once said.[189] Consequently, reporters avoid writing process and policy stories except when they are related to interbranch conflicts, rivalries among colorful personalities on Capitol Hill, or scandal. William Safire explained that editors instruct reporters to avoid "MEGOs": stories that make "my eyes glaze over."[190] David

Broder, for instance, commented that personal scandals are exciting and interesting; stories about institutional reform will put even reporters to sleep before they get to the typewriter. According to Broder, a reporter will have an easier time selling to his editor a story of petty scandal than a good many "stories of larger consequence." Junket stories sell to editors "because they fit [editors'] stereotypes of graft and sin on Capitol Hill."[191]

The press thus has difficulty conveying the complexities of the legislative process. The magnitude of coverage devoted to such exceptionally important events as legislative reorganization efforts and ethics reform never matches the number of stories devoted to a House bank scandal. To the extent that the press does cover procedural issues, it seems to do so when they are related to scandals and can be explained in terms of, and as reactions to, interbranch, partisan, or personal rivalries. Coverage of congressional activism during the Watergate crisis is a good example.

The negativity and narrow focus of coverage are particularly important because, as Herb Asher commented during a Brookings–American Enterprise Institute conference, "everything that people learn about Congress is mediated." And there seems to be a link between the nature of congressional coverage and poor public understanding of the legislative process. Charles O. Jones looked at media coverage of a particularly busy week on Capitol Hill and found that even though the legislature had undertaken some important activities, "the American people learned hardly a smidgen about Congressional action that directly affected them."[192] Dye and Zeigler described coverage of Congress as "almost without exception demeaning. As a result, people regard the *institution* of Congress with cynicism and mistrust." Furthermore, "the public knows very little about Congress in its abstract, institutional form."[193]

My findings support the contention that coverage of legislative reorganization plans, the adoption of ethics codes, and other institutional matters was sparse and lacked depth. In addition to being less exciting than petty scandal, institutional stories are more complicated for reporters and editors to understand and to write about in single news stories and columns.

Besides, the presidency is the focus of Washington journalism. Congressional lawmaking is covered from the vantage of how the legislature is responding to presidential initiatives. The press perceives Congress as generally incapable of leadership. Thus in normal circumstances Congress works best under the guiding hand of a strong president attuned to the national interest and willing to move the government in an activist, progressive direction. Members of Congress, in the minds of many reporters, are primarily concerned with parochial issues. During such extraordinary periods as the Great Society and Watergate, press coverage focused more on the presidency than on Congress.

In unusual circumstances—an executive branch scandal, an imminent war—the news media expect Congress to adopt a more independent and activist role. Congress received a good deal of press criticism during the early stages of Watergate and Iran-contra for allegedly not acting quickly or vigorously enough to investigate the scandals. Similarly, the press criticized Congress during the early phase of the 1990–91 Middle East crisis for not asserting its constitutional warmaking powers.

But there were rare conditions under which Congress received press acclaim. Efforts to reform internal congressional procedures to make the legislative process more efficient, though not thoroughly reported, were treated well: the press had frequently implored Congress to adopt substantial reforms to ethics laws. For the ten periods covered here, Congress received the most favorable coverage when it aggressively asserted its policymaking and investigatory powers.

The 89th Congress, first session (1965), comes as close as can be expected to reporters' ideal Congress. They believed Congress acted efficiently because it stretched the limits of its lawmaking powers and accepted the guiding hand of a strong, progressive president. They also supported its most activist phases during Watergate and the Middle East crisis. Congressional coverage in 1977 reinforced the view that Congress works best under the guide of a strong activist president. The failure of a Democratic president and Congress to work together effectively to enact progressive policies and reforms drew loud criticism.

The press's image of what Congress should be is clearly incompatible with the traditional role of the legislative branch. During the Brookings–American Enterprise Institute conference, one journalist argued that Congress deserves praise "when Congress acts," especially when the institution displays "heroism" and policy innovation. Several colleagues agreed. Yet the Constitution's framers designed Congress to frustrate the popular will as necessary, to *not* act in an efficient, innovative fashion. Consequently, the drumbeat of press criticism, interrupted occasionally by favorable coverage during unusual circumstances, helps explain the disjunction between the legislature's intended constitutional role and journalistic expectations. No wonder Congress is held in such low public esteem when the press criticizes the institution for behaving as the Constitution's framers intended it to and then focuses on petty scandal and members' peccadilloes to the exclusion of examining process and policy.

One reporter at the conference identified his criteria for deciding whether to write a Congress story: first, the element of drama, which satisfies the public desire for a good show; second, the chance to feature colorful legislators who can turn a good phrase or take a bold action; third, the involvement of congressional pork, which excites public concern about whether legislators are doing their jobs. The enactment of "sound public policy" was a weak fourth. This reporter's criteria do not seem at all unusual given the nature of congressional coverage I have described.

What Can Be Done?

The remedy for the inadequacies and distortions of congressional coverage is either for Congress to change or for the press to change. Neither is likely to do so very much. But both can take steps to ameliorate the problem.

Congress needs to do a better job at educating the press and the public about its activities—what it does and why it does what it does. Otherwise, journalists and the public will continue to harbor expectations—routine efficiency, activist policymaking, large-scale internal reform, strong leadership during crises and when the president is under siege—that the institution generally is not designed to live up to.

Congress also does a poor job of protecting its image. In Richard Fenno's classic argument, members "run *for* Congress by running *against* Congress."[194] In their districts they reinforce unfavorable opinions of the institution so that they can distance themselves from it and by implication assume the virtues it supposedly lacks. Even electorally safe incumbents do not educate constituents about the strengths of their institution. Instead, they attack Congress as a way of protecting themselves politically.[195] Michael Robinson and Kevin Appel have also noted that members of the legislature "complain about Congress and praise themselves as individuals."[196] And James McCartney of Knight-Ridder commented, "Congress does a lousy job in telling a reporter what goes on. The problem with Congress is that it has no organization and is just babble. It needs to present its information better, like the White House."[197]

Congress needs an office of public information, much like the White House's office of communications, devoted to dispensing information about its duties and activities. Government organizations need such entities to improve the flow of information to the public, and Congress should not be an exception. Although Congress has expanded and improved in-house media operations to help meet the needs of individual members to communicate with constituents, it has been less active in meeting more general and institutional needs.[198]

Individual members can also orient their own behavior in a way that better protects the institutional reputation. Electorally safe members—a large group indeed—have the leeway to educate constituents properly about Congress and take some responsibility for its actions.[199] Timothy Cook suggested that members can work better with journalistic definitions of newsworthiness by explaining complex issues and activities in a clear, comprehensible fashion.[200] Members could also do a better job of lowering constituents' expectations of legislative performance and could avoid perpetuating conflicts that generate short-term publicity and political gain at the expense of Congress's image.

Finally, responsibility for presenting a balanced and realistic representation of Congress lies with the journalists. In 1975 Senator J. William Fulbright wrote that "the national press would do well to reconsider its priorities. It has excelled in exposing . . . the high crimes and peccadilloes of persons in high places. But it has fallen short—far short—in its higher responsibility of public education."[201] The problem is now far worse. Much of the reporting and commentary on Congress from the prestige press has a tabloid quality. And the consequences of such Congress bashing are clear enough: public anger at the legislative branch and cynicism, the inability of Congress to do its job properly, increased rates of retirement from Congress, the refusal of many outstanding citizens to serve there, and a possible crisis of legitimacy for the institution.

It is difficult to imagine that congressional coverage will deemphasize controversy, scandal, and intrigue and focus on process and policy very soon. But reporters and editors can voluntarily do a better job of educating the public about Congress and representative government. Whether they are motivated by concern over the impact of fueling public cynicism toward the institution or by professional pride in factual reporting, fairness, and balance, journalists could truly serve the public by covering the legislative branch in a manner that befits the most representative institution of our government.

Notes

1. A book-length treatment of this topic will include several other important periods in congressional coverage: the Kefauver committee organized crime hear-

ings, the army-McCarthy hearings, Senate debate in 1957 over civil rights policy, congressional tax reform action in 1986, and federal pay raise efforts from 1988 to 1991.

2. The selection of sources is adopted from Stephen Hess's description of the news organization hierarchy in *The Washington Reporters* (Brookings, 1981). According to Hess, there is a "solar system of Washington news gathering" that includes the sun, or the "political government," and the various planets, the Washington news organizations. These organizations form "an inner ring, a ring of middle distance, and an outermost ring."

The inner ring comprises the most influential organizations, the ones most important to the government because "through them it learns what the country is learning about what it is doing." The ring includes the Associated Press, United Press International, ABC, CBS, NBC, *Newsweek*, *U.S. News and World Report*, *Time*, and the *New York Times*, *Washington Post*, and *Wall Street Journal* (p. 24). In another study, Hess showed that government press officers, in recognition of the inner ring's influence, give these organizations preferential treatment; *The Government/Press Connection* (Brookings, 1984), p. 100.

This study focuses on those inner ring sources that comprise the nucleus of Washington journalism, the print media. In *The Washington Reporters* Hess notes that Washington news has a rhythm set by the news dailies (*New York Times*, *Wall Street Journal*, and *Washington Post*). This news "travels a circuitous route back into the political government and out again to the rest of the country via the electronic media" (*Washington Reporters*, p. 96). Print journalism thus becomes the means of developing national opinion, and journalists become the molders of public perceptions of congressional performance. Television has a "secondary impact" on the government. The wire services do not emphasize interpretive reporting and news analysis as much as the major print media sources.

Therefore this study is based on the news analyses, commentaries, and editorials on Congress contained in three national news dailies and three news weeklies.

3. George C. Edwards, *The Public Presidency: The Pursuit of Popular Support* (St. Martin's Press, 1983), pp. 159, 166.

4. This background material is summarized from news reports; Congressional Quarterly, *Origins and Development of Congress* (Washington, 1976); and Walter J. Oleszek, *Congressional Procedures and the Policy Process* (Washington: Congressional Quarterly, 1978).

5. Committee on Congress, American Political Science Association, *The Reorganization of Congress* (Washington: Public Affairs Press, 1945), pp. 80–81.

6. Congressional Quarterly, *Origins and Development of Congress*, pp. 136–38.

7. Raymond Moley, "What Does Congress Represent?" *Newsweek*, May 27, 1946, p. 100.

8. "Rip Van Winkle Wakes Up," *New York Times*, March 10, 1946, sec. 4, p. 8.

9. "For a Stronger Congress," *New York Times*, July 28, 1946, sec. 4, p. 8.

10. "Make It One Package," *Washington Post*, March 12, 1946, p. 6. See also "Fiscal Controls," *Washington Post*, March 14, 1946, p. 8; and "Undermining Reform," *Washington Post*, September 30, 1946, p. 6.

11. "Unsnarling Congress," *Washington Post*, July 30, 1946, p. 10. The same day the *Post* featured a column by George B. Galloway, chairman of the Committee on Congress of the American Political Science Association, extolling the reform bill as a courageous leap in which Congress had "jumped the hurdles of timidity, inertia, and vested interests and approved modernization of much of its antiquated machinery and methods." "Reorganization Achievement," *Washington Post*, July 30, 1946, p. 4.

12. "Congress's Achievements," *Wall Street Journal*, July 30, 1946, p. 4. See also, "A Promise To Be Kept," *Wall Street Journal*, October 29, 1946, p. 6; and "Congressmen's Streamlined Job: Pensions, Pay Raise, More Help," *U.S. News and World Report*, August 9, 1946, pp. 14–15.

13. Marquis Childs, "Revamping Congress," *Washington Post*, March 16, 1946, p. 6.

14. Raymond Moley, "How You Can Get a Better Congress," *Newsweek*, July 8, 1946, p. 92.

15. Ibid.

16. One story surveyed press reactions from around the country. It found overwhelming endorsement of the reform proposals, some criticism of Congress for not reforming the seniority system and not abolishing the Senate filibuster as well as for increasing congressional pay (some thought the pay increase not substantial enough to attract top quality people to government and some extolled the ideal of public service as a reward in itself that does not need to offer financial gain). See "Changes in the Organization of Congress: Press Reactions," *U.S. News and World Report*, August 9, 1946, p. 40. One article did not express enthusiasm; it referred to the proposals as "a series of mild recommendations aimed at clearing away some of the congressional deadwood, modernizing operations and giving Congress better equipment to do its job." It noted the failure to tackle the seniority system and the House Committee on Rules. See, "Plan for Remaking Congress: Coming Fight against Change," *U.S. News and World Report*, March 15, 1946, pp. 24–25.

17. "Congress Meets the Test," *New York Times*, October 18, 1965, p. 34; and "A Salute," *Washington Post*, October 24, 1965, p. E6.

18. "The New Congress," *New York Times*, January 3, 1965, sec. 4, p. 8. See also, "Congress Gets under Way," *New York Times*, January 6, 1965, p. 38 ("the prospect is for an unusually busy and productive session in both houses"); Tom Wicker, "Johnson and Congress," *New York Times*, February 7, 1965, sec. 4, p. 5; and "LBJ and Congress: After a Fast Start, Harder Tests Ahead," *U.S. News and World Report*, March 1, 1965, pp. 52–53.

19. "Strong Start on Capitol Hill," *New York Times*, January 17, 1965, sec. 4, p. 12.

20. "The First 100 Days," *Washington Post*, April 16, 1965, p. A20. See also "Formidable Task," *Washington Post*, April 25, 1965, p. E6.

21. Tom Wicker, "Johnson's 100 Days: Domestic Achievements in Legislation Compared with Period under Roosevelt," *New York Times*, April 15, 1965, p. 22.

22. Arthur Krock, "In the Nation: At Breakneck Speed," *New York Times*, April 11, 1965, sec. 4, p. 15. See also William V. Shannon, "All the Way with L.B.J.?" *New York Times*, April 12, 1965, p. 34; "Congress: Hundred-Day Mark," *Newsweek*, April 19, 1965, p. 26; "LBJ's '100 Days'—A Record Piling Up," *U.S. News and World Report*, April 26, 1965, pp. 41–44; and "Big Week for Congress," *New York Times*, April 11, 1965, sec. 4, p. 14.

23. "Congress: Second Phase," *New York Times*, April 26, 1965, p. 30.

24. James Reston, "Washington: The Quiet Revolution," *New York Times*, August 6, 1965, p. 26.

25. Tom Wicker, "LBJ and Congress: No Rubber Stamps on the Hill," *New York Times*, August 29, 1965, sec. 4, p. 13. See also Wicker, "Politics: The Man Who Delivered the Goods," August 31, 1965, p. 32; and "Johnson and Congress," *New York Times*, June 20, 1965, sec. 4, p. 2.

26. "The President and Congress," *New York Times*, July 11, 1965, sec. 4, p. 10. See also "Big Week in Congress," *New York Times*, August 1, 1965, sec. 4, p. 10.

27. William S. White, "Johnson Program," *Washington Post*, August 4, 1965, p. A18.

28. Marquis Childs, "How LBJ Branded the 89th Congress," *Washington Post*, October 18, 1965, p. A16; and Drew Pearson, "Laws by the Loaf: President's Bread Breaking and Freshman Idealism Made 89th Congress a Smasher," *Washington Post*, October 24, 1965, p. E7. See also Tom Wicker, "Winds of Change in the Senate," *New York Times Magazine*, September 12, 1965, sec. 6, pp. 52–53, 119–20, 124; and Rowland Evans and Robert Novak, "Inside Report . . . Grumbling on Capitol Hill," October 4, 1965, p. A21.

29. Tom Wicker, "The Fruitful Session," *New York Times*, October 25, 1965, p. 41. Wicker noted that "an effective relationship does not always require Congress to put its own mark on legislation." Johnson had moved an education aid bill through Congress unchanged, overcoming the usual debate and amending of legislation.

30. "A Salute," *Washington Post*, October 24, 1965, p. E6.

31. "Congress Meets the Test," *New York Times*, October 18, 1965, p. 34. See also "Exit Congress," *New York Times*, October 24, 1965, sec. 4, p. 1.

32. "On a Note of Triumph," *New York Times*, October 24, 1965, sec. 4, p. 10. See also, "Congress Meets the Test"; "Exit Congress"; "Congress: Squaring Off over 14(b)," *Time*, October 1, 1965, p. 30; and "When Congress Got Its Back Up," *U.S. News and World Report*, October 11, 1965, pp. 41–42.

33. "From Brickbats to Bouquets," *Wall Street Journal*, October 26, 1965, p. 16. See also, "A Frenzy of Lawmaking," *Wall Street Journal*, August 4, 1965, p. 8.

34. Raymond Moley, "Laws: Then What Next?," *Newsweek*, October 11, 1965, p. 116. See also Moley, "State-Local Finances," *Newsweek*, May 3, 1965, p. 100; "Tax Help For Parents," *Newsweek*, October 18, 1965, p. 132; and "Inefficient Colleges," *Newsweek*, October 25, 1965, p. 124. Also see Henry C. Wallich, "The Powerful Society," *Newsweek*, October 4, 1965, p. 84; Henry Hazlitt, "Great Society's Cost," *Newsweek*, November 22, 1965, p. 90; Walter Lippmann, "The Great—and Good—Society," *Newsweek*, November 22, 1965,

p. 25; "Not By Popular Demand," *Wall Street Journal*, April 30, 1965, p. 16; "Restiveness on Capitol Hill," *Wall Street Journal*, July 2, 1965, p. 6; and "Pause for Digestion," *Wall Street Journal*, October 4, 1965, p. 16.

35. "Housecleaning," *Washington Post*, January 5, 1965, p. A12. See also, "Congress Looking Inward," *Washington Post*, May 12, 1965, p. A14; and "Congress Gets under Way," *New York Times*, January 6, 1965, p. 38.

36. William V. Shannon, "Congress: Reform Still Needed," *New York Times*, September 6, 1965, p. 14. See also Arthur Krock, "In the Nation: A Bureaucratic Explosion," *New York Times*, May 13, 1965, p. 36; and Tom Wicker, "Congress: What Role in the Twentieth Century," *New York Times*, August 24, 1965, p. 30.

37. These background comments are summarized from news reports; Congressional Quarterly, *Origins and Development of Congress*; and Oleszek, *Congressional Procedures*.

38. "Watchmen on the Hill," *Washington Post*, March 18, 1968, p. A16; and "Senatorial Code of Ethics," *Washington Post*, March 25, 1968, p. A14.

39. "Slow Start on Ethics," *New York Times*, March 20, 1968, p. 46; and "No Gain for Ethics," *New York Times*, March 24, 1968, sec. 4, p. 16.

40. "Senatorial Ethics," *New York Times*, November 28, 1968, p. 36.

41. "On Legislating Morality," *Wall Street Journal*, March 27, 1968, p. 16; and Jerry Landauer, "Myth of the Part-Time Congressman," *Wall Street Journal*, April 15, 1968, p. 18. See also Landauer, "Reforms to Prevent Another Dodd Scandal Urged by Ethics Unit; Senate Backing Seen," *Wall Street Journal*, March 18, 1968, p. 8; and "Quiet Burials for Congress Reforms," *Wall Street Journal*, September 6, 1968, p. 8.

42. "The Congress: Guarding the Assets," *Time*, March 29, 1968, p. 25. See also "Congress: Keeping Them Honest," *Newsweek*, April 15, 1968, p. 50.

43. The background is summarized from news reports in the three newspapers and three magazines as well as from Congressional Quarterly, *Origins and Development of Congress*; and Oleszek, *Congressional Procedures*.

44. Robert Bendiner, "Congress in the Age of Aquarius," *New York Times*, January 19, 1970, p. 46. See also, "Who Will Abolish Seniority?" *Washington Post*, February 17, 1970, p. A14; "Spotlight on Seniority," *Washington Post*, March 24, 1970, p. A18; and David Broder, "Revolt of Liberal Democrats in the House Is Long Overdue," *Washington Post*, March 24, 1970, p. A19.

45. "Rebellion in the House," *New York Times*, March 22, 1970, sec. 4, p. 16. See also, "Lights on in Congress," *New York Times*, July 22, 1970, p. 40; "The Young Liberals' Problem," *Wall Street Journal*, February 26, 1970, p. 16; Tom Wicker, "In the Nation: Opening up the House," *New York Times*, March 17, 1970, p. 42; "Uprising on Capitol Hill," *New York Times*, February 18, 1970, p. 46; John W. Finney, "Democrats in Congress See Need for a 'Revolution,'" *New York Times*, February 22, 1970, sec. 4, p. 1; and "Alternatives to Seniority," *New York Times*, February 23, 1970, p. 26.

46. William V. Shannon, "The House Decides to Stop Being So Secretive," *New York Times*, August 2, 1970, sec. 4, p. 3. See also "New Day on Capitol Hill," *New York Times*, July 29, 1970, p. 38.

47. "Down Payment on Congressional Reform," *Washington Post*, September 22, 1970, p. A20.

48. "Seniority under Attack," *New York Times*, November 18, 1970, p. 46. See also Marquis Childs, "New Ball Game for the House," *Washington Post*, November 18, 1970, p. A19.

49. David Lawrence, "Why Not Four Years for Both the President and Congress?" *U.S. News and World Report*, February 2, 1970, p. 76.

50. "Congress's Nine Old Men," *Newsweek*, February 2, 1970, pp. 20–21. See also John W. Finney, "Generation Gap in the House: The Young Want More Power," *New York Times*, March 22, 1970, sec. 4, p. 3; and Tom Wicker, "Stamping Out Seniority," *New York Times*, December 8, 1970, p. 47.

51. "Watergate: The Trial and the Senate," *Washington Post*, January 15, 1973, p. A20; and "Senate Duty," *New York Times*, May 3, 1973, p. 42.

52. Vermont Royster, "Thinking Things Over: The System," *Wall Street Journal*, May 8, 1973, p. 26; and James M. Naughton, "Congress Ascending," *New York Times*, May 12, 1973, pp. 1, 6.

53. "Congress Awakens," *New York Times*, May 20, 1973, sec. 4, p. 16.

54. "The Hearings Go On," *New York Times*, June 6, 1973, p. 46; "Watergate Pressures," *New York Times*, June 2, 1973, p. 30; and "A Proper Forum," *New York Times*, June 15, 1973, p. 36.

55. "Neglected Agenda," *New York Times*, June 18, 1973, p. 28; and "The Impoundment Battle," *Washington Post*, February 6, 1973, p. A18.

56. See, for example, Alan L. Otten, "Whose Emergency?," *Wall Street Journal*, January 18, 1973, p. 12; Alan L. Otten, "Power Plays," *Wall Street Journal*, January 26, 1973, p. 12; and Fred M. Hechinger, "Executive Obligation," *New York Times*, April 16, 1973, p. 37.

57. See, for example, Tom Wicker, "No Time to 'Get It Over With,'" *New York Times*, June 3, 1973, sec. 4, p. 17; Anthony Lewis, "Rush to Judgment," *New York Times*, June 4, 1973, p. 35; and William Raspberry, "The Senate Hearings: 'Let Them Drone On,'" *Washington Post*, June 8, 1973, p. A29.

58. "Watergate: There Is No Quick or Easy Way Out," *Washington Post*, June 6, 1973, p. A18. See also "Two Investigations; Two Different Goals," *Washington Post*, May 17, 1973, p. A26.

59. "The Senate Hearing," *Wall Street Journal*, May 22, 1973, p. 26; and "Congress and the Presidency," *Wall Street Journal*, June 4, 1973, p. 16.

60. "Congress, the Hearings and the Nation's Business," *Washington Post*, August 19, 1973, p. C6.

61. "No Undue Haste," *New York Times*, September 10, 1973, p. 34; and "The Committee's Task," *New York Times*, September 24, 1973, p. 32. See also Clayton Fritchey, "The Unfinished Hearings," *Washington Post*, August 25, 1973, p. A17.

62. "The Hearings Continue," *New York Times*, September 13, 1973, p. 46.

63. ". . . Congress Must Decide," *New York Times*, October 22, 1973, p. 30.

64. "Congress: The Do-Something 93rd," *Newsweek*, December 31, 1973, p. 12.

65. "Looking Backward," *New York Times*, July 11, 1973, p. 40; and "No Strings," *New York Times*, October 26, 1973, p. 42.

66. "Political Reversal," *New York Times*, December 23, 1973, sec. 4, p. 10.

67. James Reston, "Let's Hear From Congress," *New York Times*, November 30, 1973, p. 37.

68. "End of an Era," *Wall Street Journal*, August 16, 1973, p. 12.

69. "Impeachment," *New York Times*, October 31, 1973, p. 44.

70. Anthony Lewis, "Living with Illusion," *New York Times*, November 26, 1973, p. 31; and William Raspberry, ". . . As Congress Drags Its Feet," *Washington Post*, December 5, 1973, p. A31.

71. "Congress's Burden," *Wall Street Journal*, November 19, 1973, p. 14.

72. George F. Will, "Impeachment for the Right Reason," *Washington Post*, October 23, 1973, p. A22. See also Joseph Kraft, "Forcing Mr. Nixon Out of Office," *Washington Post*, October 23, 1973, p. A23. "There are many possible ways to achieve the one acceptable resolution of the present crisis—the forcing out of the President. The only real question is whether the country's leaders, especially in the House of Representatives, have the courage to be free men."

73. "Special Prosecutor," *New York Times*, November 2, 1973, p. 40.

74. David S. Broder, "Power: Theory and Reality," *Washington Post*, December 12, 1973, p. A30.

75. "Conscience Primer," *New York Times*, February 22, 1974, p. 32; and David E. Rosenbaum, "An Assessment of Ervin & Co.: Pathfinders," *New York Times*, April 28, 1974, sec. 4, p. 3.

76. "A United House," *New York Times*, February 7, 1974, p. 36; and "Fair Procedure," *New York Times*, May 4, 1974, p. 40.

77. William S. White, "The Decline of Congress," *Washington Post*, February 16, 1974, p. A19.

78. "Restoring the Federal Balance," *Time*, May 6, 1974, p. 14; Tom Wicker, "The Man Is Not the Office," *New York Times*, March 17, 1974, sec. 4, p. 15; "No Time for Delay," *New York Times*, April 23, 1974, p. 40; "Checks and Balances," *Newsweek*, May 6, 1974, p. 76; and Russell Baker, "Moods of Washington," *New York Times Magazine*, March 24, 1974, pp. 71–72.

79. "The Tortoise on the Hill," *Newsweek,* June 10, 1974, pp. 23–25; and "Protecting the Presidency," *Washington Post*, May 29, 1974, p. A18. An earlier critical news article is "Congress's Go-Slow Approach to the 'Nixon Problem,'" *U.S. News and World Report*, February 4, 1974, pp. 20–21.

80. Joseph Kraft, "Impeachment: Toward a Decision on the Merits," *Washington Post*, June 2, 1974, p. C7; and Joseph Alsop, "The Impeachment Timetable," *Washington Post*, May 29, 1974, p. A19. See also J. W. Anderson, "Impeachment Inquiry: Running Late," *Washington Post*, June 21, 1974, p. A22.

81. "Impeachable Offenses," *New York Times*, July 14, 1974, sec. 4, p. 16. See also "A Sense of Duty," *New York Times*, July 26, 1974, p. 32.

82. "Agony and Pride," *New York Times*, July 30, 1974, p. 32; "The Great Task Begun," *New York Times*, August 4, 1974, sec. 4, p. 16; and "Watergate Reforms," *New York Times*, July 29, 1974, p. 22.

83. William V. Shannon, "The Arithmetic of Impeachment," *New York Times*, July 27, 1974, p. 29.

84. Anthony Lewis, "The People Do Govern," *New York Times*, July 29, 1974, p. 23.

85. "The Judiciary Committee's Work," *Washington Post*, July 31, 1974, p. A20. The *Post* criticized the Rodino committee on one count—failing to place enough emphasis in the articles of impeachment on the political bribery and extortion in the case of the American Milk Producers, Inc., support of President Nixon. See "Impeachment: ITT and Milk," *New York Times*, July 26, 1974, p. A26.

86. "Congress: Reforms for Others Only," *Time*, October 21, 1974, p. 38. See also "Drawing Up a Balance Sheet on the 93rd," *Time*, December 23, 1974, p. 9. The *New York Times* had earlier urged work on many of the reforms. See "The Homestretch," *New York Times*, July 7, 1974, sec. 4, p. 14.

87. "Congress: Return of King Caucus," *Time*, December 16, 1974, pp. 17–18.

88. "A Congress That Did a Lot Is Coming Back To Do More," *U.S. News and World Report*, November 4, 1974, pp. 33–34.

89. Background information is from Mark J. Rozell, *The Press and the Carter Presidency* (Boulder, Colo.: Westview Press, 1989).

90. "The Carter Presidency," *New York Times*, November 7, 1976, p. E16.

91. Tom Wicker, "Mr. Carter's Mandate," *New York Times,* November 7, 1976, p. E17.

92. "What to Expect When Congress 'Welcomes' Carter," *U.S. News and World Report*, November 29, 1976, pp. 17–18.

93. "How Lawmakers Will Treat Ambitious White House Ideas," *U.S. News and World Report*, December 27, 1976, pp. 17–19; "Carter's Record as Governor—Clues to the Future," *U.S. News and World Report*, December 13, 1976, p. 28. See also "Will Congress Seize Reins from a Democratic White House," *U.S. News and World Report*, November 15, 1976, p. 25; "Outlook 77—A Fresh Start," *U.S. News and World Report*, December 27, 1976, p. 12; and "A New Era Begins," *U.S. News and World Report*, January 24, 1977, p. 16.

94. Stanley Cloud, "Jimmy's Mixed Signals," *Time*, October 4, 1976, p. 30; "A Carter Administration," *Time*, November 8, 1976, pp. 24, 26; "Carter!" *Time*, November 15, 1976, p. 15; "Man of the Year: I'm Jimmy Carter, and . . ." *Time*, January 3, 1977, p. 14; David S. Broder, "Carter's Dilemma," *Washington Post*, November 28, 1976, p. B7; Albert Hunt, "President Carter and Capitol Hill," *Wall Street Journal*, January 24, 1977, p. 16; "Enter Majority Rule," *New York Times*, January 3, 1977, p. 20; and Anthony Lewis, "The Long and the Short," *New York Times*, March 3, 1977, p. A33.

95. "The Congress That Startled Everybody," *U.S. News and World Report*, December 19, 1977, p. 14; and "Outlook '78—In Congress, the Mood Will Get Even Feistier," *U.S. News and World Report*, December 26, 1977, pp. 33–34.

96. Mark Rozell, *The Press and the Carter Presidency*, pp. 46–56. One article by David Broder stands out as an exception. "Much has been said, most of it critical, about President Carter's handling of Congress. Less has been said—and more is justified—about Congress's handling of the President. The end-of-the-session assessments proceed on the assumption that in the circus that is Washington, Congress is the lion act and the President's job, as the lion-tamer, is to turn those brawling 'cats' into a disciplined troupe of performers. This year, that analogy is doubly in error. It is in error, first, because these 'cats' in Congress have become increasingly immune to whip cracking. If they need anyone, it is

not the President . . . but their own leaders. Second . . . the tricks that had to be learned for the show to be a success were not things Carter could teach Congress, but things Congress could teach Carter." David S. Broder, "The Senate Has No Excuse," *Washington Post*, December 18, 1977, p. C7. See also David Broder, "Tensions between Carter and Congress," *Washington Post*, March 2, 1977, p. A19.

97. Albert R. Hunt, "President Carter and Capitol Hill," *Wall Street Journal*, January 24, 1977, p. 16; and Hunt, "Jimmy Carter vs. Congress?" *Wall Street Journal*, March 25, 1977, p. 14. See also Hedrick Smith, "Carter's Support in Congress," *New York Times*, June 18, 1977, p. 7.

98. John Herbers, "The Carter-Congress Rift May Just Have Started," *New York Times*, March 27, 1977, sec. 4, p. 4.

99. "On a Collision Course," *U.S. News and World Report*, April 18, 1977, p. 14.

100. Gerald Parshall, "Congress vs. President: Behind the Growing Feud," *U.S. News and World Report*, May 23, 1977, p. 23.

101. Lou Cannon, "The Independent Democrats," *Washington Post*, May 23, 1977, p. A1.

102. See Edward Walsh, "Carter Has Mixed Scorecard in Skirmishes with Hill," *Washington Post*, June 19, 1977, p. A14; Adam Clymer, "One Party Rules, but Two Share the Power," *New York Times*, June 12, 1977, sec. 4, p. 2; Joseph Kraft, "A Carter Base in the Congress?" *Washington Post*, June 19, 1977, p. B7; and Susan Fraker, "Shadowboxing," *Newsweek*, June 6, 1977, p. 15.

103. Thomas J. Foley, "Worst Congress in Years—Or Is It?" *U.S. News and World Report*, September 26, 1977, p. 26. See also Martin Tolchin, "Power Balance Tips to Congress from President," *New York Times*, October 9, 1977, p. 31.

104. "Carter and Congress," *U.S. News and World Report*, November 21, 1977, p. 21. See also "Congress: Showdown Ahead," *Time*, November 7, 1977, p. 19.

105. Meg Greenfield, "The Club," *Newsweek*, October 10, 1977, p. 118; and Josph Kraft, "Leadership by Reform," *Washington Post*, October 6, 1977, p. A19.

106. Thomas J. Foley, "Worst Congress in Years—Or Is It?" pp. 25–26. See also "They Are Paying the Price of Virtue," *Time*, March 14, 1977, p. 12. This story noted that a Harris survey of public attitudes toward ten national institutions showed that members of Congress ranked eighth, above only corporation executives and labor bosses.

107. Marvin Stone, "Some Old Gang?," *U.S. News and World Report*, March 14, 1977, p. 88. See also "Taking the Sugar without the Pill," *Washington Post*, February 6, 1977, p. C6; "Income and Ethics on Capitol Hill," *Washington Post*, February 8, 1977, p. A18; "The Pay Issue Persists," *Washington Post*, May 2, 1977, p. A22; "The Pay Issue in the House," *Washington Post*, June 28, 1977, p. A18; "On Ethics: Let the Third Shoe Drop," *New York Times*, February 20, 1977, sec. 4, p. 14; and "At $57,500, It's Not a Poor House," *New York Times*, March 2, 1977, p. 20.

108. "Make Me Take It," *Wall Street Journal*, February 4, 1977, p. 8. The *Journal* pointed out that members profit financially from their positions in many ways, including large capital gains on home appreciation in the Washington metropolitan area. See "The Most Expensive Loophole," *Wall Street Journal*, March 21, 1977, p. 18.

109. Charles O. Jones, "Ronald Reagan and the U.S. Congress: Visible-Hand Politics," in Charles O. Jones, ed., *The Reagan Legacy: Promise and Performance* (Chatham, House, 1988), p. 39.

110. "Where Are the Democrats?" *New York Times*, February 12, 1981, p. A26. See also Joseph Kraft, "The 'Republicrat' Debate," *Washington Post*, April 12, 1981, p. D7.

111. "Congress and the Reagan Cannonball," *New York Times*, March 22, 1981, sec. 4, p. 18. See also "The Reagan Road to Recovery," *New York Times*, February 22, 1981, sec. 4, p. 18; and Martin Tolchin, "Moving on the Fast Track," *New York Times*, February 24, 1981, sec. 2, p. 10.

112. "Riding the Congressional Horse," *New York Times*, June 21, 1981, sec. 4, p. 22. See also "Behind the Budget Battle," *Newsweek*, December 7, 1981, p. 35.

113. "Crocodile Tears," *Wall Street Journal*, June 30, 1981, p. 30.

114. "Calling a Halt," *Wall Street Journal*, November 24, 1981, p. 32.

115. David S. Broder, "Congress Has No King," *Washington Post*, September 16, 1981, p. A25.

116. Hobart Rowen, "Tough to Buck Popular President," *Washington Post*, May 3, 1981, p. G1; Haynes Johnson, "About This Matter of Summoning Spirits from the Vasty Deep," *Washington Post*, August 2, 1981, p. A3; and George F. Will, "A Day to Remember," *Newsweek*, July 6, 1981, p. 84. See also Martin Tolchin, "Democrats, Still Defensive, Hope to Generate an Offense," *New York Times*, March 29, 1981, sec. 4, p. 3; and Mark Shields, "It's Okay to Act Like the Opposition," *Washington Post*, May 8, 1981, p. A19.

117. "The Coming Budget Showdown," *Washington Post*, December 10, 1981, p. A30.

118. Steven V. Roberts, "Budget Battle: Reagan Ahead," *New York Times*, February 11, 1981, p. 28.

119. "Congressional Cop-Out," *Wall Street Journal*, September 25, 1981, p. 32. Congress did not even satisfy parochial needs very well. At the end of 1981, David Broder explained what members of Congress would face when meeting constituents in their districts. "Show a little pity for Senator Spender and Congressman Contracts. . . . This Congress has been a horror show for them. . . . Not one new program, not one new agency, not one rotten little pilot project they can pin on the wall and send out a press release to brag about. . . . [David Stockman is] whipping around the Democrats like Spender and Contracts and their staff as if they weren't the best-fed, best-paid, best-equipped Congress in the world." David Broder, "Have Pity on These Wretches," *Washington Post*, December 16, 1981, p. A31. See also "Christmastime on Capitol Hill," *Time*, July 27, 1981, p. 25.

120. "The Treason of Congress," *Wall Street Journal*, October 15, 1981, p. 28. See also "Tip's Gauntlet," *Wall Street Journal*, October 29, 1981, p. 30.

121. This background is summarized from news reports in the *New York Times, Wall Street Journal, Washington Post, Time, Newsweek,* and *U.S. News and World Report*.

122. "The Independent Counsel's Task," *Washington Post*, December 14, 1986, p. H6. See also, "Iran 2: How Best To Find It Out," *New York Times*, December 14, 1986, sec. 4, p. 22.

123. Tom Wicker, "Mr. Reagan's Choice," *New York Times*, January 9, 1987, p. A27; and Wicker, "Two Different Gates," *New York Times*, December 12, 1986, p. A35. See also Russell Baker, "Such a Swell Gang," *New York Times*, December 13, 1986, sec. 1, p. 27.

124. Linda Greenhouse, "Political Erosion: With a Shift of Gravity, Congress Begins Era," *New York Times*, January 4, 1987, sec. 4, p. 1.

125. Steven V. Roberts, "Congress Stands Ready to Test the Executive," *New York Times*, December 21, 1986, sec. 4, p. 1.

126. Norman Podhoretz, "The Imperial Congress," *Washington Post*, December 23, 1986, p. A19.

127. James J. Kilpatrick, "An Inefficient Engine Starts Again," *Washington Post*, January 4, 1987, p. C8.

128. Suzanne Garment, "We Don't Want Watergate Again, But Get It Anyway," *Wall Street Journal*, December 12, 1986, p. 28; and George F. Will, "Stonewalling on Immunity," *Washington Post*, December 17, 1986, p. A27.

129. "The Tower Report," *Wall Street Journal*, February 27, 1987, p. 14; and "The President's Speech," *Wall Street Journal*, March 4, 1987, p. 30.

130. "Reagan's Obligation," *Wall Street Journal*, May 5, 1987, p. 36; and "Not Following the Script," *Wall Street Journal*, May 12, 1987, p. 32. See also Dan Morgan and Walter Pincus, "On Tuesday, Congress Raises Curtain on Iran-Contra Affair," *Washington Post*, May 3, 1987, pp. A1, A16.

131. Charles Krauthammer, "Spectacle," *Washington Post*, May 22, 1987, p. A27.

132. Linda Greenhouse, "As the Inquiry Unfolds, Pitfalls for Lawmakers," *New York Times*, July 21, 1987, p. A6.

133. Mary McGrory, "Congress and the Constitution," *Washington Post*, June 14, 1987, pp. H1, H5.

134. Mary McGrory, "The Congressional Equation," *Washington Post*, June 23, 1987, p. A2. See also McGrory, "Who'll Break the Colonel's Spell?" *Washington Post*, July 12, 1987, pp. C1, C5.

135. David Ignatius, "Ollie's Last Laugh," *Washington Post*, July 12, 1987, pp. C1, C2.

136. Meg Greenfield, "Giving Truth a Bad Name," *Newsweek*, July 27, 1987, p. 64.

137. Tamar Jacoby, Robert B. Cullen, and Eleanor Clift, "Who's In Charge Here?" *Newsweek*, July 27, 1987, p. 18.

138. Haynes Johnson, "The Power Conflict in Iran-Contra Affair," *Washington Post*, May 31, 1987, pp. A4, A5; and Johnson, "The Healing Light of Disclosure," *Washington Post*, July 15, 1987, p. A2. See also Albert R. Hunt, "Beyond the Ollie Show," *Wall Street Journal*, July 15, 1987, p. 28.

139. Haynes Johnson, "Three Months of Hearings Fail to Crack the Case," *Washington Post*, August 4, 1987, pp. A1, A7.

140. "To Stop Elected Dictatorships," *New York Times*, August 9, 1987, sec. 4, p. 24. See also "The Iran-Contra Report," *Washington Post*, November 19, 1987, p. A22.

141. "The Iran-Contra Report," *Wall Street Journal*, November 20, 1987, p. 28. See also "Reagan's Hard Lesson," *Wall Street Journal*, November 18, 1987, p. 32.

142. "High Noon for the Constitution," *Wall Street Journal*, July 14, 1987, p. 32. See also Raymond Price, "Were the Iran-Contra Hearings Worth It?" *Wall Street Journal*, August 7, 1987, p. 20.

143. Brian Duffy, "Who's in Charge Here?" *U.S. News and World Report*, November 24, 1986, pp. 18–22; and Peter Cary, "Examining the Loose Ends in the Iran-Contra Affair," *U.S. News and World Report*, October 26, 1987, pp. 22–23.

144. Mortimer B. Zuckerman, "Implausible Deniability," *U.S. News and World Report*, August 3, 1987, p. 68. See also David R. Gergen, "Disease of Distrust," *U.S. News and World Report*, July 27, 1987, p. 64.

145. Tom Kenworthy and Helen Dewar, "Divided Congress Grants President Authority to Wage War against Iraq," *Washington Post*, January 13, 1991, pp. A1, A25; and Richard Lacayo, "A Reluctant Go-Ahead," *Time*, January 21, 1991, pp. 32–33.

146. Anthony Lewis, "War in the Gulf?" *New York Times*, October 22, 1990, p. A19; and Lewis, "War and the President," *New York Times*, November 30, 1990, p. A33.

147. George F. Will, "Mobilization's Deadly Momentum," *Washington Post*, November 15, 1990, p. A25; and Will, "Better 60-40 Than No Vote at All," *Washington Post*, January 9, 1991, p. A19.

148. George F. Will, "Once Again, Ike Was Right," *Newsweek*, January 12, 1991, p. 60.

149. Charles Krauthammer, "Make Congress Choose," *Washington Post*, November 30, 1990, p. A29.

150. Charles Krauthammer, "An Executive Declaration of War," *Washington Post*, November 16, 1990, p. A19. See also Susan F. Rasky, "Congress Asks What It Should Do in the Gulf, and How," *New York Times*, November 18, 1990, sec. 4, pp. 1–2; Susan F. Rasky, "Congress and the Gulf," *New York Times*, December 17, 1990, pp. A1, 13; Adam Clymer, "102nd Congress Opens, Troubled On Gulf but without a Consensus," *New York Times*, January 4, 1991, pp. A1, A8.

151. Nathaniel C. Nash, "Congress and the Crisis: To Intervene or Not?" *New York Times*, September 13, 1990, p. A10; and Mary McGrory, "The Hill's Own Wimp Factor," *Washington Post*, January 6, 1991, pp. C1, C5.

152. Mary McGrory, "Baker's Tempering Touch," *Washington Post*, November 15, 1990, p. A2.

153. "The Gulf Buildup," *Washington Post*, November 11, 1990, p. B6. See also "The 60-Day Clock," *Washington Post*, October 9, 1990, p. A20; "Making Timely Notice Timely," *Washington Post*, October 29, 1990, p. A14; "Calling Back Congress," *Washington Post*, November 14, 1990, p. A16; and "U.N. Logic," *Washington Post*, November 29, 1990, p. A22.

154. "Who Can Declare War?" *New York Times*, December 15, 1990, p. A26; and "Where is Congress on the Gulf?" *New York Times*, January 3, 1991, p. A20. See also "War by Default," *New York Times*, December 16, 1990, sec. 4, p. 14; Anna Quindlen, "Consent of Congress," *New York Times*, December

6, 1990, p. A27, Tom Wicker, "Bush's War Powers," *New York Times*, November 18, 1990, sec. 4, p. 17; and Wicker, "Bush Stands Warned," *New York Times*, December 2, 1990, sec. 4, p. 19.

155. "Congress's Calhoun Strategy," *New York Times*, January 7, 1991, p. A16.

156. Paul A. Gigot, "No Bipartisanship From Congress In The Gulf," *Wall Street Journal*, November 16, 1990, p. A14. See also Gigot, "As War Nears, Democrats Wiggle and Wobble," *Wall Street Journal*, January 11, 1991, p. A10; George J. Church, "The Case for War," *Time*, November 26, 1990, p. 106; and "Saddam's Protectors," *Wall Street Journal*, January 11, 1991, p. A10.

157. Robin Toner, "Mindful of History, Congress Agonizes over Going to War," *New York Times*, January 13, 1991, sec. 1, p. 12.

158. "Plan Now for Peace," *New York Times*, February 11, 1991, p. A18; and Anthony Lewis, "Presidential Power," *New York Times*, January 14, 1991, p. A17.

159. E. J. Dionne, Jr., "Foolishness Falls Victim to War Debate as Eloquence Escalates," *Washington Post*, January 12, 1991, pp. A8, A13. See also Adam Clymer, "Congress in Step," *New York Times*, January 14, 1991, p. A11.

160. David S. Broder, "Bravo, Congress," *Washington Post*, January 15, 1991, p. A21. See also Broder, "Undervalued Congress," *Washington Post*, January 30, 1991, p. A21.

161. Background is summarized from news reports in *New York Times, Wall Street Journal, Washington Post, Time, Newsweek*, and *U.S. News and World Report*.

162. David E. Rosenbaum, "Public Calls Lawmakers Corrupt and Pampered," *New York Times*, October 10, 1991, p. B17.

163. Richard Morin and Helen Dewar, "Approval of Congress Hits All-Time Low, Poll Finds," *Washington Post*, March 20, 1992, p. A16.

164. David S. Broder, "Yes, There Are Good People in Congress," *Washington Post*, November 6, 1991, p. A25. Another columnist, Michael Kinsley, decried the hypocrisy of those leading the criticism of Congress, the "columnists and commentators who make many times what a member of Congress does, and who are far more steeped in the culture of Washington than a congressman who goes home every weekend." See Michael Kinsley, "Hypocrisy from the Heartland," *Washington Post*, October 12, 1991, p. A25.

165. "Sham and Shame," *Wall Street Journal*, March 4, 1991, p. A8.

166. "Constituent Disservice," *Wall Street Journal*, April 18, 1991, p. A16.

167. "Kitegate Spills Over," *Wall Street Journal*, October 4, 1991, p. A14; and "Congress's Non-Bank Bank," *Wall Street Journal*, September 25, 1991, p. A10. See also "A New Political Ball Game," *Wall Street Journal*, October 16, 1991, p. A16.

168. "House Cleaning. Also Senate," *New York Times*, October 20, 1991, sec. 4, p. 14; and "Eating Ethics," *New York Times*, October 8, 1991, p. A24. See also "The Bouncing Bank Cleanup Lags," *New York Times*, October 2, 1991, p. A22.

169. "Listen to the Anger," *New York Times*, March 26, 1992, p. A22.

170. See generally "El Al D'Amato," *New York Times*, December 4, 1991, p. A26; "Come Clean on the House Bank," *New York Times*, March 11, 1992,

p. A22; "Not All Bounces Are Bad," *New York Times*, March 19, 1992, p. A22; and "Worse Than the House Bank," *New York Times*, March 14, 1992, p. 24.

171. "The Keating None?" *New York Times*, October 23, 1991, p. A22; and "The Keating One Hundred," *New York Times*, November 21, 1991, p. A26. See also Jill Abramson and David Rogers, "The Keating 535," *Wall Street Journal*, January 10, 1991, p. A1.

172. "Bounce the House Bank," *Washington Post*, September 23, 1991, p. A10. See also "The Speaker Has Spoken—And Well," *Washington Post*, September 29, 1991, p. C6; "The House Names Names," *Washington Post*, April 19, 1992, p. C6; and "The House Bank (Cont'd)," *Washington Post*, April 28, 1992, p. A14.

173. Nancy Gibbs, "Perk City," *Time*, October 14, 1991, pp. 18, 19–20.

174. Margaret Carlson, "The Ultimate Men's Club," *Time*, October 21, 1991, pp. 50–51. See also Eleanor Clift, "Congress: The Ultimate Men's Club," *Newsweek*, October 21, 1991, p. 32.

175. Larry Martz and Eleanor Clift, "Who Says There's No Free Lunch?" *Newsweek*, October 14, 1991, p. 30; Gloria Borger, "Blowing the Lid on Kiters Inc.," *U.S. News and World Report*, March 23, 1992, p. 36; and Gloria Borger, Stephen J. Hedges, and Gary Cohen, "Congress: Life among the Ruins," *U.S. News and World Report*, March 30, 1992, pp. 24–25. See also Tom Kenworthy, "Is the House Haunted by Midnight?" *Washington Post*, March 14, 1992, p. A4; Guy Gugliotta and Kenneth J. Cooper, "String of House Scandals Saps Public Confidence," *Washington Post*, March 11, 1992, pp. A1, A6; and Howard Kurtz, "Hill Perks: Old Story Resonates Anew," *Washington Post*, April 9, 1992, p. A4. Other news stories focused on such different problems troubling Congress as the dominance of symbolism over substance, fragmentation, lack of deference to leadership, and divided government. See Adam Clymer, "An Institution under Duress," *New York Times*, November 10, 1991, p. A23; Clymer, "Tarnished Congress," *New York Times*, November 29, 1991, p. D7; and Helen Dewar, "On Capitol Hill, Symbols Triumph," *Washington Post*, November 26, 1991, pp. A1, A4.

176. David Gergen, "Profiles in Privilege," *U.S. News and World Report*, October 14, 1991, p. 104.

177. George F. Will, "Perpetual Incumbency Machine," *Washington Post*, November 10, 1991, p. C7; and Will, "Term Limits: Antitrust in Politics," *Washington Post*, November 3, 1991, p. C7. See also his "A Case For Term Limits," *Newsweek*, October 21, 1991, p. 76; "No More Careerists in Congress," *Washington Post*, October 1, 1992, p. A27; and "What Voters Did for the System," *Washington Post*, November 12, 1992, p. A21.

178. Michael Kramer, "Shame on Them All," *Time*, October 21, 1991, pp. 46–47.

179. Stanley W. Cloud, "Bums of the Year: Congress," *Time*, January 6, 1992, p. 48. This column is accompanied by three drawings: one of a pig speaking into a group of microphones, one of the Capitol dome coming apart, and one of several hands dipping into a pile of cash.

180. Tom Kenworthy, "Keep the Bums In!" *Washington Post*, April 26, 1992, p. C5. See also Haynes Johnson, "A Bankruptcy of Principles," *Washington Post*, October 4, 1991, p. A2.

181. Mary McGrory, "Toxic Spring in Washington," *Washington Post*, April 5, 1992, p. C5. Other columnists commenting included William Safire, "Hail to the House," *New York Times*, October 7, 1991, p. A17; Paul A. Gigot, "The Voters Flex before Throwing the Bums Out," *Wall Street Journal*, March 6, 1992, p. A8; Meg Greenfield, "Everyone vs. Congress," *Washington Post*, November 5, 1991, p. A21; Greenfield, "The Judges on the Hill," *Washington Post*, October 8, 1991, p. A19; and David S. Broder, "House at Play," *Washington Post*, March 17, 1992, p. A17. A drawing of a rubber check bouncing over the Capitol accompanied the Broder column. See also Broder, "Democrats' Debit," *Washington Post*, September 25, 1991, p. A25. Political humorists took advantage of the coverage to lampoon the institution. See Tony Kornheiser, "The System of Checks and Bounces," *Washington Post*, October 6, 1991, p. F1.

182. One opinion column, by a political scientist, described the charges against Congress as "wildly distorted, patently unfair and hypocritical." See Norman Ornstein, "Congress Confidential," *Washington Post*, November 3, 1991, p. C5. I found no other article that seriously sought to set the record straight on the various charges against Congress.

183. Adam Clymer, "Congress Hunts for Way to Gain a Little Respect," *New York Times*, July 23, 1992, p. A20.

184. Charles M. Tidmarch and John J. Pitney, Jr., "Covering Congress," *Polity*, vol. 17 (Spring 1985), pp. 481–82.

185. Arthur H. Miller, Edie N. Goldenberg, and Lutz Erbring, "Type-Set Politics: Impact of Newspapers on Public Confidence," *American Political Science Review*, vol. 73 (March 1979), p. 70; and Michael J. Robinson and Kevin R. Appel, "Network News Coverage of Congress," *Political Science Quarterly*, vol. 94 (Fall 1979), pp. 412, 417.

186. Robert E. Gilbert, "President versus Congress: The Struggle for Public Attention," *Congress & the Presidency*, vol. 16 (Autumn 1989), p. 99.

187. Norman Ornstein, "What TV News Doesn't Report about Congress—and Should," *TV Guide*, October 21, 1989, p. 11.

188. Thomas R. Dye and Harmon Zeigler, *American Politics in the Media Age*, 2d ed. (Monterey, Calif.: Brooks/Cole, 1986), p. 212; and Norman J. Ornstein, "The Open Congress Meets the President," in Anthony King, ed., *Both Ends of the Avenue: The Presidency, the Executive Branch, and Congress in the 1980s* (Washington: American Enterprise Institute, 1983), p. 201.

189. Quoted in Greg Schneiders, "The 90-Second Handicap: Why TV Coverage of Legislation Falls Short," *Washington Journalism Review* (June 1985), p. 44.

190. William Safire, "The MEGO News Era," *Washington Star*, September 6, 1973, p. A15.

191. David Broder, *Behind the Front Page: A Candid Look at How the News Is Made* (Simon and Schuster, 1987), pp. 216, 227.

192. Charles O. Jones, *The United States Congress: People, Place, and Policy* (Homewood, Ill.: Dorsey Press, 1982), p. 48.

193. Dye and Zeigler, *American Politics in the Media Age*, pp. 211–12.

194. Richard F. Fenno, Jr., *Home Style: House Members in their Districts* (Little, Brown, 1978), p. 168.

195. Ibid., pp. 246–47.

196. Robinson and Appel, "Network News Coverage," p. 416.

197. Quoted in Richard Davis, *The Press and American Politics: The New Mediator* (Longman, 1992), p. 162.

198. Michael J. Robinson, "Three Faces of Congressional Media," in Thomas E. Mann and Norman J. Ornstein, eds., *The New Congress* (Washington: American Enterprise Institute, 1981), p. 64. See also the recommendations of Stephen Hess and Ronald D. Elving in their chapters of this volume.

199. Fenno, *Home Style*, p. 246.

200. Timothy E. Cook, *Making Laws and Making News: Media Strategies in the U.S. House of Representatives* (Brookings, 1989), p. 170.

201. Quoted in Broder, *Behind the Front Page*, p. 213.

5 Less News Is Worse News: Television News Coverage of Congress, 1972–92

S. Robert Lichter
Daniel R. Amundson

ONE SUNDAY in February 1993, CBS television's *60 Minutes* exposed a powerful organization that stifles reform, intimidates opponents, and generally thwarts the public interest. Unlike more celebrated exposés that left audiences throwing out Alar-coated apples or abandoning their Audis, this episode attracted little notice. There were public rumblings from what the show called "the belly of the beast," but few viewers could have been surprised by the report. After all, the target was not chemicals or dangerous cars. It was the U. S. Congress, an institution widely viewed as a hazard to our political health. Public support for Congress is at its lowest since the onset of scientific polling. Americans' disapproval of Congress now exceeds that of such targets of populist suspicion as banks, big business, labor unions, public schools, and the news media.[1]

Members of Congress may have resented the *60 Minutes* report, but they could hardly have been surprised by it. After all, they have endured far more hostile media scrutiny. In 1989 one study found that the network evening newscasts raised questions about the ethical conduct of forty-seven senators and representatives and averaged thirty-three minutes a month of airtime reporting on ethics charges.[2] That year the news ranged from charges of financial misconduct against House Speaker Jim Wright of Texas and Democratic Whip Tony Coelho of California to reports of sex scandals involving Senators Barney Frank of Massachusetts and Buz Lukens of Ohio. The relentless emphasis of the press led one member of Congress to level a charge of media McCarthyism, and a network correspondent accused his peers of going on "an ethical binge."[3]

Media bashing by legislators might be dismissed as self-interested, but many scholars agree that unfavorable or hostile news coverage has helped undermine respect for Congress. As political scientist Doris Graber summarizes, "the institution of Congress has suffered a decline in image and power. This springs partly from [news] stories that usually picture it as lobby-ridden, incompetent, and slow."[4] Observers also widely agree that television reporting has the greatest influence on public opinion. Unfortunately, virtually all of the empirical evidence comes from snapshots of relatively brief time periods that range from as little as a single month to a full year. To test the hypothesis that television news coverage has eroded Congress's public image, it would be necessary to trace coverage over a period of decades. Otherwise, short-term shifts could be attributed to particular scandals, personalities, election year politics, or other transient factors.

Studying Television's Reporting of Congress

Although a definitive study of television's images of Congress would require vast resources, it is possible to identify long-term trends by studying sample periods reiterated periodically over decades. The limiting factor in studying television news is the availability of network newscasts. The oldest continuous collection belongs to the Vanderbilt University Television News Archive, which began taping network evening newscasts in 1968. Taping procedures were standardized in 1971, and the archive began publishing indexes and abstracts in 1972. This research tool permits systematic comparisons of the amount and topical focus of coverage for more than two decades. In addition, the Vanderbilt Archive circulates video tapes of actual newscasts, permitting a more in-depth examination of the sources, issues, and evaluations contained in each story.

To give our study the greatest breadth possible with limited resources, we examined the three networks' congressional coverage during one month of each year from 1972 through 1992. We chose April to provide a reasonably typical period of day-to-day activities whose coverage can be compared over time. April is far from the cruelest month for legislators; that distinction belongs to November. Somewhat removed from both the onset of new sessions and the pressures of general elections, April's position in the calendar draws considerable coverage of the institution's ongoing operation. Congress is usually in session for much or all of the month, generating news through a wide range of hearings, caucuses, negotiations, and votes.

For each of the twenty-one years sampled, we examined the *Vanderbilt Television News Index and Abstracts* to determine the number of stories and their major topics. The results provide a broad outline of how newsworthy the networks considered Congress and what they saw as newsworthy about it. To fill in the details and provide a more precise sense of the changing tone and style of the coverage, we also conducted a much more detailed analysis of the actual footage of congressional coverage during April 1972, 1982, and 1992. For these three months we noted every source who appeared and analyzed each sound bite for any discussion of issues or evaluation of Congress and its members.[5]

Amount of Coverage

After examining April coverage from each year since 1972, we sympathized with the decisions of previous researchers to focus on relatively brief periods of congressional news. We analyzed 1,695 congressional stories over a twenty-one year period, an average of 80 a month, or just under 1 story on each network each night. The three networks offered similar amounts of coverage—522 stories on ABC, 582 on CBS, and 591 on NBC. It was obvious from the abstracts that the networks typically aired very similar stories on Congress on any given day. Statistical analysis of the variables in our study reinforced this observation. So it seems reasonable to speak of television news in general rather than concentrating on individual networks.

The two decades straddled a wide range of newsworthy events involving Congress: the Watergate investigations, the fall of Vietnam, the energy crisis, the Abscam prosecutions, the Iran-contra hearings, and the Persian Gulf War. There were six presidential elections, five different administrations, and times when each party controlled the White House and the Senate. (The Democrats remained in control of the House throughout the period.) Of course, the news also covered such recurring topics as annual budget legislation and partisan sparring over upcoming biennial elections.

Not surprisingly, changing events brought sharp variations from one year to the next in the amount of congressional news. But the trend was clear despite the temporary fluctuations (figure 5-1). Stories involving Congress peaked in April 1974 with 168, obviously reflecting the House Judiciary Committee's impeachment hearings that culminated in President Nixon's resignation that summer. The number dropped to a mere 16 during April 1990, part of the legislative lull early in the Bush administration. (By comparison, the networks devoted 66 stories to Bush's activities that month and 119 to the entire executive branch.) The vagaries

Figure 5-1. Television News Stories about Congress, 1972–92

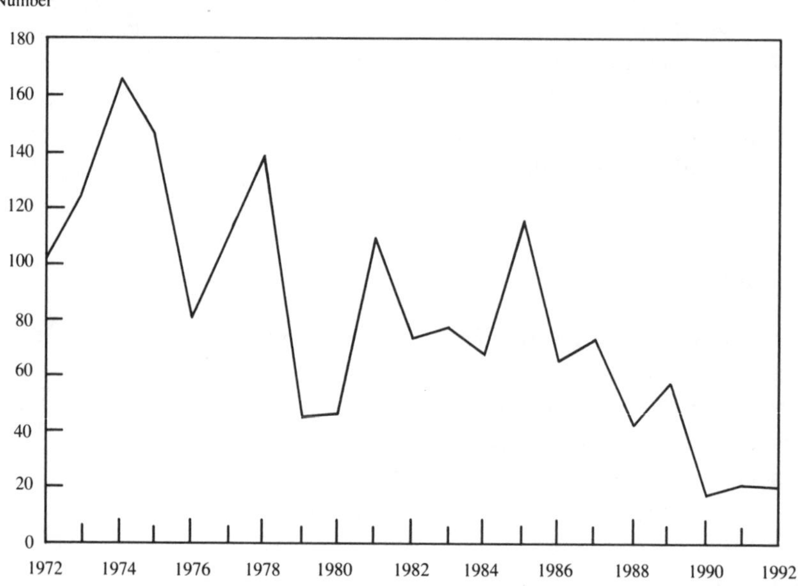

Source: Authors' calculations.

of events cannot, however, account for the gradually decreasing coverage during the two decades.

To illustrate the magnitude of Congress's loss of news coverage, we divided the study period into three seven-year intervals. The three networks together devoted more than 100 stories a month to Congress during six of the first seven years that we sampled; during the fourteen years that followed they reached that level of coverage only twice, most recently in 1985. (Readers should keep in mind that these comparisons refer only to the single month of each year that was sampled, not the entire year.) During the most recent seven-year interval the coverage never exceeded 72 stories. Thus from 1972 through 1978 congressional news averaged 124 stories a month, or about 4 a day. The most recent interval, from 1986 through 1992, saw only one-third as much coverage, 42 stories a month, a little more than 1 a day.

Ironically, this decline has occurred despite the introduction of television cameras in the House in 1979 and the Senate in 1986, which vastly expanded the store of visuals and sound bites available to the networks. During the very years that a devoted audience of news junkies became avid followers of congressional activity via C-SPAN, and individual members such as Newt Gingrich of Georgia developed national reputations by directing speeches to the viewing audience rather than to their colleagues, the major broadcast networks have lost interest in the activities of Congress.

Focus of Coverage

As the networks have paid progressively less attention to congressional activities, the focus of their interest has changed as well. We looked at the subject matter of congressional news stories and the extent to which they involved some form of political conflict.

Not surprisingly, most news about Congress has involved policy debates: 41 percent of all stories since 1972 concerned some aspect of domestic policy and 26 percent concerned foreign policy matters. Three other topics fill out most of the remaining third of coverage. Congressional investigations into alleged wrongdoing by groups or individuals other than Congress itself—corporate price fixing or overcharging, the savings and loan mess, Watergate, assassination inquiries—accounted for 15 percent of all stories broadcast. Election campaigns, including the involvement of legislators in presidential elections, took up another 6 percent. Congressional ethics drew 7 percent. (The remaining 5 percent included confirmation hearings, profiles of individual members, discussions of congressional operations, and so forth).

News about congressional ethics included both scandal coverage and general discussions of ethical standards. However, more than 80 percent of all ethics stories dealt with some specific instance of scandalous behavior, ranging from Arkansas Representative Wilbur Mills's unlikely relationship with stripper Fanne Foxe to the financial dealings of the Keating Five. And much of the generic coverage of congressional ethics was stimulated by instances or allegations of scandalous behavior.

When we once again divided the coverage into three equal time periods, we discovered that since 1986 policy coverage has plummeted to barely more than half of all stories, while scandals and other coverage concerning ethics has more than doubled to one in every six stories (figure 5-2). Although coverage of policy issues, investigations, and elections has risen and fallen over the years, coverage of ethics matters has increased gradually from 4 percent to 7 percent and then 17 percent of all news about Congress. Thus among the four major areas of subject matter, only coverage of scandal increased during each time period. As a result, scandals now stand second only to policy issues as a major focus of news

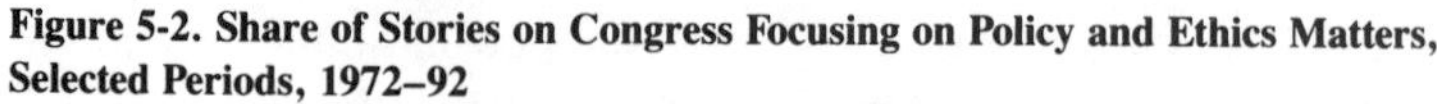

Figure 5-2. Share of Stories on Congress Focusing on Policy and Ethics Matters, Selected Periods, 1972–92

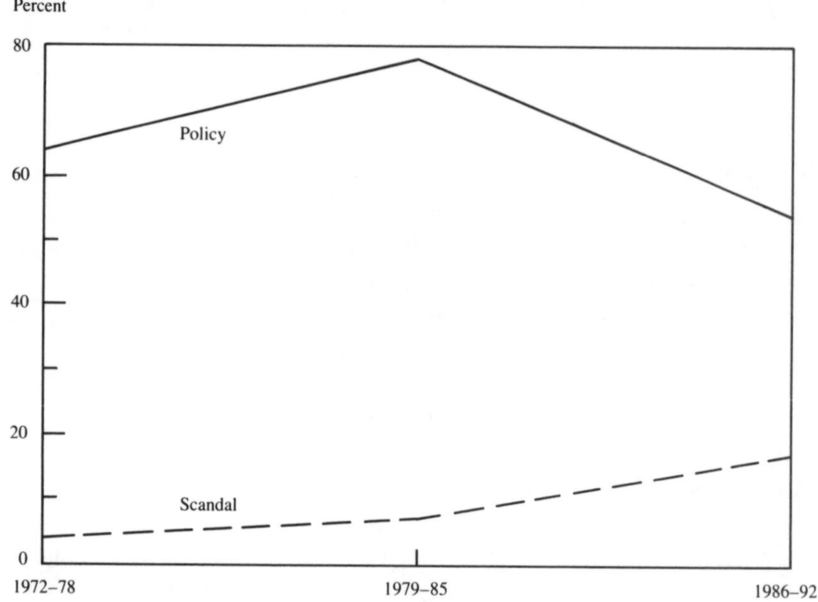

Source: Authors' calculations.

about Congress. Until the mid-1980s the networks broadcast about thirteen stories on policy matters for each report on ethical lapses. Since then the evening news has shown nearly one scandal story for every three issue stories.

As the focus of news coverage shifted from policy issues to personal scandals, story structure also changed. Our examination noted whether a story was built around conflict, either among members of Congress or between the legislature and some other political participant. Once again, a watershed was reached in the late 1980s. Before 1987, about one of three congressional stories involved some contest of wills. Since 1987 two of every three have been built around discord. In other words, the media's focus on conflict has nearly doubled in recent years. The apex was reached in 1989, when nine out of ten stories highlighted some clash of opinions or interests.

Both internal disputes and those involving other institutions have received sharply increased coverage. This upsurge reflects growing tensions between Republican presidents and the Democratic Congress in the wake of the Iran-contra affair, as well as increasingly acrimonious partisan debates in both chambers. Since 1987 nearly half of all news about Congress has chronicled tests of will with the executive branch or some other outside force. During the same period the proportion of news involving disputes among members has nearly tripled, rising from 6 to 17 percent of all stories.

Tone of the News

Although the Vanderbilt abstracts are detailed enough to indicate the amount and focus of congressional coverage, they are too abbreviated to convey the tone and style. To get a more precise picture of how Congress and its members are portrayed on the evening newscasts, we analyzed all evaluative or judgmental statements broadcast during the months of April 1972, 1982, and 1992. This procedure produced a sense of the tone of congressional coverage at decade-long intervals.

Although the amount and focus of congressional coverage changed sharply during the two decades, the tone of the newscasts was negative from start to finish and grew even more so as time went on (table 5-1). In 1972 three of every four evaluations of Congress expressed disapproval, in 1982 seven of eight, and in 1992 nearly nine of ten. The criticism was even-handed. Four of five evaluations were critical of Republicans and Democrats alike and of both the House and Senate. Judgments directed against the institution were even more unsparing than those aimed at individual members.

One other change over time is worth noting in conjunction with television's bleak portrait. The commentary on Congress and its activities has increasingly come from outside the institution. Elected representatives and their staff members have made up a steadily diminishing proportion of the sources quoted in news stories about Congress, dropping from 60 percent of all sources in 1972 and 1982 to 47 percent in 1992. (Democrats were quoted twice as often as Republicans, and senators slightly outnumbered representatives.) Members of Congress have thus been accorded fewer opportunities to speak for themselves, while their critics' voices have multiplied.

Among the frequent critics of Congress have been White House officials complaining about the lack of responsiveness to their agenda. Such comments have typically expressed the frustration of Republican administrations dealing with an institution dominated by Democrats. On April 28, 1972, for instance, Elliot Richardson, then secretary of health, education and welfare, said on the CBS evening news, "the welfare plan

Table 5-1. Tone of Television News Stories on Congress, April 1972, 1982, 1992

Item	*Positive (percent)*	*Negative (percent)*	*Number*
All statements	17	83	107
1972	26	74	38
1982	13	87	24
1992	11	89	45
Target			
Democrats	21	79	42
Republicans	21	79	19
Senate	21	79	42
House	17	83	29
Members	21	79	61
Institution	11	89	46

Source: Authors' calculations.

adopted today by the Senate Finance Committee would amount to a $9 billion step backward into the leaf-raking schemes of the 1930s . . . by the creation of a massive, permanent army of federal employees, fiddling with meaningless work or phony government jobs." Ten years later, on April 28, 1982, James Baker, Ronald Reagan's chief of staff, made a more generic complaint on ABC: "Today the president held out the hand of compromise. We had hoped for give and take [on Capitol Hill], and what we found . . . was mostly take." On April 16, 1992, George Bush's education secretary, Lamar Alexander, offered some unsolicited advice to Democratic presidential nominee Bill Clinton on the ABC evening news: "Don't complain about the president's leadership on education. Go talk to your business-as-usual friends in Congress who are blocking it and get them to pass it."

Of course, this river of rebuke was not limited to the executive branch. Legislators themselves participated. On April 16, 1982, Representative Ron Mottl of Ohio appeared on CBS to denounce a tax deduction for living expenses that Congress had just voted itself. It is, he said, "a new congressional perk which smells so foul it could only have come from the sewer." Even ordinary voters have climbed into the act occasionally, as when a tourist visiting the Capitol on April 16, 1992, told NBC's Lisa Myers, "I think they're overly ambitious to get where they want to be, and then corruption takes over." This interview appeared in a story on Congress's poor public image, to which it probably further contributed.

To document these detrimental assessments is not to suggest that network evening news should deny airtime to angry administration officials, legislators critical of their colleagues, or outraged citizens. Documenting simply shows that the selection of sound bites has accentuated the negative and left little room for approval or appreciation. In the ordeal of trial by television, the prosecution is heard more than the defense. And not only individuals but also institutions such as Congress stand in the dock for failing to serve the public interest.

Conclusion

In the past two decades the television networks have paid less and less attention to Congress, and their coverage has become progressively less policy oriented and more heavily focused on scandals and unethical behavior. The news has also increasingly emphasized conflict, both within Congress and between the institution and other participants in political affairs. Finally, our intensive analysis of one month's footage from each of the three decades shows that the tone of coverage was already derogatory a generation ago and has become worse. This holds true for evaluations of Congress as an institution and for individual members. Although Democrats have consistently dominated the focus of coverage, they have been treated as harshly as Republicans.

The long-term trend toward more adversarial coverage reflects the realities of divided government and popular disaffection with political leadership. But it also reflects the choices that collectively make up the news judgment of network journalists—daily decisions about what to cover, whom to quote, what language to use in illustrating a point. To some extent these decisions in turn reflect the tendency of journalists to emphasize conflict over concord, politics over policies, and personal foibles over institutional functions.

Reporters are often simultaneously fascinated and appalled by politics. They pride themselves on protecting the average citizen against the powerful. But they can be impatient toward the messiness and inefficiency of representative institutions, where the long-range goals of public service always seem less evident (and newsworthy) than short-term passions and partisanship. Many observers have documented the increasing tendency of contemporary journalism to conduct "a relentless critique of American . . . institutions, sometimes in the form of investigative reports, but more generally through the adversarial structure of routine coverage."[6] In this context the coverage of Congress can be seen as a particular case (though perhaps an extreme one) of a more general phenomenon.

In an era in which journalism has moved from narrating the political saga to arbitrating it, this perfectionistic approach increasingly pervades television's reporting of public life. In the stories and commentaries we sampled, it is perhaps best represented in an April 19, 1972, mournful observation by ABC's Howard K. Smith: "the debate that took place in the Senate today reveals the flaw in our system. The debate will have no effect. The president will go on with his policy. Congress will go on complaining. Divisions grow, spirit corrodes." The question remains as to whether the media are simply representing the corrosion of the national spirit or contributing to it through a jaundiced portrayal of our political institutions.

Notes

1. Based on Gallup polls from 1946 through 1992. See "Public Opinion and Demographic Report," *American Enterprise*, November–December, 1992, pp. 85–87.

2. "Keeping an Eye on Congress," *Media Monitor*, November 1989, pp. 2–3.

3. Ibid. The accusers were Representative Thomas Downey of New York and former NBC correspondent Ken Bode.

4. Doris Graber, *Mass Media and American Politics* (Washington: CQ Press, 1989), p. 265. See also the review of the literature on pp. 254 and following.

5. In formal terms, we conducted a two-part content analysis. First, taking the entire news story as the unit of analysis, we coded the number of relevant stories and the topic of each from the *Vanderbilt Television News Index and Abstracts* entries for the month of April from 1972 through 1992. Second, taking the individual source or reporter statement (the sound bite) as the unit of analysis, we coded videotapes from April 1972, 1982, and 1992 for all source appearances, issues discussed, and evaluations of institutions and individuals. Reliability coefficients were calculated after two coders independently scored each story. Reliability for topics was 96 percent, sources 98 percent, conflict in stories 90 percent, and evaluations 81 percent.

6. Ted J. Smith, "The Watchdog's Bite," *American Enterprise*, January–February 1990, p. 66. See also Thomas Patterson, *Out of Order* (Knopf, 1993); Michael J. Robinson, "American Political Legitimacy in an Era of Electronic Journalism," in Douglass Cater and Richard Adler, eds., *Television as a Social Force* (Praeger, 1975); and Larry Sabato, *Feeding Frenzy* (Free Press, 1991).

6 The Decline and Fall of Congressional News

Stephen Hess

THE LEITMOTIF in many of the hundreds of interviews that I conducted with Capitol Hill reporters during the 1980s is that their bosses—editors or producers at the home office—knew nothing about Congress. A Cox Newspapers reporter commented, "Before I came to Washington I remember the Texas papers considered Washington reporters as the enemy. They were remote entities. . . . Many at home fail to understand how Washington is covered." Another from Donray Newspapers observed, "The editors don't tell us what they're looking for and we cover issues that seem important to us but might not be to them." And from a Copley Newspapers reporter: "Most editors don't have the foggiest idea about what goes on in Washington and they don't understand things here. I'd be interested to see a survey of American editors."

A survey in October 1992 throws light on these statements. The Princeton Survey Research Associates, on behalf of the Brookings Institution, the American Enterprise Institute, and the Times Mirror Center for the People and the Press, directed a series of questions at reporters who are specialists in covering Congress ("the specialists"), another group of midlevel journalists who are not congressional specialists ("the generalists"), and a third group of news organization executives, people with titles like managing editor and executive producer ("the powers").[1]

Questions about how the media cover Congress produced a dramatic pattern of disagreement between the specialists and the powers (generalists fell in between but tended to be closer to the specialists).[2] Asked to rate press coverage of Congress in recent years, 40 percent of the powers gave positive assessments, while only 25 percent of the specialists approved. Eighty-one percent of the specialists and 66 percent of the powers faulted the press for its coverage of "the process by which policy is made in Congress." Forty-three percent of the specialists believed the media focused too much on scandals; 27 percent of the powers agreed. Forty percent of the powers and just 6 percent of the specialists credited the media with "good day-to-day coverage." Overall, 85 percent of the specialists thought that national news organizations gave too little coverage to Congress, a view shared by 53 percent of the powers.

Question: Compared to ten years ago, do you think that press coverage of Congress these days is better than it was, worse than it was, or about the same?

Rating	*Powers*	*Generalists*	*Specialists*
Better	53	33	26
Same	33	32	30
Worse	7	25	38
Don't know	7	11	6
Total	100	101	100

Perhaps, I thought, the differences in journalists' responses simply reflected whether they worked in Washington. Congressional specialists, of course, live in the capital's metropolitan area. Most but not all of the powers live in New York, headquarters of the *New York Times*, ABC, CBS, NBC, *Time, Newsweek*, the *Wall Street Journal*, the Associated Press, and Reuters. CNN comes from Atlanta. Is this another example of the so-called inside-the-beltway phenomenon? Do these responses simply mirror the perspectives of people who are too close to (or too removed from) the seat of government? So the sample was recomputed according to where the respondents lived—inside the beltway, outside the beltway. There are virtually no differences.

Rating	*Insiders*	*Ousiders*
Better	31	34
Same	34	33
Worse	24	26
Don't know	11	7
Total	100	100

There were also no differences between insiders and outsiders on assessing the media's job of covering congressional process and scandal. In fact, the two groups agreed on whether national news organizations devoted too much or too little attention to Congress.[3]

In short, then, the answers to these questions indicated that the differences between specialists and powers were rarely the differences between Washington insiders and outsiders. More likely we are observing Miles's law: where you stand depends on where you sit. For those unfamiliar with this formulation, a classic case was uncovered in a gossip column of a San Francisco newspaper by Nobel Laureate Herbert A. Simon. A functionary of the Hetch Hetchy water department sent a memo to his boss requesting more money for the waterworks. The boss went to Washington for ten days, during which time the functionary was acting manager; he received his own request and turned it down. His explanation: "from up here things don't look the same as they do from down there."[4]

Similarly, it was déjà vu for Clark Hoyt, managing editor of the Wichita *Eagle*, when he attended a 1983 conference at Harvard's Kennedy School in which journalists and members of Congress were expected to confront each other. Hoyt told his panel,

> I haven't said one word yet and I feel beat up already. I'm one of those editors out there making decisions which seem to displease both the reporters and the members of Congress. I spent seven years on the Hill covering Congress. I was intensely interested in the folkways, in the process, and in the results. I now have a very different perspective, editing a newspaper half a continent away. I am much less interested in the process.[5]

When questions in the 1992 survey turned from how journalists viewed the media's coverage of Congress to questions about Congress, there were some markedly different perspectives. The power journalists were more apt than the specialists to think that members of Congress are paid too little (40 percent versus 17 percent) and have too many perks (53 percent versus 40 percent). Much more than the specialists, the powers believed that legislators are out of touch with the needs and concerns of their constituents. Congressional specialists thought this common criticism exaggerated.

Specialists and powers also had different cures for what ails Congress. Thirty-three percent of the powers but only 15 percent of the specialists favored a line item veto for the president. Congressional term limits were opposed by 73 percent of the powers and 92 percent of the specialists. Campaign finance reform was the favorite proposal of 13 percent of the powers and 51 percent of the specialists.

What difference does it make that powers and specialists disagree over how Congress is covered? At the 1983 Harvard conference, Representative Biil Frenzel of Minnesota complained, "The press thinks it can only report events. Congress is not an event, it is a process."[6] He got no dispute from the specialists on the panel. As Jacqueline Adams, a Capitol

Hill correspondent for CBS News, observed, "You have to sell a story to the editor, and the editor wants action, not process. 'Tell me when Congress is going to do something.' They are not so much interested in a committee decision; they want final action. And that isn't what Congress is about. Congress is about process."[7] Joan McKinney, who reports for the Baton Rouge newspapers from the Senate Press Gallery, noted, "Covering the process probably is not the kind of assignment we get from home."[8]

Coverage of process, what I shall also refer to as institutional coverage, gets downplayed to the extent that key decisions on what appears in the American mainstream press have shifted from the bureaus to home offices—and shift they have in recent history. (This affects not just congressional reportage: the same can be said of presidential reporting or foreign correspondence, for example.)

Power Shifts and Other Causes

In the pantheon commemorating great battles among employees of the same organization, the internal struggles between the editors of the *New York Times* and the newspaper's Washington bureau must rate a special place. Gay Talese explained in *The Kingdom and the Power* how publisher Adolph Ochs turned over his Washington outpost to bureau chief Arthur Krock in 1932 and how Krock, "taking very little advice and certainly no nonsense from the editors in New York," ran the operation as his "private principality" until he, in turn, passed along the title and power in 1953 to James Reston, who, in turn, anointed his successor, Tom Wicker, in 1964, after which New York reasserted its supremacy.[9] For instance, "In 1965 the New York desk blocked an attempt by *The Times'* national political correspondent, David S. Broder, stationed in Washington, to cover President Johnson's speech in Princeton, New Jersey, because Princeton was part of the New York desk's territory." Broder resigned the next year to become national political correspondent at the rival *Washington Post*. In a widely bootlegged memo outlining his disputes with the *Times*, he wrote, "It was my impression that *Times* editors had a certain few stimuli to which they reacted in a political story: Instances of extremism, either of the New Left or the Radical Right; political action by southern (but not northern) Negroes; Kennedy stories of any variety. These may be the grist of political talk at New York cocktail parties, but . . . they do not begin to embrace the variety of concerns that really animate national politics."[10] By the time Talese's history of the *Times* concludes at the end of 1968, headquarters has regained control of the Washington bureau.

If the history of the *New York Times* illustrates how internal politics and personality clashes induce shifts in power away from Washington, the examples of the television broadcast networks, as described by Ken Auletta's *Three Blind Mice,* make a potent case for the importance of business economics. In rapid succession in 1986 each of the three networks was taken over. ABC was acquired by Capitol Cities Communications; Laurence Tisch's company, Loews, bought 25 percent of CBS, and he was made its president; and General Electric replaced RCA as the parent company of NBC.[11] The networks' founders had not expected their news operations to earn a profit. They could afford to view the dissemination of news as a form of public education (and public relations in a government-regulated industry). But now times were tough. And the new corporate owners were offended by the waste and redundancy they saw in the news divisions. GE commissioned a McKinsey and Company efficiency report that concluded news decisions were made with little consideration given to cost. On January 22, 1987, for instance, NBC's Washington bureau sent out thirteen crews and used film from only four. "To McKinsey's accountants," according to Auletta, "this was wasteful; to many journalists, this illustrated how news is rarely predictable, and if it were it might not be news."[12] On March 10, 1987, Dan Rather publicly scolded his new bosses on the op-ed page of the *New York Times*: "Do the owners and officers of the new CBS see news as a trust . . . or only as a business venture?"[13] An anchorman, however, was only entitled to the next-to-last word. The new owners wanted and got scaled-down news operations.

Technology also affected how much reporting was devoted to Congress. When Washington had the only coaxial cable that fed directly into the networks' New York headquarters, often more than 60 percent of the items on the evening news programs originated in the capital. Then as satellites, tape, and lightweight equipment came into affordable commercial use, the networks no longer had to rely so heavily on Washington for stories. At the same time and for the same reasons, Washington reportage became available to faraway stations for their local news programs.

The beginning of the age of communications satellites in the early 1980s coincided with a time of high profits at the stations. They were willing to spend the money to open Washington bureaus, and membership in the Senate Radio and Television Gallery rose from 750 members in 1979 to 2,300 by 1987. According to Tim Hillard, Washington bureau chief of Fisher Broadcasting, which had stations in the Pacific Northwest, "We were so enamored with the technology [that] for a year we went live every night."[14] Most of these regional operations were located on Capitol Hill and, although at their height they represented less than 10 percent of all U.S. stations, they were often considered the wave of the future.[15]

Local TV news was the medium of Congress (just as network programs favored the president). Legislators appeared in the local stories nearly three times as often as officials from the executive branch. In 1985 Jefferson-Pilot Communications' Charlotte, North Carolina, station received 15 stories a month, 182 for the year, from its Washington bureau. Freshman House member Alex McMillan was in 21 of these.[16]

But even before a recession buffeted the industry, there were signs that the local operations had had second thoughts about the value of Washington stories. In interviews with 102 stations' news directors in 1986, only 3 claimed that national coverage improved their standing in the ratings. "Government news is boring to viewers. One thing Washington is full of is talking heads and meetings."[17] By the end of the decade, Jefferson-Pilot had closed its Washington office, as had such other groups as Chronicle, Gannett, Midwest, Outlet, Storer, Gillett, H & C Communications, and Group W.

Although in some cases the primary reason for the change of emphasis was economic, and in other cases it was a personality clash or a power grab, in all cases the home office had a vision of what consumers wanted that differed from the opinions of the field office. The editor considers the Washington reporter's copy, according to a Washington reporter, "another story of government glop."[18] Some civic organizations, on the other hand, say the editors are wrong. Their argument is based largely on polling data. In 1989 the Center for Responsive Politics in Washington hired the University of Maryland's Survey Research Center to find out what the American public wanted in congressional news. When respondents were asked if they would like more stories explaining how Congress works, fewer, or about as many as they were currently getting, 62 percent wanted more, 28 percent wanted the same, and 6 percent wanted fewer.[19] Are editors and producers turning their backs on what their readers and listeners want? Or are interviewees saying what they think the interviewers want to hear?

Evidence supports the editors and producers. Since 1986 the Times Mirror Center has measured "public attentiveness to major news stories." The event that was most closely followed during this six-year period was the explosion of the space shuttle *Challenger* (80 percent of the public followed the story), then the 1989 San Francisco earthquake (73 percent), the 1992 Los Angeles riots after the Rodney King verdict (70 percent), and the 1987 rescue of a little girl in Texas who had fallen into a well (69 percent). The top Congress story—in sixty-second place—was the check-bouncing scandal in the House of Representatives, closely followed by 31 percent of the respondents. Of 294 high-interest stories tracked, ranging from the *Challenger* disaster to actor Tom Cruise's separation from his wife (a 2 percent rating), only 21 were about Congress.[20]

Even the 1989 University of Maryland poll in which respondents claimed they wanted more stories about Congress—about bills in Congress even though they might not be affected directly (53 percent), issues facing Congress (65 percent), activities of legislators from their area (59 percent)—a third of those interviewed did not know that the Democrats controlled the House of Representatives, an uninterrupted situation in Congress for thirty-five years, and only a third could correctly identify their own member of Congress.[21]

The consequences of the shift of editorial power to home offices in many cases has been fewer media resources devoted to covering Congress. This is especially the case with television. A number of investigators have charted the decline in congressional stories on the network evening news. Greg Schneiders has shown that the number of stories about Congress in 1985 was then less than half the number aired in the late 1970s, a finding later confirmed by Norman Ornstein and Michael Robinson.[22]

After a year-long study of the broadcast networks' Washington operations in 1992, Penn Kimball of the Columbia University Graduate School of Journalism concluded, "The three [ABC, CBS, NBC] now make no serious attempt to cover Congress," a determination to which the executive producers of the evening news programs fervently dissented.[23] But CNN was the only television operation to have full-time correspondents assigned to both the House and Senate.

The decline in reporting daily congressional activities has yet another cause: a startling reevaluation of what is news on the part of mainstream American publications. As late as 1982 Michael Schudson could write that "journalists accord politics a prestige that it does not have in the public mind. . . . In a sense, journalists are the patrons of political life." He concluded, "To the degree that this is so, the journalism of the national newsweeklies, most large metropolitan newspapers, and the network television news does not mirror the world, but constructs one in which the political realm is preeminent."[24] The primacy of government and politics in the news was underscored in a survey of *New York Times* and *Washington Post* front pages from 1949 to 1969: 78 percent of the national and foreign sources cited were government officials.[25] But when writing an article on what made news in 1985, I noticed that a very substantial minority of front page stories in the *New York Times* for the week of December 6–12 were not about government or politics.[26] I then went back a decade, two decades, and now have added 1992. The following table illustrates that stories about government or politics as a percentage of the front page have decreased a point a year over twenty-seven years.

Year	*Government or politics stories*	*Not government or politics stories*
1965	84	16
1975	73	27
1985	63	37
1992	55	45

Robert Lichter discovered the same trend in TV news, with the percentage about government and politics on the three networks' evening broadcasts dropping 21 points from 1975 to 1992.[27] In short, newspapers and television are now almost as likely to feature stories about business, education, health, religion, or culture as about what is happening in Congress and the other branches of government.[28]

The Nature of Coverage

The most often proved tenet of mainstream American journalism as practiced in Washington is the neutrality of the reportage. So-called watchdog groups who charge press bias in favor of the Left or Right are focusing on the exceptions. Most stories are bland and balanced. This is especially true of the hard news reporting coming from wire services, the source of most of what appears in newspapers and on radio.

A study of congressional coverage in ten metropolitan newspapers for a month in 1978 determined that most of nearly 2,300 items were neutral or balanced, even though editorials, columns, and political cartoons were included in the count. Those items that were categorized as positive or negative, however, were overwhelming negative. Seven of the papers had at least twice as many negative as positive editorials. "The press on the whole has little good to report about Congress and its membership," the authors concluded. "Whatever the merits of the criticism, such a drumbeat of negative appraisal, only occasionally counterbalanced by inherently good news or freely given editorial praise, is likely to harden the image of Congress as a defective institution."[29] In a similar study of TV network news about Congress, the investigators showed that 86 percent of the stories during five weeks in 1976 were neutral and "the majority of those stories not coded as 'neutral' were negative."[30]

"Journalists usually err on the side of negativity," Ellen Hume, formerly of the *Wall Street Journal*, has said. News is getting hit by a car, not crossing the street safely. They also view the world through skeptical lenses, or, as the *Washington Post*'s Paul Taylor put it, they are "deeply skeptical of all the major institutions of society except [their] own."[31]

At the same time that fewer stories about Congress are getting produced, a larger proportion of them are about activities that cast the institution in an unflattering light. Senator Daniel Brewster's indictment, trial, and conviction for bribery in 1969 and 1970 produced only eight stories on the three networks' news programs.[32] Today, Brewster's behavior would be of much greater interest to the networks. In June 1990, for instance, thirteen stories were related to charges against David Durenberger of Minnesota for allegedly defrauding the Senate in a travel reimbursement scheme. In July, eleven stories explored the relationship between Representative Barney Frank of Massachusetts and a male prostitute. In November twenty-four stories covered the Keating Five scandal.[33]

The coverage of Congress and its members has been caught up in the web of institution and celebrity bashing that can be seen in reporting from Hollywood, Wall Street, sports arenas, and other high-visibility locations. Larry Sabato calls this "junkyard-dog journalism," which he defines as "often harsh, aggressive, and intrusive, where feeding frenzies flourish, and gossip reaches print."[34] But coverage of congressional scandal also results from more scandals, that is, from more investigations by Congress's own ethics committees. Yet, as Suzanne Garment aptly notes, "There is simply no persuasive evidence that the increase in scandal has taken place because of a corresponding rise in corrupt official behavior."[35]

News will always remain driven by events. The amount of reportage from Congress will depend on what's going on. In this regard, 1991 was a crowded year. A new Congress began in January by debating whether the United States should go to war in the Persian Gulf and ended in the fall by deciding that Clarence Thomas should be a Supreme Court justice. ABC's top-rated evening news program mentioned Congress in 200 stories, although often the legislature was playing second fiddle to the president ("Bush will meet with Congress but he feels . . ."). Some 60 items were the television equivalent of headlines read by Peter Jennings or other anchors ("Congress passed several bills ranging from . . ."). But another 60 were full-blown Capitol Hill reports and, as expected, they were almost always about what Congress did rather than how Congress did it. Indeed, probably only 4 could be classified as institutional—"how" not "what" stories—such as Jim Wooten examining the role Congress should play in the Gulf crisis or Cokie Roberts on the Senate confirmation process.[36]

Strangely, perhaps, the *New York Times* in 1991 does not appear to be much more institutional in its reportage. I examined one hundred stories, randomly selected, and not more than five could be called process reporting. One notable example of how a newspaper can cover process was an article by Richard L. Berke with Stephen LaBaton on how banks try to lobby Congress.[37]

In their study of newspapers' congressional coverage, Charles M. Tidmarch and John J. Pitney, Jr., ask, "Is it reasonable to expect a mass circulation daily newspaper to publish, say, a 3,000-word essay on how conference committees are assembled, how strategies in conference are developed and applied, and how one might judge who the winners and losers are when the conference is done?"[38] Clearly from the news media's vantage point, the answer is an emphatic no.

A Modest Proposal

Those who are writing the obituaries of daily newspapers and television networks will be wrong again. Radio did not replace newspapers, and television did not replace radio. CBS will coexist with MTV, the *Wall Street Journal* with on-line data services. But if the present record of how the news media cover Congress as an institution is grim, the future will be grimmer. Yes, there will continue to be C-SPAN and the *MacNeil/Lehrer News Hour* for the cognoscenti, but others will find them easier to ignore as the spectrum of choice expands.[39]

Not long ago a basic home TV set brought in 7 channels. The number is now 35, approaching 50, and the nation's biggest cable company, Tele-Communications, has announced plans for a digital system that will ultimately let customers receive as many as 500 channels.[40] Fragmentation, this process is called. Many of these channels will be pay-per-view, others will be interactive shop-at-home, and still others will be used to offer the same program at different starting times (known as multiplexing). There are now channels that direct their programming to Hispanics, African Americans, youth, women, and evangelicals. New channels will target other demographically definable groups that are big enough to add sufficient subscribers to the system. Even obscure House members from urban areas, whose charms were previously unnoticed, will be useful to the twenty-four-hour all-news channels that are sprouting in Boston, Chicago, Orange County (California), Long Island (New York), and elsewhere. Les Brown, the founder of *Channels* magazine, expects there to be targeted channels arranged by ideology—liberal, conservative, ultraconservative, religious right, libertarian, and so on.[41]

The result, according to David Bartlett, president of the Radio-Television News Directors Association, is that "it will be easier for members of Congress to get into the pipeline and more difficult for them to get attention. Fragmentation means that consumers who are interested in public affairs can get more and those not interested will watch less."[42]

Fragmentation, otherwise known as specialization, has already arrived in the Periodical Press Galleries of Congress, where most of the journalists now cover Capitol Hill for *Airport Noise Report*, *Cancer Letter*, *Employee Benefits Review*, *Forest Industry Affairs*, *Government Computer News*, *Heavy Duty Trucking*, and other carefully focused publications. Increasingly such operations will be on-line computer services, which will further contribute to the atomization of news.

The more specialized and fragmented the communications system in America becomes, the less emphasis there will be on Congress as an institution.[43] Each segment of the media has its own special interest in some segment of Congress. The whole will not be the sum of the parts. It is not an integrated communications system, articulated so that all the parts are represented in proper order and proportion, and, of course, none of us are consumers of the whole, anyway.

Demands for a nonmarket media system are destined to fail in our society. As Barney Frank commented,

> Most of the press in the United States is . . . motivated in part by the need to make profits. Increasingly [press operations] are part of large corporate structures, where the people who are making the ultimate decisions have a fiduciary responsibility to their stockholders, and sometimes they feel those responsibilities more than others. They don't pick their approach to news based on some overall philosophical or charitable approach.[44]

Even the two excellent Public Broadcasting Service series on Congress, *The Lawmakers* (1981–84) and *Capitol Journal* (1985–86), were downed by market forces.

Nor can Americans realistically expect politicians to change, although we have a greater right and more leverage in demanding change. Individual legislators will continue to design communications strategies to promote themselves. Congressional committees are issues oriented. Senate and House leaders will continue to have partisan purposes. Moreover, an irony many have noted since Richard Fenno first pointed it out is that members of Congress often run for Congress by running against Congress.[45] As Oklahoma's Mickey Edwards said when he was in the House, "It would be very helpful if we let more of our colleagues know that they serve no useful purpose by denigrating an important institution in this country in order to make a few points back home politically."[46] It ill behooves some legislators to "cite 'unfair' media treatment as the cause of Congress's low public esteem."[47] But guilt, when applied to politicians or the news industry, is a low-grade instrument of change.

How, then, can the institutional Congress be heard? Let me first make clear what Congress does not need. It does not need Senate and House press operations directed by press secretaries that are similar to the White House Press Office and the president's press secretary. Daniel Patrick Moynihan once composed an Iron Law of Emulation: "Whenever any branch of the government acquires a new technique which enhances its power in relations to the other branches, that technique will soon be adopted by those other branches as well."[48] Congress, he notes, created the Congressional Budget Office to counter the competence of the President's Office of Management and Budget. But the problem is the failure to explain adequately the workings of Congress, not the media's bias on behalf of the president. Senate and House leaders have their own press operations and should be held accountable by their peers for how effectively they respond to the president.

My modest proposal is to suggest an institutional voice for Congress—actually two, one for the House and one for the Senate. Each could be called the Institutional Communications Office (of the House or Senate). Their function would be to collect and provide nonpartisan information on the operations of Congress, including important events in congressional history, statistics and precedents, and historical comparisons. These words are chosen carefully because, in fact, there are already two small offices, of excellent repute, that perform these duties (as well as some more technical duties): the Senate Historical Office (six professionals) and the House Office of the Historian (three professionals). They would be the loci of expanded and more proactive operations.

Such offices will probably find that their most active consumers are not in the Washington press corps but are journalists scattered throughout the country and even abroad. One of the findings of a study of executive agency public affairs offices in Washington was that direct dialing and long-distance telephone services have vastly expanded the demand for their services.[49] The renamed historians' offices should include several social scientists, at least one of whom should be a political scientist with a specialization in Congress, and a professional public information officer to serve as liaison with news organizations.

In addition to their present historical duties, the offices might prepare a media guide on the availability of information and experts on common institutional questions. They should reach out to the members of the foreign press in Washington, who often have difficulty understanding our nonparliamentary system. They should help make Congress more accessible to scholars, who ultimately write textbooks as well as many op-ed pieces. In collaboration with the Library of Congress, the Wilson Center at the Smithsonian, and universities around the country, they should be the catalyst for events that examine and explain Congress. They might provide regular educational programming for C-SPAN. They should expand the reach of their congressional information by making it available to computer networks. And finally, they should correct mistakes that appear in the press.

Because institutional reporting does not come comfortably to the mainstream American press, Congress must be better prepared to help explain—and defend—itself.

Notes

1. The survey, conducted from October 7 through October 29, included 47 congressional specialists, 169 generalists, and 34 powers. The generalists have titles such as Washington correspondent, news editor, and producer.

2. The survey also interviewed twenty-three radio talk show hosts. Their opinions of media coverage were most similar to those held by the generalists. Their attitudes toward Congress, however, were far more critical than those of the journalists. For example, 7 percent of the generalists believed congressional salaries are too high; 26 percent of the talk show hosts held this opinion.

3. Exceptions are assessments of specific scandals. Outsiders (and powers) are enthusiastic about how the press covered the congressional check-bouncing scandal. Insiders (and specialists) did not approve. The obverse is true of the

Keating Five coverage. Insiders (and specialists) approved how the media reported the investigation of the five senators charged with favoring Charles Keating in exchange for campaign contributions. Outsiders (and powers) were less satisfied.

4. Herbert A. Simon, *Administrative Behavior*, 3d ed. (Free Press, 1976), p. 214n.

5. Quoted in Stephen Bates, ed., *The Media and the Congress* (Columbus, Ohio: Publishing Horizons, 1987), p. 46.

6. Quoted in ibid., p. 23.

7. Quoted in ibid., p. 43.

8. Quoted in ibid., p. 28.

9. Gay Talese, *The Kingdom and the Power* (World Publishing, 1969), pp. 19, 26.

10. Ibid., pp. 384, 385.

11. Ken Auletta, *Three Blind Mice: How the TV Networks Lost Their Way* (Random House, 1991), p. 15.

12. Ibid., p. 344.

13. Dan Rather, "From Murrow to Mediocrity?" *New York Times*, March 10, 1987, p. A27.

14. Quoted in Carol Matlack, "Live from Capitol Hill," *National Journal*, February 18, 1989, p. 392.

15. See, for example, Dan Tuden, "Hometown TV Coverage Is Booming," *National Journal*, August 29, 1987, pp. 2174–75; and Peter Osterlund, "Media-Savvy Congress Turns to TV," *Christian Science Monitor*, June 3, 1988, pp. 3–4.

16. Stephen Hess, *Live from Capitol Hill! Studies of Congress and the Media* (Brookings, 1991), pp. 40, 44–45.

17. Ibid, p. 48.

18. Stephen Hess, *The Washington Reporters* (Brookings, 1981), p. 1.

19. Larry Makinson, *Dateline: Capitol Hill* (Washington: Center for Responsive Politics, 1990), pp. A-7, A-8.

20. Times Mirror Center for the People and the Press, "Times Mirror News Interest Index," press release, January 13, 1993.

21. Makinson, *Dateline*, pp. 16–17, 32–33.

22. Greg Schneiders, "The 90-Second Handicap," *Washington Journalism Review* (June 1985), p. 44; and Norman Ornstein and Michael Robinson, "The Case of Our Disappearing Congress," *TV Guide*, January 11, 1986, pp. 4–10.

23. Penn Kimball, "N.Y. to Washington: Drop Dead," *Washington Journalism Review* (November 1992), pp. 37–38, 39; subsequently expanded as *Downsizing the News* (Woodrow Wilson Center Press and Johns Hopkins University Press, 1994).

24. Michael Schudson, "The Politics of Narrative Form: The Emergence of News Conventions in Print and Television," *Daedalus*, vol. 111 (Fall 1982), p. 107.

25. Leon V. Sigal, *Reporters and Officials: The Organization and Politics of Newsmaking* (D.C. Heath, 1973), p. 124.

26. Stephen Hess, "Making News in 1985," *Baltimore Sun*, January 5, 1986, p. M1.

27. Lichter also cites a similar trend in Germany, where newscasts over new private channels devote fewer reports to political news and statements by politicians and more to human interest stories, crime, and entertainment. Robert Lichter, "The Media Elite: Masters of Our Hearts and Minds," *CEO/International Strategies* (April–May 1993), p. 36.

28. Although this development may be a response to consumer demand, journalists have also broadened political life (in the sense that Michael Schudson uses the term) to include such nongovernmental activities as education, business, and even religion.

29. Charles M. Tidmarch and John J. Pitney, Jr., "Covering Congress," *Polity*, vol. 17 (Spring 1985), p. 481. Also see Arthur H. Miller, Edie N. Goldenberg, and Lutz Erbring, "Type-Set Politics: Impact of Newspapers on Public Confidence," *American Political Science Review*, vol. 73 (March 1979), pp. 67–84.

30. Michael J. Robinson and Kevin R. Appel, "Network News Coverage of Congress," *Political Science Quarterly*, vol. 94 (Fall 1979), p. 412.

31. Ellen Hume, "The News Media and the National Interest," Andrew R. Cecil Lectures on Moral Values in a Free Society, University of Texas at Dallas, November 11, 1992; and Paul Taylor, *See How They Run: Electing the President in an Age of Mediaocracy* (Knopf, 1990), p. 23.

32. Michael J. Robinson, "Three Faces of Congressional Media," in Thomas E. Mann and Norman J. Ornstein, eds., *The New Congress* (Washington: American Enterprise Institute, 1981), p. 74.

33. All figures are from the *Tyndall Report*, 135 Rivington Street, New York, N.Y. 10002. For the charges against Durenberger and Frank, see *New York Times*, June 13, 1990, p. 1, and July 21, 1990, p. 6, respectively.

34. Larry J. Sabato, *Feeding Frenzy: How Attack Journalism Has Transformed American Politics* (Free Press, 1991), p. 26.

35. Suzanne Garment, *Scandal: The Crisis of Mistrust in American Politics* (Random House, 1991), p. 6.

36. I thank Robert Lichter and the Center for Media and Public Affairs for providing a count of congressional stories on network evening news programs in 1991.

37. Richard L. Berke with Stephen LaBaton, "A Difficult Season for Banks Trying to Lobby Capitol Hill," *New York Times*, February 19, 1991, p. D1.

38. Tidmarch and Pitney, "Covering Congress," p. 478.

39. The approximate daily weekday audiences of the major news programs: *MacNeil/Lehrer*, 2 million; C-SPAN claims 1.3 million households as a "loyal following"; CNN's prime evening news, 1 million; the three broadcast networks combined, 30 million.

40. *New York Times*, December 3, 1992, p. A1.

41. Les Brown, "Paradox of Democracy—More Channels, Less Discourse," *Media Studies Journal*, vol. 6 (Fall 1992), p. 123.

42. Stephen Hess, interview with David Bartlett, March 16, 1993.

43. There are also specialists in Congress as an institution, notably Congressional Quarterly, founded in 1945, which started with *CQ Weekly Report*; added a daily, *Congressional Monitor*, in 1981; then an on-line service, *Washington Alert*,

in 1984 that provided "bill-tracking and a dozen or so other data bases on a constantly updated basis." In 1993 it launched *HillFax*, through which "a customer can receive specific congressional information by fax within about four minutes." Neil Skene, "An Information Need," *CQ Weekly Report*, March 27, 1993, p. 717. A rival company, National Journal, publishes *CongressDaily/A.M.*, hand-delivered to subscribers by 7:00 a.m. each morning that Congress is in session, and *CongressDaily*, a Monday-Friday fax newsletter.

44. Quoted in Roger H. Davidson and Richard C. Sachs, eds., *Understanding Congress: Research Perspectives* (Government Printing Office, 1991), p. 207.

45. Richard F. Fenno, Jr., *Home Style: House Members in Their Districts* (Little, Brown, 1978), p. 168.

46. Quoted in Davidson and Sachs, eds., *Understanding Congress*, p. 57.

47. Glen R. Parker, "Can Congress Ever Be a Popular Institution?" in Joseph Cooper and G. Calvin MacKenzie, eds., *The House at Work* (University of Texas Press, 1981), p. 50.

48. Daniel Patrick Moynihan, *Counting Our Blessings: Reflections on the Future of America* (Little, Brown, 1980), p. 118.

49. Stephen Hess, *The Government/Press Connection: Press Officers and Their Offices* (Brookings, 1984). Note the pattern of calls received by one press officer at the Food and Drug Administration, pp. 51–52.

7 How the Press Views Congress

Kimberly Coursen Parker

THE NEWS MEDIA have taken a lot of heat lately for their captious coverage of political institutions and the cynical mood it has created in the public. Congress, especially, has borne the brunt of increasingly critical scrutiny that many of its defenders believe has damaged the institution and provided credibility and momentum to proposals for radical reform.

Whether or not one believes that the press has an undue influence on public opinion, there is no denying that as a whole it is and remains a major participant in the public debate on politics and governance. The plain truth is that people rely on the news media for information, and whether that information is biased or impartial, it is a vital component in their understanding of how government works.

As part of an ongoing effort to evaluate Congress and find constructive reforms to help it operate more effectively, the American Enterprise Institute–Brookings Institution Renewing Congress project has closely examined the relationships of the public and the press with the national legislature. Scholars have explored how opinions are formed and how they fit into the larger debate on congressional reform. Because media coverage of Congress is indeed influencing public opinion, directly or indirectly, it is important to learn more about how journalists themselves think of Congress. Although survey after survey has explored public opinion toward Congress and many studies have evaluated press coverage and bias, little is known about the personal opinions of those who report and analyze the news.

The conventional wisdom is that the press has grown increasingly hostile toward Congress in recent years and that its coverage, reflecting that development, has become increasingly derogatory. But although it may be true that the news media as a whole shares the public's overall assessment of Congress, there may be some news groups who do not. After all, people get their information and form their opinions based on a variety of sources: newspapers, newsmagazines, network TV news programs, radio talk shows, and many others. And within these categories members of the media differ in political allegiance, policy positions, years of experience, age, sex, and educational background.

The Renewing Congress project decided to survey journalists to help it address some of these issues. The survey attempted to step back from press coverage and other media products and explore individual knowledge and opinions. This paper draws on the findings of this wide-ranging survey, but I have focused on only a few central questions. How do journalists assess Congress as an institution? What factors influence their assessments? And do differences in journalists' viewpoints, knowledge, sophistication, and outlook with regard to Congress vary according to their job position, educational background, age, race, and sex?

Overview of the Survey

The survey was conducted for the Renewing Congress project by the Times Mirror Center for the People and the Press in October 1992.[1] The sample consisted of 331 senior members of the national news media.[2] It included people from print outlets, television, radio, and the wire services. Top executives, editors, producers, writers, and reporters were all represented. Two separate samples, one of congressional specialists drawn from the national print and broadcast media, and one of radio talk show hosts, were included in the survey. The sample was divided into five categories for the purposes of analysis: television journalists, print and other journalists, the powers that be (the upper echelon of management in the various media), congressional specialists, and radio talk show hosts.

The survey consisted of forty-eight questions on a range of issues relating to Congress as an institution, press coverage of Congress, and the prospects for and desirability of congressional reform.

Congressional Specialists and Organization Management

First, in terms of how members of the news media view the coverage of Congress, there was a dichotomy between specialists on Congress and the so-called powers that be, the top editors and news executives of national newspapers and magazines, top network news executives, executive producers of the most widely viewed news broadcasts, and nationally known columnists, anchors, and political correspondents. When asked to give their biggest complaints about the way the press covers Congress, 44 percent of the congressional specialists cited too much focus on scandals. Only 21 percent of the powers concurred. Seventeen percent of the specialists complained of too much focus on the gridlock caused by differences between executive and legislature. Only 4 percent of the powers saw this as a major problem. And 10 percent of the specialists felt the press does not understand how Congress works, compared with 4 percent of the powers.

When asked what the press does well in the way it covers Congress, 25 percent of the powers (a plurality) cited good day-to-day coverage; only 7 percent of the specialists agreed. Fifteen percent of the specialists gave the press a good grade for its coverage of politics and personalities, but only 4 percent of the powers concurred.

These two groups also differed in their assessments of Congress as an institution. When asked what Congress does best, 36 percent of the powers said, "Congress doesn't do anything well"; 15 percent of the congressional specialists agreed. Many specialists (27 percent) believed that what Congress does best is to look after voters and respond to the public. Only 11 percent of the powers offered that response. When asked what is most wrong with Congress, 54 percent of the powers cited the influence of special interests and political action committees; 24 percent of the specialists agreed. Twenty-two percent of the specialists cited bureaucratic red tape and congressional rules as the biggest problems afflicting Congress; only 4 percent of the powers saw this as a major problem.

Clearly, what you see depends on where you sit. The views of those who cover Congress day in and day out differ from the views of those who manage the media organizations and make the decisions about what stories will be covered and what tone the coverage will take.

The implications of these differing perceptions of congressional strengths and weaknesses are significant. The power of news executives and opinion leaders to set the national news agenda and dictate the extent and tone of coverage of Capitol Hill undoubtedly influences the content of that coverage.

Print and Television Journalists

Print and television journalists differed most in assessing changes in press coverage of Congress in the past ten years. When asked whether they thought press coverage of Congress today is better than it was, worse, or about the same, 27 percent of television journalists said coverage was better and 27 percent said worse. Forty percent of print journalists considered today's coverage better and 18 percent worse. Sixty-two percent of television journalists but 47 percent of print journalists believed more national coverage of Congress was necessary. Print journalists appeared more positive than the television journalists about the quality of congressional coverage.

These differences may reflect the extent to which television news has become popularized and salaciousness and scandal have become principal criteria for determining what constitutes a good story. When asked specifically about coverage of scandal in Congress, 40 percent of television journalists said news organizations give too much coverage to such stories; only 29 percent of print journalists agreed.

Rating Congress as an Institution

Respondents were asked to rate the job performance of the current Congress as excellent, good, only fair, or poor. Most of the responses were "only fair" or "poor." Television journalists rated Congress slightly better than their print colleagues. Not surprisingly congressional specialists gave Congress the highest ratings, while radio talk show hosts gave it the lowest (52 percent of radio hosts but 29 percent of congressional specialists gave Congress a rating of poor). The powers fell in between; 11 percent of them expressed no opinion. All the radio talk show hosts had opinions on this matter; in each of the other categories 3 percent had no answer.

Unfortunately, the survey did not contain a very reliable measure of the respondents' knowledge of Congress. Nonetheless, some inferences can be drawn from responses to one question. When asked whether they knew the name of their representative in the House, just 2 percent of congressional specialists and 4 percent of talk radio hosts could not recall. Among the powers, 14 percent could not name their representative, the highest percentage in the sample.

Views on Reform

There is a sharp difference, reflecting their differing attitudes toward Congress as an institution, among journalists on the matter of congressional reform. When asked what single reform would do the most to improve Congress, campaign finance reform and term limits topped the list. Most of the support for term limits came from radio talk show hosts (30 percent in favor) and television journalists (22 percent). Among congressional specialists, 51 percent favored campaign finance reform. Not a single specialist favored term limits. Again, the powers that be seemed at a loss to name specific reform proposals: 18 percent said they did not know or could not say what reform would do the most to improve Congress.

The most significant dichotomy revealed by the survey, and the topic of a more extensive analysis later, was the stark difference in opinion between congressional specialists and talk show hosts. There were occasional notable differences among the other groups in the sample, but these two were consistently at odds. This dichotomy has implications for the broader subject of public understanding of and attitudes toward Congress. Congressional specialists are much more sympathetic than others are toward the institution they cover. They have seen it up close, they know the members, they understand the constraints under which they operate, and many have developed an appreciation for its history and traditions. Some cynics may argue that these specialists have become insiders, that they have been seduced by the system. However, understanding need not mean selling out. And few can dispute that the experts' knowledge and understanding of the legislative process far surpasses that of most other journalists.

Congressional specialists surpass their colleagues not only in their experience and knowledge, but also in their education. Thirty-nine percent of them held a graduate degree, compared with less than 30 percent for the other groups. Only 17 percent of the radio talk show hosts had a graduate education. Just 5 percent of congressional specialists failed to complete college; 26 percent of the talk show hosts had dropped out.

If these differences in educational attainment, knowledge about Congress and the legislative process, and opinions on the problems facing Congress and the role it should play in the political system are indeed real and statistically significant, one can go on to discuss the broader implications for the public.

Ranking Overall Opinions of Congress

In light of the differences of attitude toward Congress on the part of congressional specialists and radio talk show hosts, I set about to isolate the effects of the two variables and determine if the differences in overall opinion were real or were caused by some other unrelated factors. Unfortunately, there was no reliable measure in the survey to indicate a respondent's overall opinion of Congress. The one question that asked respondents to rate Congress's overall performance elicited mostly negative replies and therefore was not conducive to any kind of in-depth analysis. To get around this problem, I created an index of sorts, incorporating questions about Congress, its membership, and its role in the political system.

The index of hostility, as I call it, was calculated from responses to six survey questions. They asked whether members of Congress receive too many or too few perquisites, whether current legislators have more or less integrity than those who served the institution in the 1960s and are more or less concerned with making good public policy, whether members lose touch with their constituents when they come to Washington, whether Congress or the president is more responsible for gridlock in Washington; and whether legislators should be limited in the number of terms they can serve.

For each question there were three possible reactions: a favorable, a neutral, or a hostile response. I assigned a score of zero for a favorable response, 1 for a neutral response, and 2 for a hostile response to each of the six questions. Each respondent ended up with a hostility rating that could range from zero, the least hostile, to 12, the most hostile. The sample turned out to be fairly normally distributed on the index, with most respondents falling in the middle range and few at the extremes (table 7A-1).

I next set out to discover where the groups fell on the scale. I rearranged the sample somewhat, creating four categories: television reporters and powers; print, radio, and wire reporters and powers; radio talk show hosts; and congressional specialists. Before bringing other variables into the equation, I decided to look at the relationship between the media field and the index of hostility. The mean scores for the television and print, radio, and wire groups fell almost squarely in the middle of the scale (table 7-1). Most respondents in these two categories were neutral toward Congress. The mean score for the congressional specialists, however, was well below the middle of the range, and the score for talk show hosts was well above.

The range of responses for each group shows that television and print, radio, and wire journalists include people representing nearly all possible responses. But none of the talk show hosts was in the least hostile end of the scale, and none of the congressional specialists landed in the most

Table 7-1. Hostility Scores, by Media Group

Group	*Number*	*Mean*	*Range*
Congressional specialists	29	4.38	1.00–8.00
Print, radio, and wire	95	5.83	2.00–12.00
Television	113	6.18	1.00–11.00
Talk radio	22	8.04	4.00–12.00

Source: Author's calculations based on data from the Renewing Congress project survey.

hostile range. Clearly there is a real and significant difference of opinion. Why? Are the differences between specialists and talk show hosts attributable solely to their fields, or are there other factors influencing their opinions?

I decided to see whether educational attainment, sex, race, or age were having an impact on the respondents' opinions toward Congress. Another avenue worth exploring was the possibility that the outlook of the powers that be differed somehow from that of rank-and-file journalists (48 respondents fell into the elite category and the remaining 283 in the nonelite category).

Having taken all these factors into account, I found that status as a congressional specialist or a radio talk show host was still the strongest predictor of overall feeling toward Congress. Congressional specialists were likely to be less hostile toward Congress than were radio talk show hosts. The categories proved equally strong predictors of overall score on the index (table 7A-2). Among the other variables, only level of education appeared to have any significant effect on opinions of Congress. As educational attainment increased, hostility toward Congress decreased. Sex, age, and race had no significant effect. Somewhat surprisingly, neither did elite or nonelite status. As for the other journalists, working in television, print, radio, or the wire services seemed to have no relationship to how a person scored on the index of hostility.

Radio Talk Show Hosts and Their Listeners

It is somewhat alarming to see the level of hostility expressed by radio talk show hosts. What is the reason for the hostility and to what extent it is being conveyed to the public?

According to Andrew Kohut of the Times Mirror Center for the People and the Press, the principal architect of the press survey and a veteran pollster, the opinions they express reflect public opinion on the various topics addressed in the survey much more closely than do those of the press as a whole.[3] It would of course be useful to conduct an identical survey with a sample from the general public to verify this.

In constructing the sample of radio talk show hosts, a conscious effort was made to include not just the stereotypical loud-mouthed, brash, and highly opinionated individuals, but a cross-section. With the help of the National Association of Talk Show Hosts, the top ten radio markets were identified, then within each market, association members with the largest audience were selected. Thus the sample included the likes of Diane Rehm and Derek McGinty as well as Rush Limbaugh. This diversity makes the findings even more striking.

It is hard to estimate the size of the audience or the effects of radio talk shows, but most people would agree that they have gained in popularity and influence in recent years. If people are indeed paying attention to the shows, it is important to ask on what the hosts are basing their strongly held and widely disseminated opinions. In most cases they have at best limited first-hand knowledge of Congress and how it works, and according to the survey, they are often less well educated than print and radio reporters, not to mention congressional specialists.

Talk show hosts certainly do not lack intelligence or insight, however. On the contrary, they are probably more in touch with the American people and the everyday issues and problems they deal with than are those journalists who work and live inside the capital beltway. But there is a more important point to be made here: in covering and criticizing institutions of government, journalists have a responsibility to understand the nature of those institutions and convey some of that understanding to the public.

At the time the survey was carried out, little was known about the growing number of radio talk show hosts. Since then, however, the Times Mirror Center for the People and the Press has completed a comprehensive survey of the hosts and their listeners that greatly expands our understanding of this increasingly important and influential group. I have drawn heavily on the survey in my analysis. When speculating about the power and influence of radio talk show hosts, one must first ask how many Americans actually listen to talk radio. According to the Times Mirror survey, more than 40 percent of Americans report tuning in relatively frequently to shows that "invite listeners to call in to discuss current events, public issues and politics."[4] Some 17 percent say they listen regularly, and 61 percent report having listened at least once.

Those who do listen are more often Republican and more ideologically conservative than is the population at large. Republicans are more than twice as likely as Democrats to listen regularly, and conservatives twice as likely as liberals. The survey indicates that the regular listener is most often (although some margins are thin) a white male, Republican, 50 years of age or older, college educated, with a family income higher than $50,000.[5] They listen to these programs mainly to learn how people feel about issues and to keep up with issues of the day. When offered a variety of reasons why they might tune into radio talk shows, they considered the appeal of a particular host the least important.

Who are the hosts and what generalizations can be made about them? The Times Mirror survey questioned 112 of them, two-thirds from the top twenty-five markets in the country and the other third from the smaller markets. Although conventional wisdom might lead one to believe that most radio talk show hosts are ultraconservative, the survey found that as a group they are moderate and politically independent. Sixteen percent identified themselves as Republicans, 17 percent Democrats, and the remainder reported leaning toward one or the other or having no party affiliation. Similarly, 21 percent identified themselves as firm conservatives and 22 percent as firm liberals.[6]

The hosts are well educated compared with the general public (although not when compared with their journalistic colleagues). They are fairly affluent (30 percent reported incomes in excess of $100,000), and they tend to be much less religious than the general public.[7]

In terms of the service they provide, talk show hosts see themselves more as purveyors of information than as entertainers. In fact 63 percent believe they "often play an important role in shaping or influencing public opinion" in their community. Many report bringing important local issues to the forefront, influencing the outcome of local elections, or exposing incidents of government corruption.[8]

Although they hold more moderate views than those held by the general public on many of the controversial issues of the day, their evaluations of political institutions and political figures are much more critical. This confirms the findings from the Renewing Congress survey estimating hostility toward Congress. Fifty-three percent of the hosts gave President Clinton an unfavorable rating, compared with 34 percent of the general public. The hosts were also more critical of Ross Perot, the United Nations, daily papers, network TV news, and even the church. Seventy-three percent rated Congress unfavorably, compared with 48 percent of the general public and 59 percent of regular radio listeners.[9]

Although hosts set the tone for their shows, the people who call in generally determine the content. The Times Mirror survey revealed that like the hosts themselves, these callers are hostile toward institutions of government. Sixty-four percent of callers gave Congress an unfavorable rating.[10] Knowing this, one can surmise that the content of the shows is disparaging when either the institution or its members become the topic of conversation.

The survey data have important implications not only for Congress but for American society. Radio talk show listeners are not a small or unique group. They are many, and they come from all walks of life. Talk show hosts and callers represent a wide range of interests and opinions. Nonetheless, they do share the belief that the government, especially Congress, is not to be trusted. More and more Americans seem to be tuning into these shows, and one can only assume that some of them are buying the messages the shows are sending.

Conclusions

This is a crucial time for American institutions of government, especially Congress. Press coverage of Congress has focused more and more on scandal and less and less on the legislative process. Public attitudes toward the institution have sunk to new lows. People are exasperated by the topic of Congress. In forming their opinions they appear to be paying attention to what they are hearing from myriad media outlets, but they seem sorely lacking in any real understanding of how Congress works. The danger of the situation is obvious. People are willing to support change for the sake of change; they are ready to tear down their own institutions in hopes of making them better and more responsive.

A survey of 1,000 people conducted as part of the Americans Talk Issues series and released in April 1993 showed that when presented with reforms ranging from the reasonable to the outrageous, many Americans are willing to support anything that sounds as if it would represent a change from business as usual.[11] Among proposals intended to make democracy work better and make government more responsive, cutting salaries of members of Congress was the choice of 80 percent of respondents. Offering higher salaries to encourage the best people to run for Congress was the least favored proposal. Large majorities favored limiting the terms not only of members of Congress but also of lobbyists and bureaucrats. Seventy-five percent of respondents agreed that Congress should be required to conduct scientific, nonpartisan, large-sample surveys of public opinion on all important national issues and release the results promptly so that Congress and the public will know what most

Americans want for legislation.[12] Clearly this would dilute the role of Congress as a great deliberative body; members would merely represent the whims and fancies of their constituents. Surveys such as this illustrate the danger of sustained disapproval of Congress and the reason why greater public understanding must be created.

Although better-informed members of the public once generally approved of what their institutions of government were doing, this is no longer the case. Data collected as part of the 1992 American National Election Studies show that as knowledge of politics increases, approval of Congress decreases.[13] This new trend may pose a danger to Congress because the people with the most knowledge of politics and government are the ones most likely to vote. When the relationship of knowledge and approval of Congress is considered along with findings that those who pay the most attention to politics approve least of what Congress is doing, the implications for Congress as an institution are dismal.

Meanwhile there remains a vital link between political institutions and the news media. One study conducted by the National Council of State Legislatures found that the most critical determinants for public approval of legislatures are the amount, quality, and type of news coverage they receive. One of the reasons cited for the increase in favorable evaluations of state legislatures around the country is that their activities are more visible in the media than at any time in American history. But increased exposure has not elicited more favorable responses to the national legislature.[14]

It seems ironic that at a time when public activism and interest in the political system have seemingly reached new heights, so has the level of anger and frustration with those who serve in government. Using the various technologies now available, constituents can contact their representatives in Washington almost instantaneously with complaints, criticisms, and more advice than most members can digest. The constituents are spurred to do so by radio talk show hosts who rail against the institution and its members. We need to find ways to channel those energies so that the public can work with its representatives in Congress for constructive change.

The media can contribute here, not as apologists for members of Congress or the institution itself but as informed purveyors of information. Journalists who specialize in Congress generally hold the institution in higher esteem than do their generalist colleagues. Radio talk show hosts are among the most hostile of journalists in their attitudes toward Congress. Incidentally, television journalists as a group, although not as hostile as talk show hosts, appear to be more hostile than their print and wire services colleagues. Their negative attitudes, assuming they are conveyed to the public, may be deepening general pessimism about the worth of government institutions, especially at a time when television has become the primary source of news and information for so many Americans.

What are the broader implications of the survey findings for public opinion and public understanding of Congress? It is hard to make definitive generalizations on the basis of a few limited surveys, but the findings should dispel any notion of the media as a homogeneous group. This knowledge and any additional insights it provides might prove helpful in the effort to improve reporting on Congress and the legislative process. Improved coverage could go a long way toward bringing about greater public understanding and, ultimately, raising the level of public discourse.

Appendix Tables

Table 7A-1. Index of Hostility

Cumulative value label (percent)	*Value*	*Frequency*	*Percent*
1.5	1.00	4	1.2
4.6	2.00	8	2.4
15.8	3.00	29	8.8
28.2	4.00	32	9.7
44.8	5.00	43	13.0
60.6	6.00	41	12.4
74.1	7.00	35	10.6
84.9	8.00	28	8.5
90.7	9.00	15	4.5
94.6	10.00	10	3.0
98.8	11.00	11	3.3
100.0	12.00	3	0.9
Missing	. . .	72	21.8
Total	. . .	331	100.0
Mean	6.012		
Standard deviation	2.399		
Minimum	1.000		
Maximum	12.000		

Source: Author's calculations based on data from the Renewing Congress project survey.

Table 7A-2. Influence of Eight Variables on Attitudes toward Congress[a]

Variable	*B*	*Beta*	*t - statistic*
Congress	−1.850	−.244	.0001
Education	−0.516	−.121	.0439
Sex	0.312	.054	.3719
Race	−0.090	−.020	.7405
Talk show host	1.722	.200	.0014
Elite	−0.309	−.038	.5379
Age	−0.289	−.089	.1611
Print and radio journalists	−0.261	−.052	.4125

Source: Author's calculations based on data from the Renewing Congress project survey.
a. R^2 for the entire equation was .145, indicating a moderately good fit.

Notes

1. Study performed by the Times Mirror Center for the People and the Press for Renewing Congress project, October 7–29, 1992.

2. The number of respondents giving complete responses.

3. Andrew Kohut, personal communication with author; and unpublished report of a survey by Kohut, January 20, 1993.

4. Times Mirror Center for the People and the Press, "The Vocal Minority in American Politics," July 16, 1993, p. 6.

5. Ibid., pp. 7, 8.

6. Ibid., p. 14.

7. Ibid., p. 15.

8. Ibid., p. 17.

9. Ibid., p. 21.

10. Ibid., p. 45.

11. Alan F. Kay and others, "The First ATI Survey on Improving Democracy in America," survey 22, Americans Talk Issues Foundation: Washington and St. Augustine, Fla., April 1993.

12. Ibid., p. i.

13. Inter-University Consortium for Political and Social Research, *American National Election Study, 1992* (Ann Arbor, Mich., 1993).

14. Karl T. Kurtz, "The Public Standing of the Legislature," paper prepared for the Eagleton Institute of Politics for the Symposium on the Legislature in the Twenty-First Century, Williamsburg, April 1990, rev. August 1991.

8 Brighter Lights, Wider Windows: Presenting Congress in the 1990s

Ronald D. Elving

HISTORIANS and political scientists generally agree that in qualifications and integrity the people now serving in Congress compare favorably with those of earlier eras. This benign opinion, however, is not often heard at lunch counters or on radio talk shows; and some polling data show public regard for Congress at a low ebb. If both assertions are accurate, their absolute contradiction of one another demands some explanation. Have public perceptions of Congress been misinformed by the news media and other opinion makers? Does the institution frustrate and undercut the actions of its individually sincere and capable members? Or are the members themselves responsible for, or at least complicit in, their institution's low standing? The answer to all three questions must be yes in some measure, although I will emphasize the part the institution and its members play in forming their own public image.

The Historical Institution

Through most of its history, Congress paid scant attention to presenting itself to the public. People were entitled to watch it work (within certain limitations); but few ever had the time, occasion, or inclination to do so. If government operations seemed opaque, not many seemed to mind. Now and then reformers have urged Congress to educate the public about how it worked, to expose and explain its affairs at least to the more sophisticated and educated voters. But this has always been an idealist's impulse, conceived in service to the citizenry. The idea that Congress itself might profit in some practical way from exposure and explication has not been widely discussed.

This inwardness has characterized not only the conventions of the institution but the personal style of the members as well. "For most of the twentieth century," according to Timothy Cook, "the way to get things done and to advance a career in Washington was to play an inside game, building relationships with colleagues, deferring to senior members, and bargaining, while slowly building up the legislative longevity necessary to achieve a position of power."[1] To be sure, congressional drama has not played to entirely empty seats. Congress has always been monitored by lobbyists beholden to interested parties and by reporters whose employers marketed their accounts of the proceedings in various ways. Strictly speaking, however, both the hired gun and the hired pen have performed for relatively small and special audiences (at least until the heyday of broadcast news). And while there have always been some members of Congress who have enjoyed cultivating lobbyists or reporters or both, the institutional standard has been to minimize visibility.

The successful member of the middle ranks typically kept a low profile, tending to district business while voting the party line and avoiding the press. But although still far from extinct, this semireclusive subspecies is no longer the norm. "You still occasionally hear people say 'the less I'm covered the better,'" Representative David Price of North Carolina has commented. "A generation ago, that was standard."[2]

This did not prevent certain persistent elements of the press from taking up semipermanent residence in the Capitol. The idea of a press gallery developed in the first half of the nineteenth century, when efforts were made to separate reporters from lobbyists. When the new House and Senate chambers opened in the 1850s, special press galleries provided reporters excellent seats for floor action and a commodious antechamber to which to retire during lulls.[3]

But physical accommodation was one thing, congressional openness to inquisitive reporting another. Reporters pursuing stories had few places to go for information and even fewer sources of help. Full-time press secretaries were all but unknown (in the House they were still comparatively rare as late as 1970).[4] As recently as World War II, news organizations that did not have a reporter of their own in the gallery (as well as some that did) found it difficult to obtain timely, accurate counts of floor votes (let alone those taken in committees). Leaders did not march off to explain themselves after a major event, as they do now in the radio and television correspondents' gallery. Nor did the individual members stand on the Capitol steps or grounds facing crew after crew with minicameras and microphones.

If most earlier members of Congress saw less of the press, most also saw less of their constituents. They traveled home less often and commanded little attention when they did (although some celebrity attended those from single-district states or from predominantly rural districts). Some chafed at their invisibility, but these tended to leave Congress to seek other office. Those who stayed, including those who aged into power as committee chairmen or ranking minority members, knew the value of anonymity. Spared the distress and distraction of high-powered opposition back home or high-pressure visibility in Washington, they exercised power with far greater latitude in their own sphere.

At election time, members relied on party organs to raise the money, organize the workers, and make the case to the voters. When incumbents went home to campaign, they stressed broad themes; they knew they would field few questions indeed about the provisions of bills or specific votes. When the election was over, the reelected went back to Washington and stayed there through the next session. The folks back home did not expect to see their congressman home for multiple visits each month, and the members were only compensated for a few round-trips to the district annually.

This is not to say that a Congress largely unseen was revered. Humorists from Mark Twain to Finley Peter Dunne ("Mr. Dooley") to Will Rogers satirized the manners, ethics, and perceived ineffectuality of Capitol Hill. Mark Twain referred to Congress as the nation's only "distinctly native criminal class." It has also been a scapegoat for presidents: Woodrow Wilson complained of the "little band of willful men" and Harry Truman ran against the "Do Nothing 80th Congress."

Such raillery aside, however, Congress lived rather happily through generations of comparative anonymity, making scant public relations effort and feeling little intruded upon by journalists. The average American until recently accorded Congress a certain dignity, if only because it seemed part of America's nationhood. Remote, official, and ceremonial, the institution retained the ineffable respectability of a monument. It was part of the American system; and it has been an article of civic faith that the system bloomed as the final flower of statecraft.

But judging by poll results, declining reelection rates, and dwindling margins of victory, this longstanding acceptance appears to have weakened. The ending of the cold war has eased the global political tensions that obliged Americans to stand by their institutions. And the old assumptions about the inevitable success of the American political-economic system are no longer secure. Americans no longer assume that they enjoy the highest standard of living in the world or that conditions will improve for each succeeding generation. In this context, it is easy to see how the Great Society, Vietnam, Watergate, the mounting federal debt, and various other policy disappointments and scandals have fostered cynicism and prompted a search for scapegoats. Congress has proven a reliable target in this regard for politicians of all kinds, including all three major candidates for president in the fall of 1992.

These historical developments have been accompanied by technological developments that make it far easier to observe Congress (and even to pursue it to its lair). C-SPAN now televises the proceedings of the House and Senate, along with committee hearings and related events. Members of Congress are frequent guests (and even more frequent targets) on the ever proliferating day and night talk shows on national and local radio and television. And thanks to the minicamera, satellite dishes, and uplink technologies, members from small and medium-sized cities may be as recognizable to their constituents as a mayor or a governor.[5] Meanwhile, constituents can reach out to their representatives by mail, phone, wire, and computer, and their visits to Washington (often sponsored by groups) are more common than ever. Members of Congress find themselves responding through these same tools and more, including targeted mailings and interactive television.[6]

All these lines of communication are making Congress more visible to the public, yet they do not quite succeed in making it more accessible. C-SPAN, for example, can bring the sound and fury of Congress to more than 50 million households, but it does little to make the institution and its workings intelligible. Floor debates, parliamentary maneuvers, and the wide variety of votes taken remain difficult to follow, much less understand. Meanwhile, the more obvious failings of Congress (scandal, partisan rancor, disarray) are all too readily communicated.

This may in part explain why, as new technologies bring Congress and the public together in unprecedented ways, the public's opinion of the institution has fallen to new depths. In 1992, polls found 69 percent of the public dissatisfied or angry with the House and 72 percent dissatisfied or angry with the Senate. By contrast, in the late 1940s and early 1950s, clear majorities told Gallup they had confidence in Congress.[7]

As Congress has come into the light, then, it has often found the exposure less than flattering. This may be a simple case of familiarity breeding contempt. Or it may be that greater visibility, while helping to educate some of the public about Congress, is also highlighting the institution's lingering insularity, petty corruptions, and lapses into political dysfunction. If this is the case, the solution is not to lower the light—the time for that reaction has passed—but to address the flaws it may reveal.

Making Contact

Congress presents itself to the public as an institution, as two political parties, and as individual members. But most direct contact with the public is generated by the members. Poll respondents usually recall some form of contact with their own representative, but few citizens have any sense of the caucuses that largely run both chambers of Congress, let alone any awareness of the workings of the institution itself.

The Personal Touch

The average member of Congress comes to work each day with the expectation of meeting constituents. Some of these, especially the larger organized groups, will have scheduled appointments. Others may drop by his office unannounced. Although some constituents will know the member already, most will not. And while some will pronounce themselves thrilled and surprised to catch their representative between other engagements, most will be disappointed—even miffed—if they do not get to see him. Even constituents who return more than once a year and home-state organizations that return regularly to urge the same case on the same issue expect the personal touch. This is why congressional offices devote so many hours (mostly those of receptionists, interns, and other entry-level staff) to preparing gallery passes, tour tickets, and other treats for visiting constituents. Members' waiting rooms are often so bedecked with guidebooks and tour brochures that they resemble travel agencies.

Most members of Congress are personable, and some are exceptionally charming. Others compensate for a lack of natural grace by dint of effort. Members are often prepped by aides so they can recall the names, hometowns, and concerns of the constituents they will encounter in a given day. The encounters can be distracting and draining, sapping time from committee meetings and other duties. But few members feel they can afford to deny visitors the satisfaction of a handshake and a hearing, especially when folks have come so far from home.

Members also extend themselves to greet constituents personally on home ground. The members may seem far less imposing standing alone on the hardwood of a grade school gym, but here they score invaluable points. They communicate closeness, even humility. They defend themselves directly and establish empathy. The people who come to see them, like those who visit their Hill offices, would seem those likeliest to vote. As an additional advantage, the conscientious member's itinerary can be distributed in advance to the local news media. This may generate coverage, but at a minimum it reinforces the impression that the member spends every available hour back home. Of such subliminal impressions are editorial judgments frequently formed. Senator Slade Gorton of Washington, who lost a reelection bid in 1986 because voters considered him aloof, now sends a fax of his daily schedule to the national media (as well as to Washington state reporters). Each day, the record shows him finding time in the midst of his committee and subcommittee schedule to meet with folks from back home.[8]

If constituent visits to Capitol Hill have become more common in the past generation, members' visits home have increased exponentially. And the political necessity of those visits has swollen to a degree that members from another era would not recognize. There have always been a few legislators from districts near Washington who went home frequently (a generation ago, William A. Barrett of Philadelphia returned home nightly to hold office hours), but most came to Washington early in the year and stayed until summer recess (returning in the fall to stay to the end of the session).

In recent years, however, the typical member has begun commuting two or three weekends a month, and some, including some westerners, go home every weekend. Al Gore of Tennessee made a fetish of town hall meetings when he was a young House member, and he kept it up as a young senator, attending thousands in his sixteen years in Congress. Former Representative Richard Stallings of Idaho would make his way back to Pocatello and Idaho Falls most weekends, even though it meant flying to Salt Lake City and then driving five hours to get there.[9]

Few observers would fault members for spending time with their constituents, whether in Washington or back home. But this commitment comes with high costs, including the strain on members' health and mental acuity and the lost opportunity for social interaction between members. Social occasions, planned and spontaneous, once united the members in moments of conviviality that transcended conflicts and partisan identities. Such moments are now rare.

Special Delivery

Even the most active member meets personally with no more than a few constituents. But any legislator with a good staff can reach virtually every household in his or her district through the franked newsletter, a publication up to four pages long that members may mail without cost to all homes in their district as many as four times a year. The newsletters may not solicit contributions, urge a member's reelection, or speak to issues in partisan terms. These restrictions are a challenge to the staffs who put them together, striving to promote the legislator and partisan stands on issues in terms just bland enough to pass muster with the Office of the House Clerk. But it is important to pass this test. Not only does the free mailing depend on it, but the newsletter itself has more political impact if it appears to be official and reasonably above the fray.

The great drawback of such mail is that, arriving unsolicited, it can easily be discarded unopened with the typical daily weight of junk mail. Members compensate, to some degree, by targeting their additional mailings. The best way to target mail is to answer the mail that pours into congressional offices every business day. Even machine-generated contact cards (such as those handed out in company cafeterias or union halls) often have return addresses. Once an initial letter of response has been sent, constituents' names can be filed and cross-referenced for topics of interest. "The senior offices are sending out proactive mail," Representative Steve Horn, a freshman from California, has commented. "The letters come with notes like 'Gee, I thought you might be interested in something we just did with regard to such and such.'"[10]

Staffs grind out scores of generic response letters on particular issues. They then use software programs to merge the text of these standard letters with the names and addresses of constituents who have written. These programs include blanks in the text so that keywords can be added to personalize the reply. Another personal touch is added by the office autopen, which inks in the member's signature with the look of real penmanship. Autopens are standard operating equipment in the Senate, where offices receive sacks of mail daily. Still, some House members try to answer their mail themselves and sign it personally. "I even like to add little notes at the bottom in my own handwriting, wherever I can," said Horn, who acknowledged that doing so imposes escalating time demands, even for a freshman.

One constraint on using franked mail is the bad press it has attracted in recent years, making it a target for congressional reformers who consider it a thinly veiled campaign device. The sheer volume of mail is eye catching. In fiscal year 1954, congressional mailings amounted to 43.5 million pieces. In 1984 the number was more than 924 million. The amount of mail received has also increased, but not nearly in proportion.[11]

Under pressure the House voted in 1992 to ban mass mailings outside a member's existing district. But the vote did not come until August, when many members had already targeted mailings at potential voters who, although not inside the current district, would be in the new district for purposes of that fall's election. In a similar shuffle the House voted to trim its mailing budget in fiscal year 1993 to $47.7 million. An apparent cut of 10 percent from the previous fiscal year, that amount actually represented a large increase from the $31.3 million appropriated in the previous nonelection year (1991).[12]

C-SPAN and Beyond

The event that was expected to revolutionize the presentation of Congress was the advent of gavel-to-coverage television coverage via the Cable Satellite Public Affairs Network in 1979. In political terms C-SPAN was a gift because it was to be paid for by cable operators' revenues (adding pennies a month to the basic subscription cost). Initially available to fewer than 18 million homes, it is now available to more than 55 million (although recent cutbacks are reducing the availability of C-SPAN 2).[13]

Some legislators worried that the robocameras would change Congress radically, subjecting it to some faceless editor or sinister conspiracy. Representative Jim Wright of Texas, then the House majority leader, feared the proceedings would not be "jazzy enough" for TV. And Representative Ron Dellums of California said he did not want to see "corporate America dominate these proceedings."[13] But neither the derisive nor the dire predictions were borne out. There was grandstanding, of course, but most of it closely resembled the kind for which the House had long been renowned. The Senate allowed C-SPAN in 1986 after realizing that the public was becoming increasingly aware of the House. C-SPAN may have wrought more of a change in demeanor in the Senate than in the House. Senators have discovered the use of charts and other visual aids, and the old stentorian histrionics are gradually giving way to a more professorial mode.

On balance, however, what C-SPAN has wrought is not a new Congress but a new level of public awareness of what Congress looks and sounds like. When the institution is at its best, as when it debated the resolutions to use force in the Persian Gulf in January 1991, the exposure has helped shape a favorable attitude from the public. But when it is not on its best behavior, the cameras have been telling witnesses. "C-SPAN just magnifies what's there to see," Representative Jim Leach of Iowa has said.

"The warts are more evident. Spats are not perceived well by the public, and personality spats in particular do not wear well."[15]

C-SPAN is not the only component of New Age congressional presentation, just the most obvious. House members use Capitol Hill video studios (where the Democratic Congressional Campaign Committee and the National Republican Congressional Committee have produced campaign ads since the mid-1980s) between election seasons to tape interviews. But there are also facilities through which a member may speak live, via interactive TV, with an anchor at a news network in New York or, more often, with an evening news anchor at the station back home.

On the Senate side, interactive television is provided under the auspices of the Democratic Policy Committee and its Republican counterpart, both of which use not only Senate office space but public funds. Thus when Democrat Tom Daschle cannot get back to South Dakota in time to address the Chamber of Commerce and answer questions, or when Republican Conrad Burns cannot get back to Montana to see a group of constituents scheduled to meet with him, they can be there through interactive TV. "Interactive video is the next thing," Daschle observed. "In rural areas especially. You can make a mass conference call to explain your position on Russia or abortion or whatever. In five years, it will be commonplace."[16]

Using this video conference technology, Senator Pete Wilson of California was able to meet the press in his home state on the day in 1988 when the Senate passed his amendment to cut the budget for franked mail. The video conference, of course, neatly demonstrated how one communications technique supersedes another (both at taxpayer expense). In time, perhaps holography and other forms of virtual reality will enable members to appear before their constituents in even more convincing fashion. In the interim, video conferencing and other combinations of video and telephone technology will allow members to dial their way directly into constituents' homes (perhaps to deliver a live or recorded response to a letter). They will also allow members to convene electronic news conferences and town hall meetings even while they are on call for floor votes.

Less vivid but perhaps even more pervasive is the penetration of Congress by computers. Nearly all members had computerized their offices by the mid-1980s, and the recent proliferation of modems and communication programs has linked them to the world of computer networking and information highways. Electronic mail, also known as E-mail, has begun to lend immediacy (if not always weight) to the communications that arrive on the Hill from personal computers across the country and around the world. Much of the cybernetic zeal Vice President Al Gore has brought to the White House was transported from his Senate operation. And if the average congressional office has yet to be caught up in the fervor, the time is not far off. Congress will get there, if only because the White House will.

To some degree the high-technology links between members and the public are driven by each member's desire to press his political case. But they are also driven by the public's desire to contact, react to, and communicate with Congress. Obviously, these links are limited in that they connect a member only to the economic and technical elite. But definitions of the elite are notoriously elastic, especially when the subject is electronic appliances. Modems and fax machines may still be unusual in the home, but it was not long ago that any home computer was rare. Before that, color TV, or any TV, was a measure of affluence. Even the telephone was once an instrument of the elite. Full access to the information highways and data treasures of computer networking may take less time to become common and affect the average voter than any of these predecessor technologies.[17]

No matter how sophisticated these mechanisms become, however, they are likely to remain dedicated to member-constituent contact. By its nature this contact emphasizes members' services to constituents and their perspectives on events; it does little to educate the public regarding the larger institution.

Media Relations

While using every means of self-presentation they can control, the members and committees, leaders and caucuses of Congress also try to enlist the news media—a less predictable but often effective tool for reaching the public. In recent years, elements of the party leadership and other media-savvy members have learned to manipulate news organizations—national as well as local—via the latest technology, adapting techniques (the dramatic announcement, the leaked secret report) that have existed for generations. At the same time, reporters' persistent interest in peccadilloes and the plentiful supply of petty scandals strengthens the average member's feeling that the press disrespects the institution and lacks perspective on Hill activities.

For their part, journalists who cover Capitol Hill are instinctively aware of being used to further legislative and political aims. As a rule, they resist being co-opted. But the rule is sometimes honored in the breach, as when cooperation between member and reporter might produce or promote a good story. A reporter, for example, rarely hesitates to float a trial balloon for a senator if the balloon is eye-catching enough for the front page or the lead on the evening news.

Posing for Pictures

On the night of February 17, 1993, minutes after President Bill Clinton had addressed his first joint session of Congress, a familiar ritual was replayed in the Capitol's Statuary Hall. As the new president spoke to the packed House chamber, camera crews had set up in the semicircular space that was the House's original home. Beneath the steady gaze of heroes cast in bronze along the wall, television reporters practiced their stand-up lines: "Congress may be applauding the president tonight, but there will be tougher days ahead for the president's plan here on Capitol Hill. Back to you, Steve." As soon as the president finished, senators and representatives spilled into the hallways and struggled toward the waiting cameras. As they came into sight they were set upon by eager producers, steering them toward one or another camera. When they finished their sound bites, they would thank the interviewer and move to another camera position, where other members were waiting in a queue and answering questions from print reporters (the "pencil press"). The hall quickly filled with bodies, voices, blinding glare, rising heat. The crowd around prominent members piled up like a rugby scrum.

Many members who are rarely accorded network interviews in the Radio and TV Gallery nonetheless fluttered around the hot bulbs in Statuary Hall. They did not expect network exposure here either, but they were loath to miss an opportunity to reach their constituents. Local stations come to the Capitol on such nights, using minicameras inside and mobile uplink trucks parked outside, beaming interviews live to cities large and small.

Members' interest in local coverage is, of course, far from new. Many have enjoyed excellent press in their districts and states, in part because reporters need them and in part because they work hard to keep the lines of communication open. Senator Bill Armstrong of Colorado, a conservative Republican who served three terms in the House and two in the Senate before retiring in 1990, received favorable press in his home state through most of his three decades in politics (a beating he took over an amendment to the 1986 tax reform legislation was an exception that highlighted the rule). One reason he did so well was that he set aside time each Friday to meet informally with Colorado reporters, thus guaranteeing them regular access and assuring himself of regular coverage.

But the new technology that brings local television personalities together with members of Congress creates an even cozier convergence of interest, not to mention the opportunity to speak directly into constituents' living rooms in unedited live interviews. Representative Dan Glickman of Kansas emphasized, "I am never too busy to talk to local TV. Period. Exclamation point."[18]

Some press veterans belittle cattle shows such as "Statuary Hell," regarding them as the province of drive-by journalists who come to the Hill once or twice a year. But the hour following a major speech is one of the few times when news executives everywhere want Hill reaction and the institution of Congress is in demand. Of course, what these news managers actually get is reaction from individual members. No one learns much about the institutional response or disposition, but few care. The crews are looking for good tape, and the members want little more than to be seen by the large audience still tuned in for the first minutes after the president has spoken.

There is nothing inherently wrong in this, except that an extraordinary opportunity for the public to learn something about Congress and how it works is mostly missed. "The media generally benefit public people, not public institutions," according to political scientist Michael J. Robinson. "For the most part the new media mix has rendered Congress no less safe but a little less serviceable—the members no less important but the Congress a little less viable."[19]

The Message Operation

Communications specialists who work for Congress are almost exclusively deployed by individual members. David Dreyer, a veteran of six Capitol Hill offices, including two in the House Democratic leadership, has seen the difficulty facing the institution. "Flak people," he says, are judged by one thing: "getting their bosses' names in the paper or on the evening news . . . almost always without regard to the party position on a given issue."[20] In July 1989 when Dreyer became communications director for House Majority Leader Richard A. Gephardt, he found his new boss trying to mount a sustained media offensive on a broader front. The result was a regular meeting of members and staff that became known as Gephardt's message operation or the message board. A group of Democratic House members (between twenty-five and thirty on most days the House was in session in the 101st and 102d Congresses) began to discuss coordinating their communications with the news media. A core group of staff (including George Stephanopoulos, later to become communications director for Bill Clinton) worked to form a coherent critique of George Bush's presidency and market it to reporters. After Bush had triumphed over House leaders on cutting capital gains taxes in 1989, the Gephardt people had an issue they could highlight: tax fairness. When the budget summit in 1990 led Bush to renege on his pledge of no new taxes, the Democrats claimed that fairness had carried the day.

This constituted an institutional position for Congress only in the sense that Democrats had a majority in both chambers. It was certainly not the message of congressional Republicans, nor even that of many conservative Democrats (dozens of whom had voted for lower capital gains taxes). But because Gephardt's message seemed to sum up the conflict between the president and the dominant faction of the majority congressional party, the news media treated it as an institutional voice.

A different message operation has emerged from the activities of Representative Newt Gingrich, a conservative from Georgia who became the second-ranking Republican in the House in 1989. Even before his elevation to leadership, this hyperarticulate former history professor was a leading presenter of Congress to the public. He cofounded the Conservative Opportunity Society and copioneered the use of "special orders" as an entree to cable viewers in the early 1980s. The idea was to use the deserted chamber at the end of the day as a kind of television studio, taking advantage of C-SPAN's willingness to cover the House floor until the final gavel. This tactic is still a staple for Republicans (and some Democrats), even though the camera operators have been instructed to reveal, periodically, the emptiness of the chamber.[21]

Gingrich regularly convenes an informal task force of like-minded and media-conscious colleagues to discuss tactics on upcoming bills, sometimes in coordination with business groups and other lobbies. Legislation supporting family leave, a perennial in Congress from 1985 until its enactment in 1993, was a case in point. Business lobbyists worked with Gingrich's group to crack the wall of favorable coverage that the bill received in the media.[22]

But Gingrich also uses his message operation for broader strategic objectives, primarily derogating the current Congress. For years, he and his allies have assailed not only the legislative works of Congress but its legitimacy as well. They maintain that the Democratic majority perpetuates itself through closed rules, stacked votes, and gerrymandered districts. But although their target is the Democrats, Gingrich and his confreres frame their attack in terms of the institution. The House itself, they say, is the perfect metaphor for the failed and corrupt welfare state. A pamphlet produced by this group was titled "House of Ill Repute." And when asked on NBC-TV why Republicans had not gained the majority in the House, Gingrich replied, "Because we don't tell the truth about Congress hard enough, often enough and aggressively enough."[23]

Just as Gephardt's operation altered the way the media covered tax policy, Gingrich's efforts have changed the vocabulary they use in talking about Congress and encouraged the vogue of denigratory references to the institution. The precise consequence of all this is difficult to assess. But some evidence suggests Gingrich is succeeding. Polls show respect for Congress is suffering. There has also been a modest reversal in the trend toward incumbent security. Forty-three members who sought reelection in 1992 were defeated in the primary or general election. And the number would surely have been higher if a record-high sixty-five members had not chosen to retire.

In the Senate the most successful message operations have been run by individual members committed to using the press and adept at doing so. In recent years this club has included such disparate personalities as J. Bennett Johnston of Louisiana and Daniel Patrick Moynihan of New York, Phil Gramm of Texas and Howard Metzenbaum of Ohio. Because each senator can exercise control over the floor, power is atomized. Even more than in the House, the leadership must consult its caucus, making the prospect of an institutional voice all the more remote.

George J. Mitchell of Maine, the majority leader, holds a daily "dugout session" before the Senate convenes, answering a few questions from regular correspondents in his customary lawyerly fashion. On the Republican side an informal assembly of senators will occasionally invite reporters to breakfast in the rooms of Republican Leader Bob Dole. But neither Mitchell's nor Dole's sessions are treated as news in any systematic way. Nor are they used to probe very far into the substance of pending legislation. Rather, reporters use these opportunities to press for details on scheduling or to solicit the leaders' reaction to news or statements made elsewhere.

The regular Tuesday policy luncheons held by the two parties' respective conferences (a euphemism for caucuses) in the Senate are closed to the press, as are the caucus meetings of both parties in the House. Members leaving any of these meetings are regularly buttonholed by reporters, most of whom have specific questions regarding stories they are already writing. Unless the caucus has taken a vote to fill a chairmanship or another leadership post, there is rarely any coverage of these meetings, even though they regularly discuss, and even decide the fates of, bills and other matters.

Adversarial Becomes Hostile

Through most of the nineteenth century, news columns as well as editorials were commonly written from a sharply partisan point of view. The later decades of the 1800s, however, saw the gradual elevation of middle-of-the-road journalism. The need for economies of scale has given the mass media reason to avoid giving offense. The result has been a boost for the ethic of objective journalism, in which the opinions of the reporter and editor are effaced in pursuit of fairness (and, of course, broader appeal). The twentieth century has seen countless journalists live and work within this creed despite their strong (and even extreme) political views.

At the same time, it should not be surprising that attempted objectivity, easily caricatured as holier than thou, has often caused ill feelings between journalists and the politicians they cover. Office holders have come to consider the ideal of journalistic objectivity a sham. They often ask their press secretaries about a given reporter's leanings and refuse to believe that news organizations play stories straight. The prejudices they perceive may be personal, regional, ideological, or partisan; and some members are also sensitive to what they regard as a media bias against Congress itself.

Representative Vic Fazio of California, who worked as a legislative reporter in Sacramento in the 1960s, now finds fault with his former profession. "The press are jaded, they're far more interested in how they define success for themselves and the people they work for. And the people they work for don't know what the process is about except that it's grist for the mill. They're not motivated by a desire to cover what's happening in Washington, they just want some meat—some pork stories."[24]

One need not agree with Fazio to observe that congressional reporters believe uncovering scandals will improve their visibility within their news organizations. Although some of the veterans covering Congress have no desire to go elsewhere, most of the younger reporters on the beat are restless. Those transferred from covering the president are sometimes openly resentful.

This has not always been the case. In the late nineteenth century the Capitol was the seat of government. The White House in the 1880s was still thought such a sleepy hollow that not one newspaper assigned a correspondent to cover it full time. That began to change with the arrival of Theodore Roosevelt in 1901. The refocusing was furthered by the international celebrity of Woodrow Wilson after World War I and perfected in the 1930s by Franklin D. Roosevelt, who not only handled the press with aplomb but mastered the new genie of radio.[25]

Some resentment of the media fascination with the president still colors the relationship between reporters and members on the Hill, a relationship that ranges from resentful to cordial to convivial depending on the occasion and the nature of the news at hand. Congress spends more than $1 million annually to support seven news media galleries within the Capitol building itself. There are House and Senate galleries for the daily press, a periodical press gallery for each chamber, and a radio and television gallery for each. The seventh gallery is for still photographers. In recent years most of the growth in the galleries has come from journalists for periodicals (many of which are trade newsletters), regional reporters who sometimes cover several states for smaller papers, and broadcast correspondents who work either for regional bureaus or individual local stations.[26]

If the relationship between member and media is by turns adversarial and symbiotic, it is also subject to seasons and trends. Contemporary journalists are shocked to learn that journalists a century ago often supplemented their income by serving as congressional secretaries. Maybe a future generation will be surprised to learn how many contemporary reporters have previously held jobs as staff members or campaign aides (or expect to in the future). Perhaps the most important trends and changes in recent years for politicians and journalists alike have been technological and economic. Just as campaigns have been altered by broadcast advertising (and the attendant escalation of costs), journalism has been reshaped by what is sometimes called electronic newsgathering, a category comprising not only radio and television but the ubiquitous personal computer, which creates new access to data and new ways of processing and delivering it.

At the same time, the old economies of scale that encouraged mass news media (and shrank the number of daily newspapers) are giving way at the margins. Smaller operations—local TV stations, regional reporting bureaus, newsletters, and other highly specialized publications—claim an increasing proportion of the space and attention in the galleries. Reporters for such outlets have little time for reporting larger issues or understanding institutions. Their work is carefully focused on a few committees or even a few members. Thus a growing proportion of the news from Capitol Hill is oblique to the institution or to the mission of Congress writ large.

Problems with Presentation

Congress would strike few public relations professionals as an attractive client. The institution tackles issues that are both technically daunting and emotionally exhausting. Its tradition-driven processes tend to the cryptic. It has few established means for helping the public understand its workings, and it operates at a handicap because it has no single institutional voice. Finally, Congress contributes to its own poor image with continuously self-deprecating behavior. Some of this is a by-product of the intense rivalry between the two parties. Some stems from members' desires to separate themselves from the institution, especially at reelection time. And all of it feeds upon itself, with each round of denigration making the next more acceptable.

Process: Not a Pretty Picture

As it displays itself to the public in the galleries or on C-SPAN and the conventional news media, Congress seems tortured by intentional inactivity and delay, Byzantine procedures, and anachronistic rules. The monotony is broken by intermittent outbreaks of rancor and rhetoric leading to protracted votes on incomprehensible motions. And while members worry about this impression, they resist change. Even those with a strong interest in presenting the institution favorably often bristle at suggestions for smoothing the rough spots. "Fundamentally this will and must remain an institution where there is political dissent, debate and disagreement," Speaker Thomas S. Foley told the Joint Committee on Reorganization of Congress in January 1993. "Democracy in its purest forms is often not pretty."[27]

Without disputing Foley's point, one would still expect that any government aspiring to the public trust would want to make itself as presentable as possible. And that entails hard thinking about process. In any institution, layers of tradition and precedent gradually elevate process until the product seems of secondary importance. Reform can help, but reform is never permanent. Congress passed a truly historic reform package in 1946, but many of the same issues had to be addressed a generation later in the reform bill of 1970. Now another generation has passed, and dilatory tactics, excessive emphasis on seniority, and the proliferation of committees confront both chambers again.

Congress was, of course, designed to be awkward, much as the standard typewriter keyboard was arranged to slow the expert typist (otherwise, the old manual models would have jammed). James Madison and the other constitutional framers had experienced the weight of unified authority in government and wanted none of it. Their fears created a bicameral legislature in which both chambers could claim equal power. Elaboration on this theme gave Congress committees and subcommittees, redundancy and overlapping authority, intricate leadership and seniority structures, multiple referral, conference committees and, still later, task forces and computerized efforts to amend committee-approved bills on the floor to ensure their passage.

Each element of this edifice may well be justified on constitutional grounds or in terms of its contribution. But what the public sees, fairly or not, is an institution averse to action and, at times, hamstrung by its own housekeeping. The process of governing often humbles its participants, and ordinary citizens are utterly confounded by procedures conducted in plain view. Parliamentary terms and devices are part of the problem: legislative codewords are used to describe bills and amendments at the time votes are taken. A motion to recommit or to table a bill may be plainly a killing motion to the cognoscenti, but it may be pure Greek to the uninitiated.

The complex steps and argot may be most bewildering on the House floor, where the sheer size of the body necessitates strict observation of parliamentary rules. One veteran chief of staff in the House likens its floor ritual to a Latin mass, with the legislator-priests speaking a dead language. The dialogue in committee, while less involved and encoded, still tends to exclude the audience beyond the hearing room. The same chief of staff refers to committee hearings—poorly attended, repetitive, and often pointless—as "a perfect example of a dead form."[28]

In the Senate, passing bills may be every bit as difficult, but the public may not see enough of the action to know it. The Senate does not debate and vote on rules for each bill brought to the floor (the Senate Rules Committee deals primarily with administrative matters). Instead, it improvises its way through the maze of a day's proceedings by means of off-the-floor negotiations between the majority and minority leaders, their whips, and their staffs.

What the public is likely to see in the Senate from the gallery or on C-SPAN, is the spectacle of an extended quorum call. The senator holding the floor, who may be a party leader or a senator charged with managing the bill at hand, will "suggest the absence of a quorum." The presiding officer (usually a junior senator and always a member of the majority party) is obliged to have the clerk call the roll. There follows a lugubrious recitation of the alphabetical list ("Mr. Akaka . . . Mr. Baucus . . . Mr. Bennett . . ."), during which no one answers to his or her name, including senators who are quite visible in the chamber. The clerk drones on, slowing down as he goes, never reaching the last name. Eventually, someone (often the same senator who asked for the quorum call) is ready to resume business and moves that "further proceedings under the quorum call be dispensed with."

Such quorum calls have long been recognized as useful time outs during which senators confer, bargain, arrange the next phase of debate, or agree on another course of action. Agreements are often reached in such moments to apportion speaking time or limit the number of amendments to be considered. Nonetheless, gallery tourists may be reminded of the pandas at the National Zoo, who are always officially in but generally just out of sight. On C-SPAN the tedium of these frequent intervals is relieved by classical music, which covers the sound of the roll call. All this may be perfectly legitimate in its way, but it is carried out without the slightest show of concern for the impression it makes on the public.

It is not only floor procedure that leaves the average citizen feeling shut out. The budget process, with its resolution and reconciliation and appropriation phases, weighs down even veteran Hill watchers with procedural overload. In fact, the budget process has swollen to engulf much of the calendar, energy, and character of each successive Congress. And because the result of each year's marathon is greeted with frustration and recriminations, the entire undertaking has the effect of undermining respect for the institution. The result "befuddles the minds of our citizens," Senator Pete V. Domenici, the New Mexico Republican who is his party's senior expert on budgeting, has said. "We have made our work unintelligible."[29]

If Congress has allowed complexity to proliferate, it has also failed to do much to explain itself. A case in point is the Legislative Information Office, run as a function of the Clerk of the House. Although the office serves a genuine need for information about pending bills and other matters, it is little used and little known. And it labors under restrictions that surprise even those familiar with the institution's history. LIO personnel can give a caller the margin by which a bill passed but not the number of Democrats who voted for or against. They cannot even identify a given member by party. Chief Debra Jo Turner explains that the office began in 1973, "when the leadership was very protective." The idea was to provide a source of information on legislation that would relieve members' own staffs. "It was a time when a lot of members were not so willing to be helpful," Turner says, "when their staff was smaller and they had no computers in the offices."[30]

In Search of a Single Voice

Given its past, Congress finds itself in this era of instant communication lacking the traditions, mechanisms, and mentality for effective public presentation. This means that even when Congress wants to present itself to the public, it has a hard time doing so. "After all," Timothy Cook observed, "neither chamber has anyone who can speak on behalf of all or even most of its members."[31]

Not that Capitol Hill is lacking in public relations experience; on the contrary, practitioners abound. But none is expressly employed to elucidate or defend Congress as an institution, much less to burnish its reputation. Power and position in Congress is divided between the House and the Senate and between the two historical parties. Nonelected officials, such as the powerful Clerk of the House Donnald K. Anderson, may be passionate believers in the institution, but they are viewed as products of patronage and so too beholden for quotation. Even if the outside world were ready to listen, such career employees as Anderson scrupulously avoid participation in the public debate as a matter of principle.[32]

The closest thing to an institutional response after a presidential address comes not from Congress per se but from the party that lost the last presidential election. In recent years, that meant the Democrats, which in turn meant a congressional response de facto because the Democrats controlled Congress. In February 1993, however, the job of rebutting the president belonged to the Republicans, who gave it to Robert H. Michel of Illinois (speaking for the minority party in the House, where Republican influence is weakest). Michel's remarks were not prominently featured in the next day's coverage. The *New York Times* took two fragmentary quotations, which appeared deep inside the paper with the story's jump from page 1, well below the comments of Ross Perot and former president Ronald Reagan.[33]

It might seem logical for some institutional voice to emanate from Speaker of the House Foley or Senate Majority Leader Mitchell. But although each holds a brief press availability before each day of serious floor business begins, neither is inclined to make news in these sessions. And when they do exercise their authority, they take pains to observe the boundary. They leave "the other body" largely alone. Thus neither can speak for all Democrats, let alone the whole Congress.

Whatever their personal preferences, congressional leaders find their partisan identities dominating their institutional responsibilities. The privilege of being in the leadership is conferred by simple majority vote in each party's caucus in each chamber, and it can be revoked. That means members of the leadership need to be as adept at following as they are at leading. They need to stand tall among their party's most intensely motivated members (as well as with their voting constituents back home) more than they need to broker a deal, break an impasse, and achieve a given policy objective. This pressure is all the stronger on members of the leadership who are interested in climbing still higher on the ladder.

Republican leaders Michel in the House and Dole in the Senate are even less likely to qualify as spokesmen for the institution. They are the loyal opposition in the traditional sense, resisting the program of the president and smarting at the loss of the White House. But the resentful character of the opposition to the Clinton administration has at least as much to do with the Republicans' bitter exile to semipermanent minority status on the Hill. After just two years as majority leader (1985 and 1986), Dole has endured seven years as the minority's man. And his fate seems kind compared with Michel's thirty-eight years of House service in the minority (no Republican House member currently serving has ever served in the majority).

Neither Michel nor Dole has been associated with the Republican's right wing. But in recent years, both have adapted their tone and tactics to those of their party's most implacable combatants. The adaptation dates from the spring of 1989, when Gingrich was elected House Republican whip. In leadership elections since, particularly in late 1992, confrontational conservatives who have aggressively sought to embarrass the House have carried all before them. Given this commitment to anti-Congress rhetoric, the Republican leadership is both ill-suited and disinclined to speak for the institution.

Another theoretical source of institutional image making is the office of Senate president pro tempore, traditionally assigned to the most senior member of the majority party. But these two qualifications almost guarantee that the senator in this office will be an elderly figure steeped in the clubby traditions of the pretelevision and precomputer chamber. Certainly the current president pro tem, Robert C. Byrd of West Virginia, is a case in point.[34]

Destruction from Within

Observers have long noted that the same public that despises Congress in the aggregate reelects its members individually. This seeming contradiction has also been appreciated and exploited by the members, who draw distinctions between themselves and the institution as a matter of course. "Members of Congress run *for* Congress by running *against* Congress," political scientist Richard Fenno commented in 1978.[35] And the strategy has grown ever more popular in the years since his observation. It is, according to Gary Jacobson, "especially tempting when public disdain for the Washington crowd reaches a crescendo, as it did in 1990 [and again in 1992]."[36]

The habit of Congress-bashing is bipartisan, although Republicans and Democrats do it differently. Democrats like to use Washington jokes and bureaucratic horror stories as a tactic for distancing themselves from governmental excesses or unpopular party positions. Republicans operate on a more strategic level, often making anti-Congress rhetoric the centerpiece of their campaigns.

Recently, the self-wounding rhetoric has been carried over from campaigns to the House and Senate floor debates. During the House deliberation on a constitutional amendment to balance the budget, for example, Representative Bill Sarpalius, a Texas Democrat, looked into the C-SPAN lens and said, "We are all thieves." Not to be outdone, Republican Representative Dennis Hastert of Illinois said Congress was like a nursing baby: "irresponsibility on one end and no accountability on the other."[37] Would remarks of this sort have been made under the gavel of Sam Rayburn? Probably not. But this much is certain: if such remarks had been heard on the House floor, they would not have been conveyed live and in color into millions of households nationwide.

Once again, one has to wonder to what extent the low ratings of Congress in Gallup and other polls are the result of members' crippled self-esteem. Jim Leach, the Iowa Republican, served eight terms alongside Bill Gradison, an exceptionally able and industrious Republican from Ohio who left Congress after eighteen years to become president of a health industry association early in 1993. Reflecting on Gradison's rather cheerful farewell, Leach sighed and said, "It's quite a thing when it's seen as a step up for a member to become a lobbyist."[38]

Improving Congressional Presentation

Congress has too long been content to play by itself, regarding public notice as a kind of intrusion. If Congress is hard to understand, it is in part because the institution has not done enough to explain itself. If press coverage is oblique, beside the point, and unnecessarily hostile, it is in part because Congress has done too little to maintain its credibility. And if the institutional self-image is poor, it is in part because members have worked too hard at tearing their own house down.

It may be specious to expect much improvement in congressional public standing until the nation's economic doldrums end or another crisis (such as the Persian Gulf war) suddenly casts Congress in a more heroic light. Along the way, however, there are steps Congress might take to improve its self-presentation and respond to the public's interest.

These fall into three categories. The first consists of amendments at the margin: behavioral changes requiring little or no legislative effort (and perhaps no more than a change of habit on the part of leadership). The second includes more major reforms that would require new laws, alter the way Congress does business, and hobble some of the campaign tactics that incumbents use to smooth their reelections. Such reforms might well have larger rationales, of course, but they would have corollary benefits for the presentation of the institution to the public. The third, and most ambitious kind of change, would entail more radical attitudinal changes toward presentation to the public in relation to the rest of a member's tasks. This third category is discussed in this paper's final section.

Amendments at the Margin

Minor changes in behavior could work major changes in Congress's image. Members should consider the following suggestions.

Schedule regular debates on major issues. The debate in 1991 about sending troops to the Persian Gulf elicited a moment of applause for responsible congressional behavior from both attentive observers and the general public. But the good will has since been allowed to dissipate. Congress can reinstitute formal debates on broad policy questions, however, whenever it wills. The debates could feature single champions for each side or they could involve a larger number of participants. They should be scheduled in television network prime time and be publicized by public service announcements. They need not take the place of other proceedings in committees or on the floor. (An initial experiment with two such debates on the House floor in March 1994 produced mixed results, proving little more than the importance of practice in perfecting the art.)[39]

Conduct proceedings and present legislation in plain English. There is a role for legislative language in the phrasing of legislation. But proceedings in committee and on the floor need to be intelligible to all those who are neither lawyers nor parliamentarians. The plain English version of motions, whether they are routine or unusual, could be offered before or after the parliamentary language (much as Canadian parliamentary officials conduct business in both English and French). This practice would not need to infringe on the rights of the minority party; all the motions and tactics now available would be preserved. The only difference would be the requirement that all motions be explained in terms of their practical effect.

Provide simultaneous translation and commentary on C-SPAN. The benefit of C-SPAN has always been the increased visibility of Congress at work. But that visibility is offered in such raw form as to be awkward, chaotic on occasion, and all too often incomprehensible. C-SPAN now functions like a video knothole in the congressional fence. Viewers glimpse a stiffly formal game being played by indecipherable rules. There is no play-by-play commentary. Unfortunately, the spectacle is most readily understood when it is at its unrepresentative worst.

In the 103d Congress, C-SPAN began experimenting with captions summarizing the legislation under consideration. This constituted a breakthrough even in its embryonic stage. The network should do everything it can to explain what is happening on screen through the use of subscripts, commentators, voice-overs, and recordings by clerks or parliamentary staff.

This idea has been around since television coverage was first debated. It has usually been dismissed out of distrust: members fear their motions will be mischaracterized or described in undiplomatic terms. The parties fear they may be made to look too intransigent or partisan. But if the parties can choose legislative staff and joint committee staff who work together, they can choose clerks who know how to describe a tabling motion in accurate but impartial terms. Here again, the conflict is between the anxiety of the individual member and the beneficial presentation of the institution. Congress has tended to resolve this conflict in favor of the member, a habit that lies close to the heart of the problem Congress has with its image.

Expand the means of transmitting congressional proceedings. C-SPAN now consists of two channels that are generally divided between the two chambers. But eventually, cable capability will permit scores of channels to emanate from any source. In the Senate, elaborate internal rewiring of the Dirksen and Hart Office Buildings, already under way, will soon obviate the heavy equipment C-SPAN crews now lug from hearing to hearing. The House should do the same.

In as few years as possible, any cable subscriber ought to be able to watch any official proceeding in Congress (including news conferences) simply by grazing through an array of C-SPAN options. These would include a series of programs in video form as well as text explaining congressional procedure and giving information on prominent bills. Additional information would be available by computer network and in hard copy by mail.

Multiply the opportunities for the media to hear from and question congressional leaders at length and in depth. Party leaders, committee leaders, and other pivotal figures should be expected to hold regular interviews. The morning Speaker's conference is welcome but far too brief to educate or explain. The Senate dugout session is even more limited. Both interludes should be at least twice as long. And committee leaders, some of whom could qualify as hermits, should be expected to meet with reporters regularly as well. Refusal to do so should concern the other members of the caucus when they vote on chairmen and other leaders each biennium.

Certainly these members have other duties and responsibilities to which they assign higher priority. But if Congress sincerely desires to improve its public standing, some priorities will need to change. The current generation of leaders, like their forebears, regard any conversation with reporters as carrying more potential for harm than good. They are not wrong in this assessment, particularly as long as they approach the media as defensively as they do now. But if Congress is to rise in public esteem, its leaders will need to see the benefits of mediated contact with the public. And they must be convinced that the contact is worth the risks and unhappy episodes.

At present the Speaker's conference is off-limits to TV cameras, and the Senate dugout session, which is held on the floor, is equally inaccessible. Although there are excellent reasons not to hold these brief availabilities in the broadcast studios, alternative locations could be found where pool coverage by one or two cameras would be possible.

Establish a central source of institutional information. Various ideas for congressional information offices have been proposed before, some by Foley, Gephardt, and other members of the Democratic leadership. But the more ambitious plans, including a multimedia, multimillion-dollar visitor center on the Capitol grounds, have been rejected in legislative appropriations proceedings. More modest undertakings that would not require additional personnel would probably be seen as extensions of the party leaders' present staffs (or the staffs of their appointees).

Any suggestion for an office providing press assistance also raises suspicions in the galleries. Some veteran reporters participating in a daylong conference in April 1993 sponsored by the Brookings Institution and the American Enterprise Institute believed it would inevitably become a shill for party leaders, particularly of the majority party, and a hindrance as much as a help. These concerns were deepened by Gephardt's support at the conference for the concept of an information office. Some participants suspected that an information office would become one more facet of his already extensive message operation (despite his disavowal of any such intent). Another common objection was that capable reporters prefer their own means of discovering facts, including playing off one set of sources against another. They saw little benefit in one-stop shopping for information.

Clearly, then, any central source of information would need to establish its independence from party leaders and existing communications operations. It would need to emphasize its institutional mission: the explication of the workings of Congress, overall and in as much detail as desired. The office might be assigned to explain, for instance, what Congress does in response to a presidential budget, on what timetable, and with whose involvement. This kind of information is now often lost in the crossfire of "he said, she said" newswriting in the aftermath of an event.

A central office would be able to distribute information regarding the institutional agenda, such as the statutory imperatives of the budget and appropriations. Currently, such explanations come from the members themselves (who are obviously far from neutral) or from the majority and minority staffs of the relevant committees (who work directly for the members). Perhaps such an office would be superfluous for the veterans who already navigate the hallways and folkways of House and Senate with scarcely a misdirected step. But many other Hill reporters, especially those who come to the Hill infrequently or work outside Washington entirely, need expert nonpartisan help finding the documents and understanding the procedures that would inform their coverage—especially when deadlines loom.

A central information office would risk redundancy in certain functions with the staff of the press galleries and the Legislative Information Office. The press gallery professionals act as liaisons to committee staff, administer pool reporting, and handle seating in situations where media space is limited. They are also often invaluable as guides to votes, floor procedure, precedents, and internal institutional intelligence useful for reporters at all levels of experience and expertise. But the gallery staffs are already hard pressed to accommodate the reporters who are working in the Capitol, and much of the coverage and editorial comment directed at Congress is produced by people who are strangers to the Hill, or Washington, or the galleries.[40]

A handful of out-of-town reporters use the Legislative Information Office, but most have no idea that it exists (as indeed many Washington journalists do not). The LIO functions as part of Congress's presentation of itself to the public, but only in a reactive way. Its staff of twelve fields an average of 900 to 1,100 calls daily and as many as 2,500 on the busiest days near the end of a legislative session. Having been specifically trained in Hill procedure, the LIO staff is invaluable for tracking bills, keeping reporters and others abreast of a bill's progress, and describing its status with insider understanding. But the office is strictly limited in its function. It does not have the text of bills (beyond their brief statements of purpose) and it cannot give information about individual members' votes. That is one reason that only 10 percent of its calls come from news people.[41]

Reducing the Need for Apology

Although all the suggestions I have made would help Congress improve its presentation to the public, the institution would benefit at least as much by reexamining some of the traditions and conventions that most alienate the public and most often force the institution onto the defensive.

Subject Congress to all laws, including workplace rules. Congress routinely exempts itself from the labor standards and other mandates it places on the rest of society. This has earned the institution ridicule and growing public hostility. No journalist can resist mentioning such apparent arrogance. The longstanding justification for the practice has been the need to insulate Congress from executive branch interference. There is some legitimacy in this argument, but the problem of interference could be addressed by establishing a law enforcement entity for Congress that serves as a buffer. Legislation with this intent was introduced in the 103d Congress and had more than 150 cosponsors.

Revise Senate rules so that delaying tactics can have their intended effect without amounting to minority rule. Given the sixty-seven-vote requirement for changing the rules in the Senate, it seems unlikely that further limits on cloture or other rule changes to benefit the majority will be forthcoming. But a serious debate over the merits of the filibuster and the current sixty-vote threshold for cloture would signal the Senate's interest in improving its public image. The leadership might also discourage filibusters by returning to tradition and requiring participants to hold the floor for days and nights. In this manner attention would be drawn to the filibuster and to the issue in question, and public sentiment on both could be gauged.

This would require no change in the Senate rules, yet it should discourage the casual reliance on the filibuster. George Mitchell, testifying before the Joint Committee on the Organization of Congress in January 1993, said the incidence of filibusters (real or threatened) had increased from a historical norm of roughly one a year to approximately fifty a year. Mitchell said the right to extended debate was being exercised for reasons "as trivial as a senator's travel schedule."[42]

Pass campaign financing reform that confronts public skepticism. In all likelihood the most practical route to confronting skepticism about campaign financing reform will be to court editorial opinion. The purveyors of highly ideological commentary will never be pleased with any congressional action on this issue. But a curtailing of the activities of political action committees, mixed with spending limits and some public financing, might reverse the trend toward derision among more neutral observers. The bill approved by the Senate in 1993, which included several schemes for limiting campaign expenditures (some of dubious constitutionality) never stood a chance in the House.

Adopt a commitment to ethics that confronts public skepticism. The scandals that boil up around Congress involve personal ethics, yet the public has come to believe Congress as an institution is corrupt.[43] And changes in that belief are not likely soon: in 1993 continuing ethics investigations kept the pot boiling. The year began with Senator Bob Packwood of Oregon under heavy assault from women's groups after the *Washington Post* published accounts of sexual harassment from nearly thirty women. Senator Dave Durenberger of Minnesota was indicted by a federal grand jury for, among other things, allegedly billing the Treasury for the lease of a condo he actually owned.[44] Former Representative Nicholas Mavroules of Massachusetts pleaded guilty to fifteen counts of misusing his office for personal gain and went to jail. In midsummer, news came that Ways and Means Chairman Dan Rostenkowski, who symbolizes the House to many, would probably be indicted for receiving cash illegally from the House Post Office. (Rostenkowski was indicted on seventeen charges, including embezzlement and misuse of government funds, on May 31, 1994.)[45]

The irony is that these scandals occur in an era of rising ethical standards. Congress has come a considerable distance just since the 1970s. The recent decision to ban honoraria (in exchange for pay raises) was only one of a series of renunciations of outside income. Both party caucuses in the House have adopted rules forcing chairmen and ranking members to step down if indicted, although when the Republicans adopted theirs in 1993, they exempted Representative Joseph M. McDade of Pennsylvania, a Republican already under indictment.

In time these reforms may help people believe Congress is ethical, but in the interim they would mostly remind the public of existing ethics abuses and abusers. And when the decision was made to grandfather McDade under the old rules, the spectacle inspired cynicism as much as confidence. This case illustrates the persistent awkwardness of ethics proceedings on the Hill. As long as ethics cases continue to devolve into referendums on the popularity of the members involved, the public is not likely to revise its opinion of Congress.

Communication and Effectiveness

Until 1929 the Senate routinely closed debates on treaties and nominations. Progressives such as Senator Robert M. La Follette, Jr., of Wisconsin believed this tradition had run its course. But Senator Thomas Heflin of Alabama rose to defend the old ways and suggested that the press gallery be abolished.[46] Heflin's motion might indeed attract votes in Congress today, in either chamber and from both parties. But La Follette was closer to the trends. Officials often prefer the candor and flexibility of private meetings, yet most politicians now need to be news: widespread name recognition is necessary for members' reelection or promotion to higher office. There is also a conflict between the public's interest in access and the public's interest in efficient and effective policymaking.

It may well be that Congress will never earn the respect, far less the admiration, of the public until people believe it has addressed in a meaningful way the vital matters of the end of the twentieth century: the federal budget deficit, health care coverage, unemployment, defense conversion, trade, immigration, education, crime, welfare, AIDS. To tackle so many difficult issues, Congress needs to become far more effective as a lawmaking institution. And to do that, it must improve its capacity for compromise and accommodation, both of which are more easily accomplished in private than in public.

But the need for more openness and accountability is also real, and ignoring it for the sake of getting things done will continue to have consequences, not only for the institution of Congress but for its parties and members as well. Although individual incumbents still do better in polls than Congress as a whole, the gap has begun to shrink. Reelection margins for incumbents were notably depressed in 1990 and 1992, and the 1992 election cycle set a record for retirements from the House.[47]

What is needed is a general reweighing of the balance between discretion and disclosure. By precedent and predilection Congress has tended too often to circle the wagons as a preemptive reaction. Some of the most severe bruises it has suffered in recent years were made worse by members' and leaders' attempts to evade responsibility for their actions. In 1988, for instance, when an independent commission recommended a 51 percent pay increase, members were initially prepared to accept the raise without a vote. When the size of the raise spurred an outcry, the next strategy was to hold a vote the day after it had taken effect. But in February 1989, after an outpouring of rage from the media and the public, the leadership and the members backed down (a smaller raise was approved in November). The resulting rancor contributed to the downfall of Speaker Jim Wright later that spring, fueled the movement to limit terms, and fed various kinds of anti-Congress agitation into the 1990s.[48]

In 1990 the General Accounting Office began warning members about abuse of the House Bank. The reaction from House leaders was to keep the matter private and admonish members to stay within the rules. When the GAO published its report in September 1991, the House closed the bank and started an Ethics Committee investigation. Five months later the strategy was to name just two dozen abusers of the bank and bury the names of some 300 others who had overdrafts. That strategy fell through, but not before aggravating an already angry wound.[49]

Despite the drubbing Congress took for the pay raise and the House bank and the House Post Office affairs—or perhaps because of it—

obfuscation was once again the order of the day when the legislative appropriations bill for fiscal year 1993 came to the floors of the House and Senate. Once again, it was difficult to parse the bill so as to tell how much was spent on staff or travel. Even members' own salaries and fringe benefits were not readily identifiable line items.[50]

Congress reflexively guards information as if it were proprietary. Even the reports done by the Congressional Research Service cannot be shared with the public or the news media, lest the service be perceived as serving someone other than Congress. And as noted earlier, the House Legislative Information Office may not tell a caller anything that relates to party, even the party affiliation of a member.

In the period immediately after Watergate, Congress seemed willing to forgo its habitual secrecy. Disclosure laws bared not only amounts and sources of campaign funding but the personal finances of members. Committees opened their hearings and critical markup sessions where bills are amended for floor consideration. Under Chairman Al Ullman of Oregon even the Ways and Means Committee opened its doors. Since then, however, the trend has been reversed. Ullman's successor, Dan Rostenkowski, put together the big tax bills of the 1980s in executive session, and this has once again become standard operating procedure.

Opening meetings and releasing documents may not increase public respect for the institution in any immediate or direct way. Indeed, after an initial round of laudatory editorials, there might well be adverse consequences. The public would likely see staged markups, with members voting to ratify deals reached in private before the meeting. The public would also see committee rooms filled with lobbyists, whose presence may well tip votes in favor of special interests. Members frequently justify closed meetings by saying they want to talk to each other with "the lobsters" out of the room.

Assuming such unintended consequences would occur, they would parallel those that have followed ethics reforms. Raising standards of ethics often calls attention to practices otherwise little noted by press or public. Tougher procedures for dealing with ethical abuses may magnify minor offenses and prolong the embarrassment for all concerned. In such cases members (and Congress itself) would suffer for their attempts at bettering the institution and its standing.

Advocates of openness must count these costs. When in 1992 a revolt among junior Republicans forced the House to release the names of all who had overdrawn their accounts at the House bank, some members paid with their jobs. Some of the victims, far from being the profligates and scofflaws suggested in media coverage, were among the hardest working and most conscientious members. And when the House eventually finds itself compelled to release the results of its investigation into the House post office, it can scarcely expect favorable news coverage.

Nonetheless the protection of individual members should not be more important than the protection of the reputation and standing of the institution itself. That is the fundamental cost-benefit analysis that Congress, its leaders, and its members must recalculate. Congress is no longer isolated enough from the public to avoid attention to its internal struggles and its more secretive practices. And the sacrifices that are made in extirpating the less defensible of these practices constitute a payment toward greater respect for the institution in the longer term.

Some of Congress's obscure traditions are rooted in defensible policy considerations and not just in political anxiety. One example is the 1932 rule against naming those members who sign a discharge petition (forcing to the floor a bill that has been bottled up in committee) until they constitute a majority of the House. But when they are viewed in the context of Congress's many efforts to shield itself from scrutiny, such practices suggest a fortress mentality.[51]

Congress's efforts to protect itself and its members must be judged by some sensible standard that balances the needs of the leaders and members against the responsibilities of representative government. Are the long-range interests of the institution best served by avoiding embarrassment for current members? Or are they better served by trusting the public to see how the institution works and running it so as to withstand the scrutiny?

The process of redefining acceptable secrecy has already begun, and there will always be disagreement over proper standards. But surely the standard should strive to differentiate between secrecy for demonstrable policy-related purposes and secrecy enforced to protect members from political, personal, or legal exposure.

Conclusion

Historically, Congress has been a public institution that conducted much of its business out of public view. In recent years the institution has been emerging from its cocoon consciousness; but the metamorphosis is far from complete. Congress still regards public communication as a political tool to be used by individual members and the two parties, and not for the larger purposes of the institution as a whole. "We have to look at what the image is [and at] how we come across," Representative David Price of North Carolina once said. "We need to convey some kind of reasonable sense of how the place works—what it's about."[52]

To be sure, the tarnished congressional image is more than a matter of myopic public relations. Better presentation alone cannot erase serious inadequacies of ethics or performance; that task can ultimately be accomplished only by better performance. All the same, Congress has a separate (if related) burden of perception. Many of the popular notions of failure and corruption on Capitol Hill are more caricature than reality, and even the more responsible news media often overstate the case (as in the furor over "bounced checks" or "check kiting" at the House bank). When such episodes occur, the institution is largely powerless to correct misimpressions or alter the direction of the story. It is at these times that more effective presentation could help Congress contend with its critics. To use an analogy: the quality of a restaurant's food may be its premier concern, but presentation can either heighten or lessen that food's appeal.

Within Congress, unfortunately, there is nothing resembling consensus on either the cause or cure of the institution's poor public standing. Some point to the frustration that has festered in Congress since runaway budget deficits in the 1980s choked off the creation of new programs and forced the government to turn in upon itself. Others attribute the problem to gridlock between the branches during the years they were controlled by separate parties (1981–92). Gridlock, they say, convinced the public that Congress could not come to grips with economic, social, or cultural issues.

It has also been argued that Congress is caught up in a cycle of declining public confidence that afflicts other branches and levels of government, schools, big business, organized labor, the media, and established religion. Here, too, the prescription tells Congress to stick to its knitting, pass legislation in cooperation with the Clinton administration, and watch for a new dawn of public faith. Such hopes are based in precedent: after the passage of the Civil Rights Act of 1964, the Gallup Organization found Congress's standing with the public was soaring. And when the Senate investigated Watergate in 1973 and the House followed with impeachment hearings in 1974, the nation watched and accorded the institution greater respect.[53]

But waiting for Congress's reputation to be saved by works alone does nothing to address the crisis of confidence now impeding its work. It will take time for the institution to address problems, and still more time for solutions to be found. In the interim the institution would be well served by a new attitude toward its public presentation. Congress needs to order its own affairs not only with concern for its institutional traditions, prerogatives, and dignity but for public opinion and comprehension as well.

To make a difference, such a change in attitude must be visible in members' relationship to the institution. Those who care passionately about their own press clippings but feel free to denigrate the institution should reconsider their long-term interest. In some instances a member will be called upon to sacrifice his or her personal advantage for the sake of some larger whole—a committee position, a party vote, or even a matter of institutional loyalty. Members need to accept more of these sacrifices, and those who refuse should be taken to task by their peers.

Distasteful as some in Congress may find this idea, the disadvantages must be weighed against the cost of remaining a culture apart. If Congress insists on shuttering its windows whenever it fears the light, it may find that the traditions, prerogatives, and dignity it seeks to protect have been forfeited to the erosion of public confidence.

It has been observed that greater familiarity at least risks greater contempt. But it can also be argued that respect breeds respect, while secretiveness surely begets distrust. By embracing change in its manner of presentation, Congress can signal its intent to alter its relationship with the public. Although good intentions alone will not restore an institution's standing, they can constitute a first step; and in this case they may be a necessary precondition for reviving the nation's faith in its legislature. Such an effort would not in itself constitute a revival, nor would it be sufficient cause for revival. But without it, Congress has little immediate hope of refurbishing its public image.

Notes

1. Timothy E. Cook, *Making Laws and Making News* (Washington: Brookings, 1989), p. 167.

2. Ronald D. Elving, interview with Representative David Price, April 2, 1993. Price was a professor of political science at Duke University before his election.

3. Donald A. Ritchie, *Press Gallery: Congress and the Washington Correspondents* (Harvard University Press, 1991), pp. 4–5, 26–27, 60–61.

4. Cook, *Making Laws and Making News*, p. 73.

5. Bob Benenson, "Savvy 'Stars' Making Local TV a Potent Tool," *Congressional Quarterly Weekly Report*, July 18, 1987, p. 1551.

6. Stephen Frantzich, "A New Congress for a New Era: The Promise of Technology," paper prepared for the Renewing Congress Project of the Brookings Institution and the American Enterprise Institute. A look back at the precom-

puter world of mail can be found in Michael J. Robinson, "Three Faces of Congressional Media," in Thomas E. Mann and Norman J. Ornstein, eds., *The New Congress* (Washington: American Enterprise Institute, 1981), pp. 60–61.

7. Poll by Gordon S. Black conducted in the third week of May 1992. *Polling Report*, vol. 8 (June 22, 1992), p. 1. Also see a poll conducted by Lou Harris January 22–23, 1993, *Polling Report*, vol. 9 (March 8, 1993), p. 4. For comparison, see polls conducted by the Gallup organization in August 1947, July 1948, August 1953, and August 1954; George H. Gallup, *The Gallup Poll: Public Opinion 1935–1971* (Random House, 1972), vol. 1, pp. 665, 744; vol. 2, pp. 1161, 1263.

8. Fax press release from the office of Senator Slade Gorton to the author, May 14, 1993.

9. Phil Duncan, ed., *Politics in America 1992: The 102nd Congress* (Washington: CQ Press), p. 1382; and Ronald D. Elving, "Idaho," *Congressional Quarterly Weekly Report*, February 27, 1988, p. 411.

10. Ronald D. Elving, interview with Representative Steve Horn, April 16, 1993.

11. Thomas E. Mann, Norman J. Ornstein, and Michael J. Malbin, eds., *Vital Statistics on Congress 1989–90* (Washington: CQ Press, 1990), pp. 164–65.

12. Beth Donovan, "Legislative Funding Total Is Less Than Last Year's," *Congressional Quarterly Weekly Report*, October 10, 1992, p. 3130.

13. Thomas J. Meyer, "No Sound Bites Here," *New York Times Sunday Magazine*, March 15, 1992, p. 46. The figure is also cited in Frantzich, "A New Congress for a New Era," p. 9.

14. *Congressional Record*, June 14, 1978, pp. 17664–65.

15. Ronald D. Elving, interview with Representative Jim Leach, March 24, 1993.

16. Ronald D. Elving, interview with Senator Thomas A. Daschle, April 14, 1993.

17. Frantzich, "New Congress for a New Era."

18. Quoted in Benenson, "Savvy 'Stars' Making Local TV a Potent Tool," p. 1553.

19. Robinson, "Three Faces of Congressional Media," p. 96.

20. Ronald D. Elving, interview with David Dreyer, April 14, 1993.

21. Duncan, *Politics in America*, p. 369.

22. Ronald D. Elving, interview with Mary Tavenner, business lobbyist who headed the informal coalition of opponents to the Family and Medical Leave Act from 1987 through 1993, August 30, 1993.

23. Newt Gingrich, "Meet the Press," December 1, 1991, transcript p. 5.

24. Ronald D. Elving, interview with Representative Vic Fazio, April 2, 1993.

25. Ritchie, *Press Gallery*, p. 218.

26. Ronald D. Elving, interview with Patrick Towell, chairman of the Standing Committee of Congressional Correspondents, April 15, 1993.

27. Beth Donovan, "Congress' Mandate for Change Rests with New Joint Panel," *Congressional Quarterly Weekly Report*, January 30, 1993, p. 204; see also prepared testimony for Speaker Thomas S. Foley, January 26, 1993.

28. Ronald D. Elving, interview with Joe Crapa, chief of staff to Representative David Obey of Wisconsin, April 7, 1993. Crapa has been a House staff member since 1975, when he became the first staff director for the caucus formed by Democrats in the Watergate Baby class of 1974.

29. Quoted in Hook, "Extensive Reform Proposals Cook on the Front Burner," p. 1579.

30. Ronald D. Elving, interview with Debra Jo Turner, August 16, 1993.

31. Cook, *Making Laws and Making News*, p. 7.

32. Ronald D. Elving, interview with Donnald K. Anderson, July 16, 1993.

33. Thomas L. Friedman, "A Split Congress Sits Back and Listens and Waits," New York Times, Feb. 18, 1993, p. A17.

34. Janet Hook, "Byrd Will Give Up Senate Majority Leadership," *Congressional Quarterly Weekly Report*, April 16, 1988, p. 975.

35. Richard F. Fenno, *Home Style: Members in Their Districts* (Boston: Little, Brown, 1978), p. 168.

36. Gary C. Jacobson, *The Politics of Congressional Elections* (HarperCollins, 1992), p. 90.

37. Peter Carlson, "The Least Exclusive Club in the World," *Washington Post Sunday Magazine*, Nov. 4, 1990, p. 42.

38. Ronald D. Elving, interview with Leach, March 24, 1993.

39. Laura Michaelis, "Decorum Is in Short Supply at First 'Oxford' Debate," *Congressional Quarterly Weekly Report*, March 19, 1994, p. 652.

40. Ronald D. Elving, interview with Jerry Gallegos, deputy superintendent of the House Daily Press Gallery, September 9, 1993.

41. Ronald D. Elving, interview with Debra Jo Turner, chief, and Robert Neill, assistant chief, House Legislative Information Office, August 16, 1993.

42. Helen Dewar and Kenneth J. Cooper, "Mitchell Seeks Rule Changes to Cut 'Delay and Deadlock,'" *Washington Post*, January 27, 1993, p. A4.

43. John Harwood and David Rogers, "House Lists Overdrafts by over 300 of Its Members as Polled Public Wishes a Plague on Both Parties," *Wall Street Journal*, April 17, 1992, p. A12.

44. *Congressional Quarterly Almanac, 1993*, (Congressional Quarterly, 1994), pp. 55–63, 68–74.

45. Phil Kuntz, "Rostenkowski on Trial: Assessing the Charges," *Congressional Quarterly Weekly Report*, June 4, 1994, pp. 1439–46.

46. *New York Times*, May 24, 1929; and *Congressional Record*, 71 Cong., 1 sess., pp. 3048–55; cited in Ritchie, *Press Gallery*, pp. 177–78.

47. Herb Asher and Mike Barr, "Popular Support for Congress and Its Members," in this volume.

48. "Congress Hikes Pay, Revises Ethics Law," *Congressional Quarterly Almanac*, vol. 45 (Washington: CQ Press, 1989), pp. 51–54, 56–57, 60.

49. "Voters Enraged over House Bank Abuses," *1992 Congressional Quarterly Almanac*, vol. 48 (Washington: CQ Press, 1992), pp. 23–42.

50. "Congress Looks at Its Own Bottom Line," *1992 Congressional Quarterly Almanac*, p. 633–34.

51. Phil Kuntz, "Anti-Secrecy Drive Putting Democrats on Defensive," *Congressional Quarterly Weekly Report*, September 11, 1993, pp. 2369–70.

52. Ronald D. Elving, interview with Price, April 2, 1993.

53. Harris Polls for the years from 1963 through 1981 show congressional approval peaking at more than 60 percent in 1965. Roger H. Davidson and Walter J. Oleszek, *Congress and Its Members* (Washington: CQ Press, 1981), figure 5-2.

Index